# K'iche': A Study in the Sociology of Language

## SIL International
## Publications in Sociolinguistics

## Publication 6

Publications in Sociolinguistics is a serial publication of SIL International. The series is a venue for works covering a broad range of topics in sociolinguistics. While most volumes are authored by members of SIL, suitable works by others will also form part of the series.

**Series Editor**

M. Paul Lewis

**Associate Editor**

Gloria Kindell

**Volume Editor**

Marilyn A. Mayers

**Production Staff**

Bonnie Brown, Managing Editor
Margaret González, Compositor
Hazel Shorey, Graphic Artist

# K'iche': A Study in the Sociology of Language

M. Paul Lewis

SIL International
Dallas, Texas

© 2001 by SIL International
Library of Congress Catalog No: 2001090110
ISBN: 1-55671-120-4
ISSN: 0-0895-9897

Printed in the United States of America
All Rights Reserved

09 08 07 06 05 04 03 02 01    10 9 8 7 6 5 4 3 2 1

No part of this publication may be reproduced, stored in a retrieval system, or transmitted in any form or by any means—electronic, mechanical, photocopy, recording, or otherwise—without the express permission of SIL International, with the exception of brief excerpts in journal articles or reviews.

Copies of this and other publications of SIL International may be obtained from

International Academic Bookstore
SIL International
7500 W. Camp Wisdom Road
Dallas, TX 75236-5699

Voice: 972-708-7404
Fax: 972-708-7363
Email: academic_books@sil.org
Internet: http://www.sil.org

# Contents

| | |
|---|---|
| List of Tables | ix |
| List of Figures | xi |
| List of Maps | xi |
| Acknowledgments | xiii |
| 1 Introduction | 1 |
|    1.1 Preconquest Mayan society | 2 |

### 1.2–1.5 Postconquest Guatemala

| | |
|---|---|
| 1.2 The colony | 4 |
| 1.3 The period of independence and the liberal revolution | 8 |
| 1.4 The period of *indigenismo* | 11 |
| 1.5 Post-*indigenismo* | 15 |
| 2 Maintenance and Shift of Language and Identity in K'iche' Communities | 21 |

### 2.1–2.3 Bilingualism, language contact, and language choice

| | |
|---|---|
| 2.1 Bilingualism and language shift | 22 |
| 2.2 The analysis of language choice | 22 |
| 2.3 Bilingualism and diglossia | 23 |

### 2.4–2.8 Ethnocultural identity and language

| | |
|---|---|
| 2.4 Ethnicity and language | 25 |
| 2.5 The language-in-culture nexus | 28 |
| 2.6 Language and culture continuity | 29 |

|       |                                                   |     |
|-------|---------------------------------------------------|-----|
| 2.7   | Causes of language and culture shift.             | 30  |
| 2.8   | Summary.                                          | 31  |

### 2.9–2.12 Ethnolinguistic vitality theory

|       |                                                   |     |
|-------|---------------------------------------------------|-----|
| 2.9   | Objective ethnolinguistic vitality                | 34  |
| 2.10  | Subjective vitality factors.                      | 37  |
| 2.11  | Multiple identities and boundary maintenance      | 38  |
| 2.12  | Synthesis.                                        | 40  |

### 2.13–2.15 The description of Guatemalan communities

|       |                                                   |     |
|-------|---------------------------------------------------|-----|
| 2.13  | Distinctive community types                       | 43  |
| 2.14  | Ethnic identity maintenance                       | 45  |
| 2.15  | Summary.                                          | 47  |
| 3     | Research Project Design and Methodology           | 49  |
| 3.1   | General description                               | 49  |
| 3.2   | Selection of the communities                      | 51  |
| 3.3   | Language use data.                                | 54  |
| 3.4   | Data collection                                   | 54  |
| 3.5   | Unit of observation                               | 55  |
| 3.6   | Language use observation data forms               | 56  |
| 3.7   | Sampling method                                   | 56  |
| 3.8   | Sample size.                                      | 57  |
| 3.9   | Data recording and analysis methods               | 58  |
| 3.10  | Community resource data                           | 67  |
| 3.11  | Statistical analysis procedures                   | 69  |
| 4     | Community Resource Profile Data Analysis—the Towns| 71  |
| 4.1   | Analysis of community resource profile data      | 71  |

### 4.2–4.5 Chichicastenango

|       |                                                   |     |
|-------|---------------------------------------------------|-----|
| 4.2   | Demographic factors.                              | 73  |
| 4.3   | Institutional support factors                     | 76  |
| 4.4   | Status factors                                    | 88  |
| 4.5   | Subjective factors.                               | 91  |

### 4.6–4.9 Cunén

|       |                                                   |     |
|-------|---------------------------------------------------|-----|
| 4.6   | Demographic factors.                              | 93  |
| 4.7   | Institutional support factors                     | 96  |
| 4.8   | Status factors                                    | 100 |
| 4.9   | Subjective vitality factors.                      | 101 |

### 4.10–4.13 Joyabaj

|       |                                                   |     |
|-------|---------------------------------------------------|-----|
| 4.10  | Demographic factors.                              | 104 |
| 4.11  | Institutional support Factors                     | 104 |
| 4.12  | Status factors                                    | 109 |

4.13 Subjective factors . . . . . . . . . . . . . . . . . . . 109
### 4.14–4.17 Sacapulas
4.14 Demographic factors. . . . . . . . . . . . . . . . . . 111
4.15 Institutional support factors . . . . . . . . . . . . . . 112
4.16 Status factors . . . . . . . . . . . . . . . . . . . . . 115
4.17 Subjective factors . . . . . . . . . . . . . . . . . . . 115
### 4.18–4.21 San Andrés Sajcabajá
4.18 Demographic factors. . . . . . . . . . . . . . . . . . 117
4.19 Institutional support factors . . . . . . . . . . . . . . 118
4.20 Status factors . . . . . . . . . . . . . . . . . . . . . 122
4.21 Subjective factors . . . . . . . . . . . . . . . . . . . 122

5 Community Resource Profile Data Analysis—the Cities . . . . 123
### 5.1–5.5 Santa Cruz del Quiché
5.1 Demographic factors. . . . . . . . . . . . . . . . . . 124
5.2 Institutional support factors . . . . . . . . . . . . . . 124
5.3 Status factors . . . . . . . . . . . . . . . . . . . . . 129
5.4 Subjective factors . . . . . . . . . . . . . . . . . . . 129
5.5 Two rural communities . . . . . . . . . . . . . . . . 130
### 5.6–5.9 Totonicapán
5.6 Demographic factors. . . . . . . . . . . . . . . . . . 132
5.7 Institutional support factors . . . . . . . . . . . . . . 133
5.8 Status factors . . . . . . . . . . . . . . . . . . . . . 137
5.9 Subjective factors . . . . . . . . . . . . . . . . . . . 138

6 Language Use in the Seven Communities. . . . . . . . . . . 141
6.1 Language use in Chichicastenango. . . . . . . . . . . . 143
6.2 Language use in Cunén. . . . . . . . . . . . . . . . . 159
6.3 Language use in Joyabaj . . . . . . . . . . . . . . . . 170
6.4 Language use in Sacapulas . . . . . . . . . . . . . . . 178
6.5 Language use in San Andrés Sajcabajá . . . . . . . . . 187
6.6 Language use in Santa Cruz del Quiché . . . . . . . . 197
6.7 Language use in Totonicapán . . . . . . . . . . . . . 206

7 Integration of the Two Data Sets . . . . . . . . . . . . . . 217
### 7.1–7.4 Ethnolinguistic identity measures
7.1 Demographic factors. . . . . . . . . . . . . . . . . . 218
7.2 Institutional support factors . . . . . . . . . . . . . . 222
7.3 Status factors . . . . . . . . . . . . . . . . . . . . . 226
7.4 Subjective vitality factors. . . . . . . . . . . . . . . . 229

|       |                                                        |     |
| ----- | ------------------------------------------------------ | --- |
| 7.5   | Language maintenance indices                           | 231 |
| 7.6   | Summary                                                | 239 |
| 7.7   | Conclusions                                            | 242 |

Appendix: Community Resource Profile Questions . . . . . . . . 247
    Demographics and boundary maintenance-related questions . . 247
    Status related questions . . . . . . . . . . . . . . . . . . . 249
    Subjective vitality related questions . . . . . . . . . . . . 254

References . . . . . . . . . . . . . . . . . . . . . . . . . . . 257

## Tables

| | | |
|---|---|---|
| 3.1 | Tally of observations by community. | 58 |
| 3.2 | Formality level of situation/location categories. | 65 |
| 6.1 | Speech transactions in Chichicastenango by race and sex of speaker and interlocutor | 145 |
| 6.2 | Maximum likelihood analysis-of-variance: Race and sex data from Chichicastenango. | 146 |
| 6.3 | Tally of language use for SEX*RACE*IRACE in Chichicastenango | 146 |
| 6.4 | Tally of language use for RACE*ISEX in Chichicastenango. | 148 |
| 6.5 | Tally of language use for SEX*ISEX in Chichicastenango | 149 |
| 6.6 | Tally of language use for ISEX*IRACE in Chichicastenango. | 150 |
| 6.7 | K'iche' language use by age group in Chichicastenango | 152 |
| 6.8 | K'iche' language use by domain in Chichicastenango | 155 |
| 6.9 | Language use by formality level in Chichicastenango | 158 |
| 6.10 | Speech transactions in Cunén by race and sex of speaker and interlocutor. | 160 |
| 6.11 | Maximum likelihood analysis-of-variance: Race and sex data from Cunén. | 161 |
| 6.12 | Tally of language use for SEX*RACE*ISEX*IRACE in Cunén. | 162 |
| 6.13 | K'iche' language use by age group in Cunén | 164 |
| 6.14 | K'iche' language use by domain in Cunén | 167 |
| 6.15 | K'iche' language use by formality level in Cunén | 169 |
| 6.16 | Speech transactions in Joyabaj by race and sex of speaker and interlocutor. | 171 |
| 6.17 | Maximum likelihood analysis-of-variance: Race and sex data from Joyabaj | 172 |
| 6.18 | Tally of language use for RACE*IRACE in Joyabaj | 172 |
| 6.19 | K'iche' language use by age group in Joyabaj | 174 |
| 6.20 | K'iche' language use by domain in Joyabaj. | 175 |
| 6.21 | K'iche' language use by formality level in Joyabaj | 177 |
| 6.22 | Speech transactions in Sacapulas by race and sex of speaker and interlocutor | 179 |
| 6.23 | Maximum likelihood analysis-of-variance: Race and sex data from Sacapulas | 180 |
| 6.24 | Tally of language use for race in Sacapulas | 181 |
| 6.25 | K'iche' language use by age group in Sacapulas. | 182 |
| 6.26 | K'iche' language use by domain in Sacapulas. | 184 |
| 6.27 | K'iche' language use by formality level in Sacapulas | 186 |
| 6.28 | Speech transactions in San Andrés Sajcabajá by race and sex of speaker and interlocutor | 188 |

6.29 Maximum likelihood analysis-of-variance: Race and sex data from San Andrés Sajcabajá . . . . . . . . . . . . . . . . . 189
6.30 Tally of language use for SEX*RACE*ISEX*IRACE in San Andrés Sajcabajá . . . . . . . . . . . . . . . . . . . 190
6.31 K'iche' language use by age group in San Andrés Sajcabajá . 192
6.32 K'iche' language use by domain in San Andrés Sajcabajá . . 194
6.33 K'iche' language use by formality level in San Andrés Sajcabajá . . . . . . . . . . . . . . . . . . . 196
6.34 Speech transactions in Santa Cruz del Quiché by race and sex of speaker and interlocutor . . . . . . . . . . . . . . 198
6.35 Maximum likelihood analysis-of-variance: Race and sex data from Santa Cruz del Quiché . . . . . . . . . . . . 199
6.36 Tally of language use for SEX*RACE*ISEX*IRACE in Santa Cruz del Quiché . . . . . . . . . . . . . . . . . . 199
6.37 K'iche' language use by age group in Santa Cruz del Quiché. 201
6.38 K'iche' language use by domain in Santa Cruz del Quiché . . 203
6.39 K'iche' language use by formality level in Santa Cruz del Quiché . . . . . . . . . . . . . . . . . . 205
6.40 Speech transactions in Totonicapán by race and sex of speaker and interlocutor . . . . . . . . . . . . . . . . 207
6.41 Maximum likelihood analysis-of-variance: Race and sex data from Totonicapán. . . . . . . . . . . . . . . . . . . 208
6.42 Tally of language use for RACE*IRACE in Totonicapán . . . 208
6.43 Tally of language use for SEX*ISEX in Totonicapán. . . . . 210
6.44 Tally of language use for SEX*IRACE in Totonicapán. . . . 210
6.45 K'iche' language use by age group in Totonicapán . . . . . 212
6.46 K'iche' language use by domain in Totonicapán . . . . . . 214
6.47 K'iche' language use by formality level in Totonicapán . . . 216
7.1 Summary of demographic factors . . . . . . . . . . . . . 219
7.2 Summary of institutional support factors. . . . . . . . . . 224
7.3 Summary of status factors . . . . . . . . . . . . . . . . 227
7.4 Summary of subjective vitality factors. . . . . . . . . . . 230
7.5 Summary of language use by age groups . . . . . . . . . 232
7.6 Summary of language maintenance indices by domain . . . 234
7.7 Global language maintenance indices . . . . . . . . . . . 238

## Figures

| | | |
|---|---|---|
| 6.1 | Interaction of RACE*SEX*IRACE in Chichicastenango. | 147 |
| 6.2 | Interaction of RACE*ISEX in Chichicastenango | 148 |
| 6.3 | Interaction of SEX*ISEX in Chichicastenango. | 150 |
| 6.4 | Interaction of ISEX*IRACE in Chichicastenango | 151 |
| 6.5 | Language use by age group in Chichicastenango | 152 |
| 6.6 | Language use by domain in Chichicastenango | 156 |
| 6.7 | Language use by SEX*RACE*ISEX*IRACE in Cunén. | 163 |
| 6.8 | Language use by age group in Cunén | 165 |
| 6.9 | Language use by domain in Cunén | 168 |
| 6.10 | Interaction of RACE*IRACE in Joyabaj | 173 |
| 6.11 | Language use by age group in Joyabaj | 174 |
| 6.12 | Language use by domain in Joyabaj. | 176 |
| 6.13 | Interaction of RACE in Sacapulas | 181 |
| 6.14 | Language use by age group in Sacapulas. | 183 |
| 6.15 | Language use by domain in Sacapulas. | 185 |
| 6.16 | Interaction of RACE*SEX*IRACE*ISEX in San Andrés Sajcabajá | 191 |
| 6.17 | Language use by age group in San Andrés Sajcabajá | 192 |
| 6.18 | Language use by domain in San Andrés Sajcabajá | 195 |
| 6.19 | Interaction of SEX*RACE*ISEX*IRACE in Santa Cruz del Quiché. | 200 |
| 6.20 | Language use by age group in Santa Cruz del Quiché. | 202 |
| 6.21 | Language use by domain in Santa Cruz del Quiché. | 204 |
| 6.22 | Interaction of RACE*IRACE Totonicapán. | 209 |
| 6.23 | Interaction of SEX*ISEX in Totonicapán | 210 |
| 6.24 | Interaction of SEX*IRACE in Totonicapán | 211 |
| 6.25 | Language use by age group in Totonicapán | 213 |
| 6.26 | Language use by domain in Totonicapán | 215 |
| 7.1 | Global language maintenance indices | 240 |
| 7.2 | Comparative language use by age groups | 241 |

## Maps

| | | |
|---|---|---|
| 1 | The K'iche' Speaking Area of Guatemala | 52 |
| 2 | The K'iche' Varieties Included in this Study | 53 |

# Acknowledgments

The production of a volume such as this one is the result of thousands of hours of praying, planning, consulting, organizing, data collecting, analysis, editing, proofreading, and typesetting. It is therefore quite misleading to have only a single name on the cover and title page. The original research which this book reports on involved more than forty-five people during nearly four very intense years of planning, field work, and evaluation. The analysis, which resulted in my dissertation, took another four years. It has taken almost five additional years of editing and revising to bring this book to publication.

The largest vote of thanks continues to be to the members of the Quiché Survey Team, my SIL colleagues in Guatemala: Charissa Crossley, Ed and Mary Fox, Jo Ann Munson, Marty and Diane Quigley, Paul and Anne Stevenson, Nancy Suiter, Mae Toedeter, and Reg and Ivy Willems. In addition, we had the excellent assistance of Federic Hernández Zapeta, Basilia López Vicente, Domingo Tix Yac, Francisco Valeriano Bach, Josefa González Cortéz, José Nas León, Miguel Francisco Menchú, María Isabel Ordoñez, Manuel de Jesús Bach Cabrera, Manuel Pelíz Pacajoj, Miguel Santos Hernández, Nicolas de León Colaj, Pablo Pérez Cortéz, Pascual Urizar León, René Montenegro B., Santiago Camajá Hernández, Santos Elías Zapeta, Tomás Tian Chicoj, and Vicente González M. *Sib'alaj mal tiox chiwe iwonojel!*

The survey team also benefited from the wise counsel and guidance of our colleagues in Guatemala: Wesley Collins, David and Carol Fox, David and Marilyn Henne, Merieta Johnson, Catherine Langan, Mary Shaw, Helen Neuenswander, Neville and María Theresa Stiles. Deborah Hatfield also contributed by pointing us to much useful literature on language maintenance and shift. Charles Ferguson and Shirley Brice Heath were inspirational in encouraging me to begin the graduate study program at Georgetown University that produced the dissertation on which this volume is based. Ralph Fasold, Peter Patrick, and Roger Shuy patiently guided me through the production of the dissertation and contributed much to the quality of the analysis and its presentation. Their willingness to read, comment, and ask penetrating questions have contributed greatly to the refinement of my thinking as well as to the development of the content of this volume.

More recently, Millie Larson, Gloria Kindell, Marilyn Mayers, Mary Ruth Wise, and others in the editorial department have assisted greatly in the preparation of this manuscript and provided encouragement to keep on. Matt Benjamin willingly produced the maps which have enhanced this volume. Others in the International Sociolinguistics Department of SIL International have borne with me as I have stolen hours from them to dedicate myself to getting this book done.

A special word of thanks and a debt of love is due my wife Adalee, who has never had doubts about this even when I did, and my children, Katie, Ellie, Jed and Sara, who have put up with a too preoccupied father for most of their lives.

The greatest thanks of all must go to Him who has done marvelous things, the Creator of the K'iche's, who, I trust, delights in these feeble efforts to understand the world He has made. To Him be all the glory forever and ever. Amen.

# 1
# Introduction

Guatemala is a small mountainous country located in Central America. It is the ancestral homeland of descendants of the Mayan civilization and has become the homeland of the descendants of the Spanish conquistadors who arrived almost five hundred years ago. The arrival of the Spaniards was a catastrophic event in its effect on the social processes of Mesoamerica and of Guatemala in particular, with its inevitable clashes of culture and language. "The key division is ethnic, between Mayan-speaking Indians and Hispanicized, Spanish-speaking ladinos" (Nyrop 1983:xxiii). Other divisions within Guatemalan society, e.g., Roman Catholics versus Protestants and wealthy elite versus impoverished masses, correlate with the more basic ethnic and cultural division.

The language use situation among the K'iche' (alternately spelled Quiché, cf. Lewis 1993), one of the largest Mayan groups in Guatemala, is unclear. In spite of five hundred years of Spanish dominance, with increasing pressure to use Spanish in more formal and public domains and economic pressures which favored assimilation to the cultural patterns of Spanish speakers, until the early 1980s, it was generally assumed that K'iche' was being maintained. This assumption was supported by the existence of large numbers of monolinguals and by the relative lack of participation of Mayans in Spanish-dominated domains. Fishman (1967; 1968/1972) has labeled such a situation as diglossia[1] without bilingualism and characterizes such

---

[1]The term diglossia is used in sociolinguistics to refer to a situation where different linguistic varieties co-occur throughout a speech community, each with a distinct range of social functions. See chapter 2 for a fuller discussion of this concept.

circumstances as prone to rapid linguistic change when social changes take place which allow access to the dominant linguistic variety. Social changes within the last sixty years began with the shift to the policy of *indigenismo* in the 1940s and the more recent shift to Mayan nationalism in the 1980s. In this study, I propose that the stable diglossia without bilingualism is eroding and that this is related to social changes taking place accompanied by a shift in Mayan identity.

The question must be raised, however, as to why language shift is beginning now, even though it appears that the motivation to learn Spanish has always been strong. It seems that Mayans have changed their evaluation of the importance of acquiring proficiency in Spanish. This represents a fundamental shift in Mayan values, i.e., an identity shift which amounts to a realignment of core cultural values such that success is no longer measured in terms of the traditional Mayan standards (the ability to work, to respond to community needs, to participate in communal obligations, etc.). Rather, it now uses a new set of standards which include many of the values of the ladino world, not the least of which is a higher level of formal education and the resulting economic rewards derived therefrom.

In order to understand the processes of change which are taking place in language use, it is also necessary to understand the processes of change which are at work in the social, political, and economic domains. A brief summary is given here of the historical development of modern K'iche' society with particular focus on the relationship between social, economic, and political trends along with the changes in formal language policy. Modern-day Guatemalan cultural ways have deep roots and a historical base helps in understanding the dynamics of the events unfolding today.

## 1.1 Preconquest Mayan society

Preconquest Mayan society reached its peak in the first few centuries A.D. and is known as the "Old Empire". During this time, the Mayans developed their skills in architecture, mathematics, and astronomy although they used no beasts of burden, no metal tools, and did not develop the wheel. The majority of the people lived in the rural areas, and the cities were reserved as religious and ceremonial centers. Land tenancy tended to be communal rather than individual.

For reasons that have never been clearly determined, the Old Empire declined and the major city centers were abandoned. Mayan culture reemerged in what archaeologists have termed the neoclassical period with its largest and most important centers located in the Yucatán, which became the new locus of Mayan high culture and development. The neoclassical period, however, showed the influence of the great cities of the Aztec empire in Central Mexico. Some of this influence was the result of invasions and conquests that resulted in intermarriage between the conquerors and the conquered. According to their own traditions, the Quichés were one such invading group.

The Quichés were the creators of a powerful kingdom centered at their capital city, Utatlán, in Guatemala's northwestern highlands which was located well south of the more prominent neoclassical cities. From Utatlán they extended their influence over a wide area and maintained both friendly and unfriendly relations with other Mayan groups around them. The oral traditions of the Quichés attest to their having Toltec origins and refer to a long migration which eventually brought them to the Guatemalan highlands where they conquered the local peoples and established their kingdom.

As might be expected, pre-Columbian Quichean culture was preoccupied with conquest and waging war. Perhaps this militaristic orientation also resulted in concerns with social ranking between commoners and aristocracy and a highly ritualized religious system which included human sacrifice. There was also a preoccupation with calendrics and the symbolic spatial orientation of objects according to the four cardinal points as evidenced in surviving religious practices and legends.

Like the political and social history of Guatemala, the history of language policy in Guatemala parallels the economic and political developments in the region. While there have been some speculations about the sociolinguistics of pre-Columbian Mesoamerica (e.g., Fought 1985), it is difficult to arrive at any evidence as to what the language policy was prior to the arrival of the Conquerors. Certainly, the strong influence of the Aztec civilization on the Mayan, resulting in considerable linguistic and cultural borrowing, can be well attested.

## 1.2–1.5 Postconquest Guatemala

The history of postconquest social and language policy in Guatemala is more amenable to documentation. My analysis divides the history of Guatemalan language planning and public policy into three major periods with a fourth period beginning in the late 1980s. The first three are all periods where acculturation and eventual assimilation to Spanish were the goals. The methodology used to achieve the goals of integration and assimilation differed in each of these periods. Where either a carrot or a stick could be used to motivate, sadly, more often than not, the stick was the motivator of choice during the two initial periods. The third period attempted to use more benign methods, with telling results. The fourth incipient period seems to be one of Mayan reaction to the success of the assimilationist goals under the benign policies of *indigenismo*. It is marked more by goals of dissimilation and language maintenance, in spite of, or perhaps because of, the increasing threat of language shift and even, in some cases, language death.

## 1.2 The colony

"[B]y the time the Spaniards arrived the various political entities in the Highlands were in a state of continuous war with each other. The Spaniards and their Mexican allies were at first regarded not as a threat by some city-states but rather as allies in these internecine wars" (Nyrop 1983:6). In 1523 Pedro de Alvarado, a subaltern of Hernán Cortéz, led a small contingent of Spanish forces in an attack on the Quiché kingdom. In 1524, in a much-celebrated battle near present-day Quezaltenango, the Quiché king's grandson, Tecum Uman, and his forces were defeated by the Spanish invaders. Utatlán fell shortly thereafter.

The effects of the Spanish conquest upon the Quichés were massive and devastating. Carmack (1981:7) marks the fall of Utatlán as the beginning of radical cultural changes for the Quiché. The warlike aristocracy was, for the most part, eliminated in the fighting with the Spaniards. Consequently, the elaborate cultural and religious hierarchy centered in the citadel city of Utatlán was demolished and only remnants of that cultural heritage survive in contemporary Quiché cosmology, social organization, and cultural practices.

By 1527 Guatemala was recognized by the Spanish crown as a captaincy general which allowed it to have its own governor but maintained its subordinate position under the viceroyalty of New Spain. In 1544 all of Central America from Panama north to southern Mexico was combined to form an *audiencia,* and the capital was established at the site of present-day Antigua Guatemala in 1549 (Nyrop 1983:7).

The early years of colonization did not go well. Hawkins (1984:47) argues that the ruling ideology of the colonial period in New Spain, as the province was called, was one which viewed the Mayans as "barely human infidels...the opposite of all things Spanish and properly elite." Mayans were viewed as a source of labor by the secular authorities while the Church viewed them as savages in need of the civilizing effects of Christianity.

## 1.2 The colony

The Spanish made heavy demands for tribute which resulted in revolts which were quashed mercilessly. "The most insistent problems were holding the Indians in subjection and creating means to induce them to work so as to produce a surplus beyond what was needed for their own subsistence" (Jones 1940/66:13). The *encomienda* system, which had been used in the Caribbean and in Mexico, was brought to Guatemala as well. It granted rights to favored subjects of the crown as rewards for their participation in the conquest. As part of each grant, the Mayan population was divided among the various Spanish grantees and required to provide labor for that grantee, the *encomendero,* in return for meager payment. The *encomendero* was also obligated to provide the Mayans with the benefits of Spanish civilization including the introduction of Christianity. In practice, the payment offered them was "often so low that the Indian could hardly maintain himself and the duty of the *encomendero*...was often forgotten" (Jones 1940/66:14). The result was a virtual system of slave labor which was made even more onerous by the bureaucratic ineptitude with which it was administered. The *encomienda* grants overlapped, and Mayan laborers were assigned to more than one *encomendero* resulting in impossible obligations being placed upon them.

With the establishment of the *audiencia,* administrative and judicial authority was centered in a single capital city, known today as Antigua Guatemala. This change in governmental organization in part was to improve the efficiency of the governance of the colony but also was a means of facilitating the administration of the Mayans. The power of the state began to extend outside of the capital and the need to control the Mayans who were scattered over the countryside was more keenly felt. Over time, the crown asserted its political control over the colony by making the *encomiendas* non-heritable beyond the second generation. As the second inheritors died the *encomiendas* reverted to the crown. "As the *encomiendas* passed to the crown, the basic two-level political structure of township versus central government was established" (Hawkins 1984:57).

Both the state and the Church had interests in handling the Mayans more effectively. "Both powers agreed that they should be forced to live in towns with straight streets to make them more sociable" (Jones 1940/66:17). This policy, called *reducción,* marked the beginning of the Guatemalan *municipio,* a unit of government similar to the county or township in the United States. It still continues to be the basic building block of Guatemalan government and has come to be the basic social unit of Mayan society as well. Goubaud Carrera (1945/64:23) speaks of a

Guatemala which is a mosaic made up of more than two hundred ethnic entities each of which is more or less different from all of the others. He states:

> *Componen este mosaico unas doscientas entidades étnicas indígenas, que se diferencian en mayor o menor grado entre sí, pero que por tal diferenciación deben considerarse como grupos étnicos distintos. Cada uno de estos grupos étnicos indígenas, constituyen una comunidad social, un conjunto de costumbres, actitudes, sentimientos y modalidades del pensamiento que son comprartidos en una forma convencional, por el grupo de personas que ocupan una área geográfica, un territorio.*

> This mosaic is composed of some two hundred indigenous ethnic entities, that differentiate to a greater or lesser degree among themselves, but which ought to be considered distinct ethnic groups. Each one of these indigenous ethnic groups constitutes a social community, a collection of customs, attitudes, feelings, and ways of thinking that are shared by convention by the group of people who occupy a geographic area, a territory. (my translation)

The social community based on geographic and territorial proximity is the *municipio* which was the creation of the Spanish colonizers.

> The *reducción* program benefited virtually all Spaniards and was greatly desired by them. For the priests, *reducción* provided a compact, easy means of reaching the people to be Christianized. For the Spanish crown, *reducción* facilitated the administration of the Indians and the collection of the tribute to be sent to Spain. For the Spaniards born in the New World...*reducción* removed the smallholders from the land. These lands could then be appropriated. (Hawkins 1984:58)

In part to avoid the potential abuses which might result, *encomenderos* and eventually all Spaniards were forbidden to live in the Mayan towns (Jones 1940/66:18). Even though this regulation was regularly disregarded, the *municipio* became the societal unit with which Mayans came most closely to identify and also the means by which the Spaniards and the Mayans came to be isolated from each other. "They [the *municipios*] undoubtedly also helped to keep the population divided into classes with limited contact with each other and with conflicting interests" (Hawkins 1984:18). Goubaud Carrera (1945:23) observes the continuance of this locally oriented social organization when he says that the territory in

## 1.2 The colony

Guatemala that constitutes the indigenous social community is the municipality.

While the forms of Spanish government were imposed and nominally accepted in these indigenous communities, the actual day-to-day life and customs of the Mayan citizens were little changed. Hawkins (1984), however, argues that Mayans took the social forms brought to them by the Spanish and made use of these forms to create a new identity. He states:

> More important, Alvarado and his band introduced the Spanish cultural categories that the aborigines would adopt, the Iberian status ideology that the aborigines would invert, and many of the symbolic oppositions that aborigines would employ to define their existence with the imposed institutions of enslavement. In the process, the aborigines would make themselves Indians. (Hawkins 1984:49–50)

Hawkins, whose work represents a paradigm shift in the work on Mayan social history and relations and is too far reaching to be adequately summarized here, takes the position that much of what is now considered to be Mayan culture is really Spanish culture as adopted and reinterpreted by the postconquest Mayans.

The Church had greater success in making inroads into the cultural life of the Mayans partly because of the efforts of Bartolomé de las Casas and other clerics to convince the Spanish crown that the protection and preservation of the Mayans was necessary. In 1542, the New Laws were issued which greatly restricted the activities of the *encomenderos* and benefited the clergy and indirectly the Mayans as well. Though their evangelization was nominally successful, the Christianity of the Mayans is an extremely syncretistic variety in which the forms of Christianity were adopted without affecting the essential content of the Mayan cosmology.

Jones (1940/66:20) asserts that the primary points of contact between Spaniards and Mayans during the colonial period were labor and taxation. Though the *encomienda* system faded and was replaced by other mechanisms for extracting labor from the Mayan population, labor assumed greater and greater importance as the primary means by which the Spanish government could gain revenue. Other taxes came into being as the demands for funds increased, all of which weighed heavily on the impoverished Mayan population. As the Spanish crown recognized that the economic fortunes of Guatemala were not going to equal those of the other more profitable colonies, demands for other types of revenues increased and concern for the overall development of the colony declined.

The initial period of language policy, immediately following the conquest, was marked by a policy of oppression with the advantages of education being offered to the sons of the Spanish nobility and only in Spanish and Latin. Heath (1972:7) has noted that the general policy of the Spanish crown was to work towards the elimination of the indigenous languages in the colonies out of a concern for the efficient administration of colonial affairs. Though there were apparent exceptions to the policy of elimination—Fray Bartolomé de las Casas, a Dominican, and later, Hermano Pedro, a Franciscan monk, were notable for their interest in providing education for both Spanish and Mayan, rich and poor, men and women—the goal of the policy was to eliminate the need to deal with the indigenous peoples through any language other than Spanish. The *criollos,* Spaniards born in the New World, and many of the friars who lived among the Mayans consistently resisted any efforts to teach Spanish to them as a way "to protect their positions and put the prelates from Spain at a distinct disadvantage among the Indians" (Heath 1972:34–35). As long as they could be kept speaking their own language, they would be more humble. Hawkins (1984:44) also concludes that the linguistic diversity among the Mayan groups assisted the Spaniards in maintaining control by keeping them divided among themselves.

### 1.3 The period of independence and the liberal revolution

The second period of language policy in Guatemala began after independence from Spain in 1821. The language policy of the new republic became one of extermination. The goal of the government was to exterminate the indigenous languages through repressive legislation and harsh social policies. Skinner-Klee (1954:20) says that the *Decreto del Congreso Constituyente* of October 1824 mandated "the 'extinction' of the indigenous languages due to the fact that they were so 'diverse, incomplete, and imperfect', and 'insufficient for enlightening the people or perfecting the civilization'."[2]

This statement reflects the general problem faced by the newly independent Guatemala and which continued for many years following independence. With an economy based on cheap manual labor there existed strong incentives to maintain a situation which would keep the Mayans subservient and available for use. On the other hand, the promoters of independence and the liberals to follow could not envision a civilized and enlightened society without the assimilation (or elimination) of the indigenous cultures. This double vision resulted in the punishment of the Mayans for retaining their languages and cultural norms while at the same time denying them access to the means of assimilation. Thus, while the

---

[2]This is Richards' translation (1989:97).

## 1.3 The period of independence and the liberal revolution

pressure to assimilate was strong (whether by the carrot or the stick), the opportunities for assimilation were few.

At the beginning of this period the federation of Central America was rife with divisions. The conservatives favored a strong central government arguing that the division of power between the various regional states was inefficient and too expensive. The liberals, on the other hand, argued that tyranny was the result of a strong central government and that the model of the United States was the one to be followed. These philosophical divisions overlapped and coincided with regional divisions and doomed the regional federation from the start. What followed was a period of unrest and dissension as government after government was unseated, fell from power, and failed to bring about the unity that had been envisioned for the region. Guatemala was seen as the most powerful of the member states and so was opposed by most of the other member states on the basis of regional jealousy.

It was not until the rise to power of José Rafael Carrera that a strong central, albeit dictatorial, authority was established. It was during his tenure in office that all hopes of a federated Central America were dashed when in 1847 he declared Guatemala to be absolutely independent. Although he resigned the presidency in 1848 and went into exile, there was no one who could replace him and within the space of a single year there were three successors to the Guatemalan presidency. One year later, the illiterate and superstitious Carrera returned to Guatemala, became the head of the army, and by 1850 was once more established in the presidency. With strong support from the conservatives, Carrera undid many of the actions of the liberals and received much support from the aristocracy and the Church. In 1854 he was declared president for life and given the power to name his successor.

Carrera's more than thirty years in power are characterized by a strong sense of Guatemalan nationalism. He put down a revolt by the northwestern highland provinces, called Los Altos, which was an attempt to create a sixth Central American republic. His policies were hostile to the neighboring republics as he attempted to consolidate the strength and position of Guatemala. Identified as being a mulatto and as having Mayan blood, Carrera, in spite of his conservative supporters, was characterized as being hostile to whites. Perhaps this bigotry was overlooked since most of those who were the victims of his brutality were members of the now out-of-favor liberal party.

When Carrera's chosen successor, Vicente Cerna, proved to be weak and ineffectual the situation became ripe for a revolution. The Liberal Revolution, which is much-celebrated and remembered in Guatemala today, took place in 1871 and brought to power two famous heroes in Guatemalan history. Spanish-born Miguel García Granados was a London-educated moderate liberal. Justo Rufino Barrios, the most famous and revered of all Guatemala's presidents, was the second leader of the revolution and perhaps the more dynamic of the two. Granados was named the provisional president and Barrios assumed a military position giving him control of the highlands. One year later, in 1872, Granados called upon Barrios to assume the acting presidency while Granados went off to defend the cause of liberalism in Honduras (Jones 1940/66:49). When popular elections were held in 1873 Barrios was elected to the presidency where he would serve for the next twelve years. Barrios' leadership style was autocratic and not very much in keeping with the principles of liberalism. His primary point of agreement with the liberals was in maintaining the dream of a united federation of Central America. The social reforms which he instituted by decree consisted primarily in the reduction of the influence of the Church and its elimination from any official role in public life. He expelled the Jesuit order, confiscated Church properties, abolished monasteries, and opened the borders of Guatemala to Protestant missionaries. Barrios established freedom of religion, a policy which is a source of much pride to present-day Guatemalans.

Barrios also greatly strengthened the role of the departmental (provincial) governments giving them wide-ranging powers. This level of government became the key means by which the central government's authority is administered outside of the capital. It sets the departmental authorities over the municipal governments which, though under the control of the central government, continue to be in large part more local, and hence, Mayan, in their orientation.

Barrios felt strongly that the key to the development of Guatemala rested in an increase in European immigration. "The natives he considered an inferior race to be exploited, though he sought to draw them to the ladino standards of life and lent his support to plans for giving them common schools" (Jones 1940/66:56). Barrios seems to have been primarily concerned with agricultural development and was convinced that without the maintenance of the existing system of cheap, forced, Mayan labor such development would not be achieved. It was Barrios who encouraged the introduction of coffee as an export crop. This decision revolutionized the Guatemalan economy, but also institutionalized even more strongly the need for cheap manual labor. When Barrios died the inevitable vacuum of power was created and there followed a succession of weaker, less notable men whose governments were marked by partisan fighting. The notable exceptions to this pattern are the two or three

## 1.3 The period of independence and the liberal revolution

strong-handed presidents who assumed dictatorial powers. All of these were liberals at least in name and paid lip-service to the principles of the liberal revolution.

Over all, the liberal revolution brought about few changes in policy towards Mayans. The liberals were ruthless in their efforts to achieve agricultural productivity and drove the Mayans from the most profitable lands thus making them even more dependent on the landholders for employment. In a situation reminiscent of the pre-Civil War South in the United States, as coffee and other export crops increased in importance, the need for laborers increased as well and government regulations effectively served the needs of the agricultural sector at the expense of the Mayan population.

## 1.4 The period of *indigenismo*

The third period of language policy began in the 1940s when the government created the *Instituto Indigenista Nacional* (hereafter IIN) which was given responsibility for overseeing Mayan affairs. This shift in policy was the result of the overthrow of the dictator Ubico and the beginning of the sweeping changes instituted during the ten-year tenure of Juan José Arévalo and Jacobo Arbenz Guzmán. Stewart (1984:23) characterizes this period as one marked by "new initiatives in all areas of public life and oriented towards balancing to some degree the inequities that burdened the masses in the past in the interests of a small group." A new constitution granted the vote to illiterate males and literate females, both groups that had previously been denied suffrage. This action effectively granted the vote to Mayan males since most of them at the time would have been illiterate and thus denied access to the polls. Illiterate females remained without the right to vote, an estimated 76 percent of Guatemalan women at the time (Nyrop 1983:23). Under Arévalo there were many social reforms including the abolishment of the vagrancy laws (which were used to force Mayans to work for little pay), the establishment of the right of laborers to organize unions and strike, and the passage of minimum wage laws. These were the first real efforts to provide Mayans with civil rights. One-third of the budget was allocated for social welfare projects, among these a national literacy campaign. It was during this time that the IIN was also established and the policy of *indigenismo* was adopted. Education, health, hospitals, as well as roads and bridges were funded. Carmack (1981:347) observes that the postconquest community life of the Quichés "was not drastically changed by the forces of modernization" until this period in Guatemalan history.

The elections which followed Arévalo's term in office resulted in an even more marked shift away from the traditional liberal approach to social policy. Jacobo Arbenz Guzmán was elected with the support of many groups which represented students and workers and which were opposed to the interests of the extremely powerful North American businesses which had become well entrenched monopolies in Guatemala. Arbenz attempted to reduce the monopoly of these corporations by establishing Guatemalan competitors. He also began a major program of agrarian reform. All of this met with opposition from United Fruit and its political allies in both Guatemala and the United States and resulted in the now-infamous CIA-backed coup of 1954 which established military and military-backed governments which ruled Guatemala until the late 1980s.

The changes in language policy introduced by the Arévalo and Arbenz governments reflected the growing trend in Latin America begun at the Congress of Interamerican Indianists held at Pátzcuaro, Mexico in 1940. This approach was formalized and given endorsement by the Pan American Union and thus became the pattern in many countries in Latin America (Whetten 1961:69). The movement connected with this congress, known as *indigenismo,* took a much more benign though still assimilationist view of indigenous language and cultural problems and resulted in changes in language policy in both Mexico and Guatemala. These changes led to the idea of promoting and preserving indigenous languages and cultures while at the same time promoting the integration of the indigenous peoples into the national society.

Goubaud Carrera (1964:144), the first director of Guatemala's IIN, described this change of affairs as follows:

> *Los principales aspectos que caracterizan a este nuevo período, en Guatemala, pueden resumirse de la siguiente manera: 1o, una mayor expresión de acción política por parte del indígena; 2o, una orientación de la política oficial hacia un incremento de bienestar general del pueblo; y 3o, un reconocimiento formal y general de que la cultura indígena es un factor importante en la cultura moderna del país.*

> The principal aspects that characterize this new period in Guatemala can be summed up in the following way: (1) a greater expression of political action by the Indian; (2) an orientation of official policy towards an increase in the general welfare of the people; and (3) a general formal recognition that the indigenous culture is an important factor in the modern culture of the country. (my translation)

## 1.4 The period of indigenismo

In the history of Guatemalan social policy, it can be observed in case after case that changes in policy which tend to benefit Mayans come as the result of external pressures. The shift to *indigenismo* is one such change. Motivated by the worldwide trend to value indigenous peoples and their cultures, Guatemala could not long maintain its feudal policies with regard to the Mayans who lived within its borders.

Chiodi (1990:207) observes that for Guatemala, the presence of the Mayans always has been a source of shame and resentment, "a stain on the country, the original sin of a country that longs, at least in principle, to be part of the Western world".[3] Chiodi's perspective is that for a nation which wishes to be accepted as a modern nation in the Western world, the continuing existence of the Mayan languages and cultures was and still is perceived by many Guatemalans as a failure to achieve the levels of modernization which would make it a member of the larger community of developed nations. Chiodi (1990:208) cites Tumin (without bibliographic reference) expressing a similarly pessimistic conclusion when he states:

> *La futura transculturación será una calle de una sola vía, a lo largo de la cual la cultura indígena desaparecerá lentamente del paisaje. En otras palabras, es escasa la esperanza, si hay alguna, de que surja una unidad nacional que mezcle los "mejores" elementos de los dos principales patrones culturales que existen ahora en Guatemala.*

> The future transculturation will be a one-way street, along which the Indian culture will slowly disappear from the scene. In other words, there is little hope, if any, that a national unity will emerge which will mix the "best" elements of the two principal cultural patterns that now exist in Guatemala. (my translation)

Whether so cynical a view is justified or not, the IIN, particularly after the political changes that took place in 1954, has always been hamstrung in its efforts to benefit the Mayans by lack of funds, personnel, and administrative priorities. Chiodi (1990:passim) points out that in spite of the fact that Mayans represent a majority of the population in Guatemala, neither the IIN, the *Seminario de Integración Social,* an agency similarly dedicated to the "social integration" of the Guatemalan population, nor even the state-funded (though autonomous) Universidad de San Carlos, have had any kind of effective programs to deal with or even study Mayan affairs. Although as early as 1935 there were efforts to begin programs to

---

[3]My translation of *la mancha del país, el pecado original de una nación que anhela -así por principio- a sentirse parte del mundo occidental.*

teach Spanish to Mayan children, official recognition of this process came in 1945 when President Arévalo inaugurated a congress for Mayan teachers. In 1949 the first National Linguistic Congress was held at which alphabets for the Mayan languages were approved and the principles for future orthography design were laid down. These principles were based on an ideology of assimilation in which it was felt that the highest good could be achieved if the Mayan populations acquired Spanish and were facilitated in that acquisition by the orthographies used to represent their own languages. Stewart (1984:25) notes that the first Linguistic Congress was called "in order to standardize the graphemic representations of the various languages." The standard to which these "standardized" alphabets were to adhere was Spanish. (See Lewis 1993.)

Among the early attempts at castilianization was a pre-primary program of instruction which used only monolingual Spanish-speaking teachers. This program was aimed at teaching the children enough of the Spanish language so that they could begin their elementary education using the official language. The program has been characterized as a failure at least in part because of its use only of Spanish as the medium of instruction (Richards 1989:98). To remedy this situation the program was re-instituted in 1965 as a bilingual program, and the teachers were instructed in the use of bilingual methodology. The staff of this program were themselves bilinguals and were, at least in theory, assigned to a school located in their own language area. The goals of this program included castilianization of the children and the teaching of reading and writing. Stewart (1984:28) states, "The program has been a qualified success" and cites a study which shows that students who have been through the program are more successful than those who have not. Morren (1988:354) also comments, "Using bilingual promoters, who usually are native speakers of the Mayan vernacular and speak Spanish as a second language and therefore are culturally and linguistically perceived as 'insiders' by the target community, proved to be much more successful than anything previously attempted."

During the military regimes beginning in 1954, the reforms of all types were neglected or suppressed and replaced by apathy and indifference (Stewart 1984:23). The success of the bilingual castilianization program, however, could not be ignored. In 1980 an experimental bilingual education project was begun. This project went well beyond the castilianization goals of the previous programs and created fully bilingual curricula for the early elementary grades in the four major Mayan languages, Quiché, Mam, Cakchiquel, and K'ekchí'. "The evaluation results showed that students attending the pilot schools aggregately demonstrated lower dropout

## 1.4 The period of indigenismo

and higher promotion rates, higher reading scores, and higher achievement scores in the subject areas of mathematics, social sciences, and natural sciences" (Richards 1989:100 reporting from Troike 1984).

The success of this experimental project led to the formal institutionalization of bilingual education as a "program" of the Guatemalan Ministry of Education in 1984. Also, the rewritten Constitution of 1985 states: "the intention to recognize, respect and promote the multicultural and plurilinguistic nature of Guatemalan society and, furthermore, mandate[s] that in communities that have a majority population of Mayan-language speakers schooling should be imparted bilingually" (Richards 1989:101). This marks a change in philosophy from the purely assimilationist goals of the previous programs.

From the days of the colonists to the period of independence and on into more recent times, in spite of changes in form, there have been few changes in substance for the indigenous peoples of Guatemala. Until the late 1940s, Jones' observation held true:

> To a remarkable degree the Indians continue a people apart, little touched by the changes going on around them and caring even less about adopting the features of modern life which have come to their doors. Their attitude toward the ladinos is still one of aloofness, and the ladinos, notwithstanding gestures toward incorporating them in the nation, have had therein little success and it seems little real desire to bring it about. (Jones 1940/66:312)

The introduction of *indigenismo,* however, and the more recent amplifications of the recognition of Mayans and Mayan languages and cultures as being a valued part of Guatemala's cultural heritage have led to a breaking down of the walls between ladino and Mayan.

### 1.5 Post-*indigenismo*

The change in philosophy reflected in the Constitution of the Republic, revised in 1985, the Literacy Law of 1986 (Congreso de la República de Guatemala, 1986), the 1987 alphabet reform (Congreso de la República de Guatemala, 1987), and the creation of the Mayan Language Academy in 1990 all came about as the result of a political coup d'état. Though some might see the military coup of 1982 as just more of the same military regime infighting for power, the change in government which placed Brigadier General Efraín Rios Montt in the Presidential Palace was the culmination of the fundamental dissatisfaction of a generation of younger Guatemalans, even those within the military, with the military's apathetic approach to social policy. Rios Montt was himself replaced by yet another general, Oscar Humberto Mejía Victores in 1983, but the process of democratization had begun and continued on to its conclusion with the democratic election of a civilian government. Though military hegemony remained for several more years and continues to have a strong influence on the civilian governments that have been elected, Guatemala was once more on a path leading to renewed enthusiasm for social policies which would attempt to redress the inequalities in Guatemalan society.

The legislative changes which have resulted undoubtedly mark the beginning of a fourth period in language policy for Guatemala. While still in its infancy, the defining features of this new period can be identified by a *de jure* recognition of the role of Mayans as full and equal participants in Guatemalan society and the assumption by the Mayans of their rights and responsibilities to be fully self-determining in regard to matters dealing with their language and culture.

Undoubtedly, the spawning ground for this emergence of Mayan nationalism has been the access to education and the benefits of modern society granted to Mayans as a result of the policies of *indigenismo*. Where in the past Mayans had been virtually locked out of the educational and economic systems (except as manual laborers), *indigenismo* and the castilianization programs have enabled a few, but enough, Mayans to be successful in gaining not just an elementary education but in some cases education through the tertiary level both in Guatemalan and foreign universities. Though Spanish (and English or French) have become the languages used by these Mayans for education, they have not been so far removed from their roots that they have forgotten about their native languages, though indeed many no longer speak them. In many cases, under the influence of university training, many educated Mayans have returned to their homes with a strong conviction that their culture and language needs to be preserved. This proto-elite, born out of the "kindness" of *indigenismo,* has now become the vanguard for a strongly vocal Mayan nationalist movement which uses Mayan languages and language policy as the symbol of its struggle.

A second source of this growing nationalism is the growing pressure from international social policy to favor pluralism and to disfavor monoculturism. Multilingualism and multiculturalism are now widely seen as resources and strengths. International organizations (and funders of aid programs) favor policies which will foster multilingualism and the self-determination of ethnic minorities. Under this influence, Guatemalan policy makers, some of whom are Mayans, are now also adopting more

## 1.5 Post-indigenismo

open and pluralistic policies than have ever been seen in the history of Guatemala.

If the policy of *indigenismo* was the ideology which provided access for Mayans to the benefits of the ladino culture and economy, the programs of *indigenismo* and PRONEBI, the bilingual education program, have been the instruments in bringing about access for Mayan children to education and access for educated Mayans to positions where they can be influential in the formation of policy. Richards (1989:107) observes that the textbook writers of PRONEBI were the ones who "provided the organizational impetus to form an Academy of Mayan Languages". The establishment of a Mayan elite has been the most important development in the process of moving from an ethnic movement to a full-blown ethnic nationalism.

The changes instituted in the 1940s constitute a watershed for the Mayans and were the first real changes in social policy since the arrival of the Spanish Conquerors more than four hundred years earlier. Those changes made it possible for Mayans to be successful in receiving an education. Though the numbers are not large, a sufficient number of Mayans have been able to achieve success in Spanish-dominated society. These examples of success have been the catalysts that have increased the momentum of ladinoization which, though continuous from the arrival of the Spaniards, had never before been a serious threat to Mayan identity and solidarity. Now, however, many scholars and many Mayans themselves are alarmed at the rate at which younger Mayans, with the encouragement of their parents in many cases, are abandoning their traditional ways and languages in order to participate more fully in what until now were not perceived as advantages of the ladino lifestyle. This change in perception is the result of a shift in identity, which is the result of the widespread social changes which began with the shift to a policy of *indigenismo*.

Modern-day Mayans are quiet, gentle, friendly people in spite of their warrior forebears. They have developed to perfection the art of survival through passivity. Their skills were also well developed for maintaining cultural identity in the face of considerable contact with outsiders. These skills served them well in their contact with other Mayans and when confronted by the Spanish invaders. They have continued to serve them well through the postconquest period in the face of a hostile and dominant ladino society. The passive resistance of Mayans to all attempts from the conquerors to get them to be productive laborers was one of the major frustrations to the authorities of both the colonial period and the period of independence. Only when confronted with a less hostile adversary has the strategy of passivity proven to be less effective in maintaining Mayan solidarity.

Another important factor to be taken into account is the development of the *municipio* as the basic sociopolitical unit of Mayan society. These town centers provided the social cohesion so that the people of each *municipio* would become a separate ethnicity with their own lore and traditions, their own religious cults, and their own distinctive dress. Under the oppressive policies of the colony and the young republic, these ethnicities could harden their boundaries, reenforce their own value systems, and passively resist the impossible demands placed upon them to assimilate.

Under the policies of the social reformers, more and more young people began to abandon the unifying and contrastive distinctives of their ethnicity and acquired education and position in the dominant society. This constitutes a basic shift in values and identity which now accepts what had been denied by the Mayan ethnicities since the end of the colonial period: ladino education has value, ladino occupations are valid, and a person can find value and be successful through the mechanisms of ladino society.

This newly begun fourth period of social and language history in Guatemala is characterized by efforts to retain and maintain Mayan identity and language in the face of this identity shift. The focus of this new movement, however, is no longer centered on the maintenance of distinctive, *municipio*-based, ethnicities, but rather on the creation and promotion of a larger regionally based Mayan nationalism. Where the local ethnicities were solidarity (and thereby, survival) oriented, Mayan nationalism is power (and revitalization) oriented. Mayan culture is being remade under the categories of a new ladinoized identity.

This brings us back then to the final important characteristic of Guatemalan social history, one perhaps even more basic than either of the first two, i.e., the opposition between Mayan and ladino. The widely held view is that since the Conquest there have been two separate societies co-existing in Guatemala—distinct, disconnected, unintegrated. The focus of much government planning and practice from the Conquest onwards was on achieving an integration of the two, albeit by means of the extermination of the "inferior" Mayan cultures. The society of Guatemala could also be viewed as a continuum rather than as two distinct and separate societies. Mayan cultural behaviors and ladino cultural behaviors represent the extremes of status at either end of this continuum. The two societies have indeed become integrated with each maintaining itself intact in terms of form. The meaning attached to those forms, however, have been those assigned by the conquerors. Indigenous culture is lower status and ladino culture is higher status. What is revolutionary about the rise of Mayan nationalism is the rejection of the Spanish-imposed ideology and the promulgation of a new ideology

## 1.5 Post-indigenismo

which attempts to redefine certain aspects of Mayan culture as having greater value in the overall social system. This revolution, however, still retains ladino values as the standard by which the meaning of cultural behaviors is determined.

The two most recent periods in language policy in Guatemala are those in which the greatest amount of change has taken place since the Conquest. As we consider the data on modern-day language use in seven K'iche' communities, we will see how important these key characteristics are to the analysis of the interplay between social change, identity shift, and language shift.

# 2

# Maintenance and Shift of Language and Identity in K'iche' Communities

In the introduction, I examined the historical developments which have led to the current language situation in Guatemala, and I alluded to the role of social and political changes in bringing about the linguistic changes which are now occurring. In this chapter, after placing the topic of language use and language contact in the context of research on bilingualism, I examine some of the threads of research relating to language and identity and to language shift and identity shift. In particular, I focus on the work of Joshua Fishman, who has approached the topic from the perspective of the sociology of language. I also focus on the work of Howard Giles and his colleagues who approached the topic from the perspective of social psychology, and elaborated ethnolinguistic vitality theory. Finally, I attempt to synthesize these approaches and make application of the theory to the investigation of language and identity shift in the K'iche' situation.

### 2.1–2.3 Bilingualism, language contact, and language choice

The literature on bilingualism and language choice is large and cannot be adequately summarized here except in the most cursory way. Romaine (1989:8) cites Mackey (1968:554) to point out that bilingualism is not so much a matter of language itself, i.e., the linguistic codes, as it is a matter of the use of those linguistic codes. Understanding the relationship between bilingualism and individual and societal language choice is of primary importance, as well as the effect of the contact of two linguistic groups on each other in their language use patterns.

## 2.1 Bilingualism and language shift

Fasold (1984:216) notes, "bilingualism is not a sufficient condition for [language] shift, although it may be a necessary one." The acquisition of a second language can be seen as the acquisition of domains of use for that language by an individual. This represents not only a change in the linguistic competence of the individual but also a change in the social meaning of the use of that language for that individual in that society. Individuals make use of all of the varieties of language within their linguistic repertoire in intricate and complex ways that are determined by a number of interrelated and overlapping considerations. Fasold (1984:213) makes the observation, "Language shift and, the other side of the coin, language maintenance are really the long-term, collective results of [individual] language choice." Thus, societal bilingualism is very much related to bilingualism in the individual, and societal choices of language can be seen to be influenced by many of the same factors that affect individual language choice.

## 2.2 The analysis of language choice

Herman (1961) hypothesized that language choice is affected by three factors which overlap and have varying potency in affecting a speaker's choice of linguistic code in any situation. They are (1) personal needs, (2) the immediate situation, and (3) the background situation.

Herman subsumes under personal needs the degree of comfort one feels in using a particular language as well as pressure placed on a speaker by the group. The immediate and the larger background situation are two levels of situational forces. The immediate situation takes into account the face-to-face demands of a particular situation. The background situation deals with other groups and larger societal concerns that are not immediately apparent in any given situation. While the dynamics of language choice identified by Herman are true of individuals making real-time language-use decisions, they can be extended as well to entire groups. They can also be shown to be at work in the long-term language maintenance and shift decisions of an entire cultural group.

## 2.3 Bilingualism and diglossia

In a considerable extension and refinement of the term DIGLOSSIA, first proposed by Ferguson (1959), Fishman (1967) made the distinction between BILINGUALISM, the use of two or more languages by an individual, and diglossia, the use of two or more languages within a society. Fishman used the term diglossia to refer not only to the use of multiple languages at the societal level, but more importantly, to the compartmentalization of roles or functions for each of the languages (see Fasold 1984).

Broad diglossia exists in a society when each of the linguistic varieties is assigned a specific role or is used for a delimited set of functions. Fishman proposed that multilingual (i.e., language contact) situations can be characterized by the logical combinations of the presence or absence of bilingualism (an individual phenomenon) and diglossia (a societal phenomenon). Fishman (1967, 1968/1972) recognized that the existence of bilingualism and diglossia is the direct result of a variety of nonlinguistic factors. While the nonlinguistic factors may vary from situation to situation, individuals and social groups respond to them by assuming a specific sociopsychological orientation, an identity. Paulston (1987) has analyzed the changes in the self-perception of social groups in terms of these nonlinguistic factors showing that language maintenance can be quite directly related to group self-perceptions.

When language groups are in contact with one another, investigators would like to be able to predict the outcome of such contact situations. Fishman (1967, 1986) described the potential outcomes of the various kinds of situations which result in language contact and makes predictions about expected language maintenance results for each of the quadrants in the matrix produced by the interplay of bilingualism and diglossia. The four possible combinations are (1) both diglossia and bilingualism, (2) bilingualism without diglossia, (3) diglossia without bilingualism, and (4) neither diglossia nor bilingualism. For each situation Fishman posits a degree of stability based on the interplay of individual bilingualism (or its absence) and societal diglossia (or its absence).

In situations where there is both diglossia and bilingualism there are individuals who use more than one language or variety, and there is societal compartmentalization of the roles for each of the varieties that the members of that society use. This tight compartmentalization of roles maintains the use of each language variety. This sociological perspective complements what investigators of bilingualism have also observed: "Theories of bilingualism thus argue that there must be a series of areas of life in which one language, for bilingual speakers, is the only accepted medium of communication" (McAllister 1984:321). It is not compartmentalization alone, but also access to the various roles assigned to each linguistic variety which characterizes a society in which both diglossia and bilingualism occur. If a large segment of the population is denied access to the roles in society wherein the use of a particular variety is appropriate, that segment will not acquire proficiency in the variety associated with those roles. A society that does not provide the means for individuals to acquire proficiency in a second language cannot be considered a society where there is both diglossia and bilingualism.

In the second possibility, where there is diglossia but not bilingualism, there exist two or more linguistic varieties within the society but relatively few people who speak both. Frequently, this is the kind of situation where two or more ethnolinguistic groups have come to be united within political boundaries. The interaction between the groups is largely by means of interpreters. With access denied to the prestige roles in society, the masses have neither adequate means nor adequate motivation for bilingualism. Here the compartmentalization of roles is so strong that the boundaries between the groups become impassable. Thus, the factors that ensure diglossia inhibit bilingualism. Fishman predicts that such societies are likely to experience severe strains centered around language as social patterns are altered by the forces of industrialization, universal education and literacy, modernization, and democratization with their emphasis on the participation of the masses in more areas of society.

The third possible situation is that of bilingualism without diglossia. It exists where there are individuals who use more than one linguistic variety but where there are no societal norms as to which language is appropriate to use with which interlocutor concerning which topics, under what circumstances. Fishman states that this situation will only occur under circumstances accompanying "rapid social change, great social unrest,...widespread abandonment of earlier norms before the consolidation of new ones" (Fishman 1968/1972:145). Furthermore, it seems that in this kind of situation bilingualism is acquired at an early age and in the home and neighborhood. The variety brought home from work and school is acquired as a second language. In these situations societal institutions tend to promote monolingualism in the second language. Thus, industrialization and modernization will further motivate members of the society to abandon their traditional sociocultural patterns in order to acquire the patterns (and the language) of the institutions which control the means of production. Fishman (1968/1972:149) suggests that under these unstable conditions language interference as well as language shift and language loss should be an expected outcome. The result is that "the language or variety which is

## 2.3 Bilingualism and diglossia

fortunate enough to be associated with the predominant drift of social forces tends to displace the others" (Fishman 1968/1972:149).

The fourth situation described by Fishman's framework is that in which neither diglossia nor bilingualism is present. Such situations are extremely rare, if they exist at all. In order for there to be no role compartmentalization (diglossia), the speech community would have to be one in which no significance was attached to differences in linguistic varieties.

## 2.4–2.8 Ethnocultural identity and language

Just as the literature on bilingualism and language contact phenomena is large, so there is an equally large literature which examines the relationship of ethnic identity to language from a variety of disciplinary perspectives. Where linguists have attempted to examine the effect of ethnic diversity on language, sociologists, anthropologists, and social psychologists have looked at the effect on society of multilingualism as a marker of ethnic diversity. Sociologists and other social scientists have attempted to describe and refine the definition of ethnicity and group identity[4] and to identify the dynamics of situations where distinct ethnic groups come into contact with each other.[5] Sociologists of language and linguistic anthropologists have attempted to examine the relationship between language and identity.[6]

## 2.4 Ethnicity and language

The study of ethnicity and ethnic identity has resulted in there being two approaches to the definition of ethnicity. These two approaches, identified as objectivist and subjectivist by Ross (1979) differ, among other things, over what they see as the relationship of language to ethnicity.

**2.4.1 The objectivist view.** "Objectivists...view language as one of the primary defining characteristics of ethnic identity" (Ross 1979:3). The connection between ethnic identity and language choice can be seen as a means of using language to symbolize an identity. Pool (1979) states

---

[4]E.g., Lieberson 1961; Fishman 1965; Tajfel 1981, 1982; Paulston 1987.
[5]E.g., Banton 1983; Barth 1969/70; Grassi 1977; Inglehart 1972; Lieberson 1970; Tajfel 1978, 1981, 1982; Lukens 1979; Hidalgo 1986.
[6]E.g., Fishman 1965, 1977, 1986, 1989; Lieberson 1970; Lamy 1979; Eastman 1981; Milroy 1982; Edwards 1985; Fishman 1986; Gudykunst 1988.

rather clearly the issues involved in the relationship between ethnic identity and language as a marker of identity.

> Let us suppose that in a certain society there are several groups of people who agree on the question of who belongs to which group. In addition to this societal identity consensus, let us further suppose that the members of each group normally speak a language peculiar to that group alone or at least differentiating that group from each of the others in that society. In such a society, what happens to someone whose language or identity changes? (Pool 1979:6)

From this perspective the connection between language and identity seems rather obvious and straightforward when viewed as a static phenomenon. Hispanics are those who speak Spanish, Americans are those who speak an American variety of English, K'iche's are those who speak K'iche', and so forth. But as Pool's question indicates, the connection between language and identity is a dynamic one. What of the child of Hispanic parents who does not speak Spanish, or the American-born child of Australian parents and countless other such situations where the circumstances are in transition or on the fringe? From the macro-sociolinguistic perspective, what of whole societies which are experiencing such changes of language or identity or both?

Few societies, in fact, are static. In almost all cases, identity groups are in contact with others and in many cases overlap. Individuals are rarely members of a single group. Even in monolingual situations, class, age, or gender may serve to stratify the society. A young K'iche' man will have multiple group memberships—as a youth, as a male, as a K'iche', as a Guatemalan—which overlap and interact.

Some of the intersecting and overlapping identity roles available to the group may have other linguistic codes associated with them. Pool points out that in some cases the identity may have not just one associated language but also a second (or third) language as well. "Identity is related to how well a person knows another language, not just which language he mainly speaks" (Pool 1979:15).

The objectivist view sees language as being one of the crucial distinctive cultural behaviors out of which the sense of group identity grows.

Combs (1977), an anthropologist, sees the language choice made by a social group as being related to a basic set of core values which he calls the "inner layer" of the culture. "The inner layer is the heart of the culture, that which makes it distinct from others, and is peculiar to that people" (Combs 1977:225). Inner layer features of a culture are the basic motivating values of a group of people, are more difficult to observe, and are more resistant to change. Language is part of the basic core of identity and not part of the more easily disposable outer layer features of culture such as types of housing, clothing styles, means of subsistence, and principal foods. "The 'outer layer' of the culture is mainly of an adaptive nature, and relates to physical environment" (Combs 1977:225). Outer layer features are more readily observable and are "generally the most expedient adaptations to the physical environment" (Combs 1977:226). Combs asserts that a society which is changing its core values, e.g., kinship system, ceremonial system, political/power system, cosmology, and/or language is a society which is less stable than one which is simply making adjustments to meet a changing physical environment. Changes which affect the inner layer features, particularly to the degree that they are embraced by younger people or at least not resisted by the elders can be indicators of a basic shift in the culture itself, an identity shift. If the objectivist view is correct, language shift is an indicator of such an identity shift.

**2.4.2 The subjectivist view.** The subjectivist view of ethnic identity sees the origin of identity not in the differing cultural behaviors, but in a more basic sense of "groupness" which is the source of the differentiation in behavior. According to this view, the external forms which serve unifying and separatist functions (Garvin 1956) are changeable or even disposable. They serve as symbols of the more basic group feeling. Language serves as a marker of an individual's ethnic identity whether or not the individual has competence in the language or even regularly uses it. From the subjectivist point of view, it is the basic sense of ethnic identification which is important and which may acquire different representations in cultural and linguistic behavior over time. The link between language use and ethnic identity, while not causal as in the objectivist view, is still strong and important.

Subjectivists view language shift as only one of many possible changes in overt behavior which may or may not indicate a more radical change in the core of the ethnocultural identity. Objectivists, on the other hand, see a language shift as a radical change in the core identity of the ethnoculture. It can be inferred then that a change in language use can be related to an underlying change in identity for the objectivist but as a change in the value or meaning given to the use of the languages in question for the subjectivist. When a group "loses" a language, it does not necessarily lose its identity, its sense of being a group, but the change in language is certainly an indicator of a change in the way the group wishes to relate to its physical and social environment. The fact that a group might feel a need to change its associated language is certainly evidence that there have been changes in the environment which require new survival or advancement strategies to be developed.

## 2.5 The language-in-culture nexus

The difficulty with both the objectivist and subjectivist views of ethnic identity is that they attempt to define the relationship between language and culture in a very static and monoplex way. Fishman (1991) clarifies this oversimplification by examining language shift and its relationship to identity to determine the best strategies for reversing the language (and culture) shift. He emphasizes that language and culture are inextricably intertwined using the term "language-in-culture nexus" to refer to not just language itself but the roles and meaning of the use of a language variety within a given cultural system. While it may be theoretically or conceptually helpful to separate language from culture, they are not completely distinct phenomena and cannot be teased apart from each other without doing damage to the data. Fishman describes three major ways in which languages are connected to ethnocultures, i.e., indexically, symbolically, and in a part/whole fashion (Fishman 1991:20).

The first of these, the indexical linkage, is the inextricable connection between the words of the language and the things of the culture. While a culture can be relinguified with a new linguistic code, the process "exacts a very substantial cost in time, effort, and attrition before fully adequate new lexical associations, fully adequate new verbal-cultural replacements or substitutions, and fully adequate ethnolinguistic symbolic structures and identities are fashioned" (Fishman 1991:26).

Language is also symbolically linked to culture, that is, the language and the culture come to "stand for each other in the minds of the insiders and of outsiders too" (Fishman 1991:22). Thus, the language of a culture comes to have the prestige, or lack thereof, of the culture itself. If a culture is despised, so is its language. If a culture is esteemed, so is its language. Furthermore, the language of a culture that is oppressed comes to be associated with not only the stereotypical characteristics of that culture but with the characteristics of the state of being oppressed. No matter what the characteristics of the culture in objective terms, if it is subjectively perceived to be lacking in prestige, or modernity, or usefulness, the language with which it is associated will similarly be perceived as embarrassing, old-fashioned, or impractical.

The third way in which language and culture are linked is in a part/whole relationship. Language and culture are, in part, the same thing. A culture without a language is only a partial culture and a language without a culture is impoverished, at best. "So much of any culture is primarily verbally constituted: its songs and its prayers, its laws and its proverbs, its tales and its greetings, its curses and its blessings, its philosophy, its history and its teachings, and on and on, encompassing almost all of non-material culture" (Fishman 1991:24). Sociolinguistics, particularly the ethnography of speaking, is dedicated to describing and understanding the ways in which language is culture.

## 2.6 Language and culture continuity

The connection between language and culture is not straightforward. Fishman makes the contrast between identity continuity and ethnocultural continuity. Identity, the sense of being a group, can be maintained even after the language traditionally associated with that group has been abandoned and even after the core content of the ethnoculture has been radically changed. Ethnocultural continuity is less easily maintained, however, since linguistic discontinuity results in great cultural disruption and dislocation. The difference between these two can be likened to the difference between organic continuity and genetic mutation. In a living organism cells are continuously dying and being replaced, yet the organism does not change in its essential nature. Technically, it has changed from its original form since none of its original organic material may still be present, but it is still considered to be the same organism it always was. When a mutation takes place, however, the new cells which replace the dead ones are genetically different and the organism undergoes a change in its essential nature. In just this way, ethnocultural continuity can be seen as organic continuity, while identity continuity (with loss of ethnocultural continuity) parallels the process of mutation.

Fishman identifies several dimensions along which the interpenetration of language and culture can be measured in order to determine if language shift is actually occurring. Included among these are (1) the differentiation between speaking, reading, and writing; (2) the connection between attitude, volition, competence, and performance; and (3) a description of the sociocultural contexts and role relations in which a language is being used.

Each of these dimensions provides insights into patterns of language use. If a language is used for literary purposes it has a hardier profile than a language which can be understood by a sizable population but is rarely spoken. Similarly, a language which is spoken willingly by speakers with an intact competence in the language is in a stronger position than a language where people may have some level of competence but no willingness to use the language, or where, in spite of some remnants of linguistic competence, there are simply no culturally appropriate opportunities for linguistic performance.

The third category, that of sociocultural contexts and role relations is discussed more fully since it is the area of principal focus of this study of language use among the K'iche' of Guatemala and provides the rationale for the data gathering methodology which was adopted. Sociocultural contexts are "...all of the interactions that are rather unambiguously related (topically and situationally) to one or another of the major institutions of society: e.g., the family, the work sphere, education, religion, entertainment and the mass media, the political party, the government, etc. These are referred to as 'domains' " (Fishman 1991:44). Role relations are the relationships between participants in interactions such as husband-wife, parent-child, and employer-employee. Various role relations are more commonly associated with certain sociocultural contexts (domains) and are characterized by different status levels for each of the participants. The measurement of these factors is crucial to the study of language shift. "It is exactly such variation, both from person to person and from situation to situation for the same person, that must ultimately be sketched out, across a large and representative sample of persons and, optimally, for two periods in time (but minimally for one), if the L[anguage] S[hift] picture...is to be clarified" (Fishman 1991:45).

## 2.7 Causes of language and culture shift

More to the point, Fishman describes a number of factors which contribute to the motivation for language-in-culture shift. "The location of shift in the total 'sociocultural space' of a speech community is an indication of just where the stresses and strains of cross-cultural contact have eroded the ability of the smaller and weaker to withstand the stronger and larger" (Fishman 1991:55).

Government policy is one area where pressure can be exerted to promote language shift. The historical pattern in Guatemala of repression and extermination was not particularly effective and has been reversed in this century under the worldwide trend toward multiculturalism. Even under modern totalitarian regimes, language repression has not been reinstated primarily because of the pressure of world opinion.

More important factors which Fishman identifies as contributing to language shift are: physical and demographic, social and cultural dislocations, all of which work in various ways to erode the boundaries of the minority group and make it susceptible to language shift.

Physical and demographic dislocation refers to population transfer. Such population transfer can be brought about through natural disasters (famines, earthquakes, floods), warfare, genocide, invasions, loss of natural resources (deforestation, soil exhaustion, erosion, toxic contamination), and through economic pressures brought about by industrialization and modernization.

Social dislocation refers to the inequalities experienced by members of ethnolinguistic minority groups who are frequently disadvantaged in terms of education and economic opportunity. Such social dislocation, says Fishman, is commonly marked by "briefer school attendance and by lower income, by lower literacy in any language and by poverty, by lack of social graces as defined by the majority population, and by lack of conveniences of everyday life that are so common among the majority population" (Fishman 1991:59). The result of such a situation is that the rewards of society are only available through the language and culture of the majority group. Shift to the majority language (and culture) is rewarded. Maintenance of the minority language and culture is not.

Cultural dislocation is the destruction of the means of maintaining a distinct ethnolinguistic identity. This may be through harsh governmental prohibitions but more frequently occurs in more subtle ways through the processes of modernization and democratization. Where the majority rules, the minority will always be disadvantaged. Unless there are safeguards which protect the language-in-culture rights of the minority, cultural dislocation will further erode the vitality of minority ethnolinguistic groups.

## 2.8 Summary

The goal of research into ethnic identity and language must not be to determine a single identity for a group, but rather to determine which of the multiple identities available to a group is most salient for that group under what circumstances, and to identify the language which is associated with that identity. From either the objectivist or the subjectivist point of view, language shift is an indicator of a consciousness that adjustments need to be made to fit a changed or changing environment. Depending on the theoretical perspective taken, these adjustments can be viewed as either a change in the core of the culture, or as a simple matter of expediency. Language shift can be identified by (1) the differential in usage of a language between speaking, reading, and writing, (2) the degree of willingness (volition/attitude) and ability (competence/performance) to use the language, and (3) a description of the sociocultural contexts and role relations in which a language is being used. Furthermore, an identification of any of the sources of physical, demographic, social, or cultural dislocation can be of predictive value in estimating the vitality of an ethnolinguistic group.

## 2.9–2.12 Ethnolinguistic vitality theory

The work of Howard Giles, Richard Bourhis, and their colleagues is a well-developed inquiry into the ethnolinguistic identity factors that influence a group's resistance to language shift. Working from the perspective of social psychology, these investigators begin, not by looking at the dynamics of group relationships as do sociologists, but with a careful, and often experiment-based, investigation of the dynamics of individual contact situations. From the data about individual behavior, extrapolations are made to group behavior which is then empirically investigated as well. As a result, social psychologists tend to have less to say specifically about language maintenance or shift than about the language use patterns of individuals. The theory has been refined from earlier work dealing with Accommodation Theory, which demonstrated the tendency of individuals to either converge or diverge in their linguistic behavior, to more recent work which presents a more comprehensive theory of group behavior and which deals more directly with language maintenance or shift as the group analogs of individual divergence and convergence.

Ethnolinguistic Identity Theory (EIT) has its roots in Social Identity Theory developed by Henri Tajfel and his colleagues. This approach emphasizes the notion that individuals perceive themselves as being members of a group and define their social identity in terms of their group membership(s). Each individual attempts to maintain (or achieve) a positive social identity by emphasizing the characteristics of their group which will be evaluated positively. Language is an obvious group characteristic and the in-group/out-group distinction is an important factor in affecting how individuals use their language repertoires. The relative evaluation of the in-group vis-à-vis the out-group is another way of talking about ethnolinguistic vitality.

Ethnolinguistic vitality is a broad concept which includes social, cultural, economic, political, and linguistic factors as a means of estimating the relative robustness of an ethnic group's identity in situations where the group is in frequent contact with another group or groups. Giles et al. (1977) cited in Bourhis, Giles, and Rosenthal (1981:145–146) have defined vitality as "that which makes a group likely to behave as a distinctive and active collective entity in intergroup situations." From the subjectivist point of view, EIT can be seen as an attempt to measure the inner, less-observable sense of group identity shared by the members of an ethnic collectivity using external, observable cultural behaviors. It provides an index of the sense of groupness which is called ethnic identity. Implicit in this is the assumption that there is a scale of increasing (or decreasing) ethnic strength which can be used to measure the sociocultural health of ethnic groups. It also recognizes the multiple group memberships which are possible for an individual and is an attempt to measure the relative strength of an individual's attachment to those competing identities and to identify the most salient group focus.

The most notable difference between the Ethnolinguistic Identity Theory presented by Giles and Johnson (1987) and earlier models of EIT is the addition of subjective vitality factors to supplement the objective indicators of vitality identified in the earlier work. The most recent restatement of the theory (Giles 1991) integrates data from other disciplines with EIT. It then arrives at a more precise specification of the interrelationships between the various factors and attempts to give the theory more predictive power in terms of language contact outcomes.

EIT attempts to account for the factors which influence the maintenance of language in contact situations from the perspective of social psychology. It is useful in integrating and identifying the parameters of ethnolinguistic contact which are significant in the study of language maintenance and also provides a means of making connections and parallels with the work of Paulston (1987), Milroy (1980), and Lepage and Tabouret-Keller (1985).

Giles and Johnson (1987) take a bottom-up approach by looking at microlevel phenomena involving individual reactions to speech contact situations. They state, "This theory was originally formulated to address the issue of who in an ethnic group uses what language strategy, when, and why, in interethnic encounters" (Giles 1987:69). These observations provide insights into the factors which motivate individuals to either maintain their language through divergent speech behaviors or to shift through convergent speech patterns.

The factors affecting language contact outcomes can be categorized in a variety of ways. EIT makes a primary distinction between objective ethnolinguistic vitality and subjective ethnolinguistic vitality. Objective factors are those concerned with the measurement of structural variables in the society which could influence the vitality of an ethnolinguistic group. They include environmental factors such as demographic factors, social-structural factors, and political-legal factors,[7] as well as intergroup dynamics such as access to language acquisition, sociocultural status, cultural core values, and interactional norms.

Subjective factors are those concerned with the perceptions of the members of a group regarding their own group's relative strength and prestige in relation to another group with which they have contact. Such perceptions affect the outcome of language and culture contact situations. The subjective perceptions of both the in-group and the out-group are important.

## 2.9 Objective ethnolinguistic vitality

Three general categories of objective vitality factors have been identified: demographic, institutional support, and status factors. They correspond well with Fishman's major language-shift-supporting areas of dislocation: physical/demographic, cultural, and social. These broad categorizations take into account sociostructural factors relating to group size and distribution, political and economic dominance, institutional support, boundary maintenance, and relative status and prestige.

**2.9.1 Demographic factors.** The demographic factors include the size and distribution of the contact groups. Obviously, a small group might be expected to have a more difficult time maintaining its identity and language when confronted with a larger, more powerful prestigious group. Two groups of more or less equal size and prestige are more likely to come to a standoff in a contact situation.

Giles, Bourhis, and Taylor (1977) identified eight subcomponents of demographics which are divided between two larger subcategories: group distribution and group numbers. Group distribution entails three subcomponents: (1) national territory, (2) group concentration, and (3) group proportion. National territory "is related to the notion of ancestral homeland" (Giles 1977:312). Group concentration deals with the relative population density of a group since "widespread diffusion of minority group members as individuals may discourage group solidarity" (Giles 1977:313). Group proportion refers to the number of speakers "belonging to the ethnolinguistic in-group compared with that belonging to the relevant out-group..." (Giles 1977:313). A lower proportion is likely to lead to lower ethnolinguistic vitality than a higher one.

---

[7]Giles, Coupland, Williams, and Leets (1991) while recognizing the threads of research begun by Giles and Bourhis, also trace the development of EIT from the work of de Vries (1984) where these terms are used to describe what are referred to by the others as objective vitality factors.

## 2.9 Objective ethnolinguistic vitality

Group number factors include five subcomponents: (1) absolute numbers, (2) birth rate, (3) mixed marriages, (4) immigration, and (5) emigration. The relationship of each of these to ethnolinguistic vitality is straightforward. A group with one million speakers is likely to be stronger than a group with only three living speakers left. The birth rate of the group in relation to the birth of the out-group can be a predictor of future, vitality. The rate of exogamous marriages can be an indicator of vitality though their significance on language and ethnicity needs to be evaluated carefully. Immigration and emigration patterns need to be evaluated and the significance of the patterns must be interpreted. "Migrants can either contribute to the strengthening of a linguistic subordinate group by assimilating into it, or they can contribute to its weakening by assimilating into the linguistic dominant group" (Giles 1977:315).

Fishman's (1986) sociological analysis notes the differences between the immigrant minority ethnolinguistic group and the conquering minority ethnolinguistic group. Though both are few in numbers relative to the out-group, the balance is changed by the distribution of economic and political advantage. Even so, the outcome is not assured in favor of the group with positive status. (For example, French did not become the dominant language in Great Britain following the Norman invasion, but Spanish did become the language of power in Spanish America).

Fishman also uses the size of the group as an important prerequisite for the existence of a variety of roles and functions for which there will be appropriate language varieties. Without a large and diverse population there will not be sufficient compartmentalization. Without compartmentalization there can be no diglossia. Without diglossia the balance between language varieties is lost and a readjustment of language use patterns is inevitable.

Group size and distribution are not the only factors that need to be considered. Small groups which densely populate a delimited geographic area may be more able to maintain their identity than groups which are widely spread and their individual group members are isolated from other group members. Rural groups who remain intact are more likely to be successful than urban groups which have numerous out-group contacts. In this regard, an ideological orientation towards separation (boundary hardness) facilitates the isolation and the identity maintenance of the group. Examples given by Fishman are the Old Order Amish and the Hasidim (one a rural group, the other urban) who not only through geographical location but more through ideology have maintained their isolation from the larger society and its erosive effects on identity and language.

The work of Milroy (1980) points out the important role of social networks as norm enforcement mechanisms. Where populations are close-knit and involved in dense and multiplex social ties, there is a greater likelihood that language norms will be enforced whether these norms promote maintenance or shift. Widespread population groups, where social ties are neither dense nor multiplex, experience a relaxation in the stringency with which behavioral norms are enforced. When the system of sanctions and rewards is weakened, there is a greater likelihood that behaviors will change as group members respond to the values (and rewards) of the out-group behaviors. Other tensions placed on close-knit groups are urbanization, industrialization, universal education, and other network-erosive phenomena.

**2.9.2 Institutional support factors.** Institutional support factors are those which relate to the kind of recognition and use given to a language or variety in education, media, government, religion, and other societal institutions. Giles, Bourhis, and Taylor (1977:315–316) observe that institutional support can be either formal or informal. Informal support refers to the extent to which a minority group has organized itself in terms of pressure groups, and formal support is that built into the institutional structure itself. The kinds of institutions are many and diverse. It would seem likely that some are more crucial indicators than others, e.g., education. The use and support of a language in education at all levels is not only an objective indicator of vitality but also is influential in the shaping of subjective perceptions of ethnolinguistic vitality. The language of religion is an indicator that also should be considered carefully.

Societal institutions also play a role in situations of bilingualism without diglossia as promoters of monolingualism in the second (dominant) language. The assignment of specific roles or functions for each variety explains how the compartmentalization results in a specific variety being deemed appropriate for education, religious practice, media use, governmental operations, etc. It is these institutions of society which are the essence of what constitutes a domain. They are both the loci of language use and the reinforcers of what is deemed to be the appropriate use of language in any given domain.

The relative prestige of the institution can be influential upon the perceived status of the language variety associated with it and may influence whether or not it is acceptable for a specific function. The roles assigned to a language may be affected by ideological pressures, as is the case in many bilingual education programs with assimilationist ideologies or in vernacular language schools where the purpose is language and identity maintenance. In most cases, institutional support is both a reflection of and a reinforcer of status.

**2.9.3 Status factors.** Status factors are those which deal with the relative prestige of the linguistic variety. The language may be acquired because of compartmentalization of roles where a particular variety is recognized as the High (H) variety and assigned functions which are associated with more prestigious activities. This prestige is derived from the prestige ascribed to the *speakers* of the language, not from any particular linguistic features of the language itself (though many speakers attribute greater beauty, eloquence, simplicity, etc., to H varieties). Fishman (1991) makes reference to this in noting that while a domain of use is related to and defined by societal institutions, it is also characterized by the role relationships that exist between the interlocutors. The prestige of the speakers is related to their economic, social, and political positions. Giles, Bourhis, and Taylor (1977) identified four kinds of prestige: economic, ascribed (social), sociohistorical, and language. Economic status is the degree of participation in and control of the economy that a group has achieved, particularly over its own economic destiny. Social status parallels economic status in many cases and can be defined as group self-esteem which includes subjective vitality factors. It can also be the status ascribed to a group by members of the out-group and therefore also has an objective component. Sociohistorical status refers to the history of the group and the perception of the group past as being more or less "glorious". The presence or absence of historical rallying points or the existence of a history that is perceived as shameful or embarrassing are factors which affect the sociohistorical status of an ethnolinguistic group. Finally, language status refers specifically to the perceived status of the languages in contact. A language which has been standardized may have greater status than one that has not been standardized and thus may contribute to the overall perceived vitality of the group which associates with that language.

## 2.10 Subjective vitality factors

A group's own self-perception of its vitality apart from the objective indicators can be analyzed as subjective vitality factors. In several studies, the importance of this subjective evaluation was greater than that of the objective measures. Thus, groups which perceive themselves to be successful tend to behave in ways which reinforce that success. Groups which perceive themselves to be failing may react by engaging in language and identity maintenance efforts or by shifting to behaviors which conform more to societal out-group norms.

## 2.11 Multiple identities and boundary maintenance

An additional factor is the sharpness of focus of an individual or group on a single, most salient identity from among the multiple, other-group allegiances which exert their influence on the individual or group. If the in-group is relatively homogeneous and there is a considerable focus on a single ethnic identity and allegiance to that identity, the adoption of their linguistic norms is more likely. If, however, group members feel multiple allegiances to other group identities, their identity will be more diffuse, less focused, and they will be less likely to respond to group norm enforcement mechanisms.

Giles and Johnson (1987) explain that groups not only have a core identity but they also have boundaries which they attempt to maintain. Individuals must cross these group boundaries when they pass from one group identity to another. Such perceptions of hard boundaries make ethnic identification easier and make the in-group membership more focused. Although individuals may have multiple group memberships, the development of certain intergroup boundaries into hard and impassable ones makes the group membership associated with those particular boundaries more salient. Other group memberships still exist but become less salient because the distinctions between them are not in focus.

Boundary maintenance factors include the relative hardness or softness of group boundaries as measured by the degree of access to the full range of role repertoires of the society. Both diglossia (compartmentalization) and bilingualism (access) are important contributors to stability in language contact situations. Just as compartmentalization is an important status factor, so access is an important boundary maintenance factor. Where group boundaries are rigid and unyielding, there is likely to be forced language maintenance, but also increased pressures for social change which will break down those boundaries.

Giles and Johnson (1987:72) sum up EIT in five propositions which affect the degree to which an individual (and the number of individuals) in the in-group diverges (i.e., engages in language maintenance behaviors) from a member of the out-group. These controlling factors are:

(1) the degree to which the individual identifies himself with, and the strength of his identification with, a group identity which is strongly associated with a particular language;
(2) the degree to which the individual or group makes insecure social comparisons of themselves with the out-group;
(3) the degree to which the group members perceive their own group's vitality to be high;

## 2.11 Multiple identities and boundary maintenance

(4) the degree to which the group perceives its own boundaries to be hard and impassable; and
(5) the degree to which the group has strong feelings of identification with few other social groups.

"It is our contention that ethnic minority groups experiencing such a psychological climate would not only be very likely to *maintain* their ethnolinguistic identity and diverge from an out-group speaker, but would also be less disposed to acquiring native-like proficiency in the dominant group's tongue and be extremely keen to maintain use of the ethnic tongue within the family context and beyond and expend energies in this direction" (Giles 1987:72–73).

The interplay of these five propositions can lead to different sociopsychological configurations in terms of language maintenance behaviors which they describe. The configuration identified by Giles and Johnson as "group conformity" corresponds in many respects to what Paulston identifies as "ethnicity". Group identification is moderate because it is "just taken for granted" (Paulston 1987:35). Few other group memberships are perceived as being significant and, in cases where the group is dominated by another, comparisons with the other group will be insecure when the dominant group's value system is used to make the comparison. In such situations, boundaries are hard and closed since group membership can only be achieved by birth. Group members will see themselves as belonging to a strong, vital group and such a group is likely to experience moderate language shift.

Similarly, what Giles and Johnson identify as a configuration of "ethnic solidarity" corresponds to Paulston's "ethnic movement". This is a more active orientation towards language maintenance marked by strong identification with the ethnic group, "ethnicity turned militant" (Paulston 1987:38). Here the emphasis is on boundary maintenance, either because the boundaries are perceived to have softened and opened, posing a threat to the maintenance of an otherwise high vitality; or because in spite of hard, closed boundaries, vitality is perceived as being low and thus in danger.

Paulston identifies even stronger forms of maintenance-oriented social configurations naming them "ethnic nationalism" and "geographic nationalism". Giles and Johnson, however, look in the other direction at factors leading to language erosion and identify the configuration related to language shift which they term "conformity to societal norms". In Paulston's terms this would be the loss of ethnicity.

Giles et al. (1991) present a model which "captures the intergroup arena of minority language situations, recognizes outcomes and processes beyond survival, attends to 'cognitive climates' as a mediator of minority language status...and emphasizes the interactional dynamic nature of the entire process" (Giles et al. 1991:116). They also show how these multiple factors can be summed up in terms of two continuous variables: dependency and solidarity.

> Dependency relates to the extent to which you are dependent on your ethnic in-group for identity definitions and so refers to the number of social group options available to you. Solidarity relates to the degree of identification and affect subjectively associated with membership of one's in-group. (Giles et al. 1991:119)

Giles et al. (1991) recognize the importance of how interactions are subjectively classified by the participants as being interpersonal or intergroup. Interpersonal interactions are more controlled by the "moods, temperaments, and personalities of those involved" while intergroup interactions are "based entirely on the interactants dealing with each other as representatives of different social categories" (Giles 1991:120). They see these as being two separate continua rather than the poles of a single continuum since interactions may have varying degrees of interpersonalness and intergroupness at the same time.

## 2.12 Synthesis

It is clear from the survey of the literature that the sociology of language and social psychology are looking at the same phenomena and arriving at quite similar conclusions regarding the extralinguistic factors which are influential in the maintenance or shift of both language and ethnic identity. While the sociology of language is concerned with group behavior, social psychology begins with individual behavior. Both have identified similar sets of factors which influence both levels of behavior and which can be taken into account in the analysis of the K'iche' situation.

The situation in Guatemala seems to be a case of diglossia without bilingualism. The severe strains predicted for such a situation are increasingly evident as the effects of *indigenismo* and political and social liberalization become increasingly widespread. The social changes of the last sixty years have destabilized the diglossic situation and opened the doors for a larger number of Mayans to acquire proficiency in Spanish and to participate in ladino culture. The situation is becoming more and more one where there is bilingualism without diglossia. The rapid social change and the disruption of Mayan social and cultural life, brought about by modernization

## 2.12 Synthesis

and by physical and demographic dislocations, seem to have accelerated the processes of language and culture shift.

It is difficult, however, to predict the final outcome of the changes that are taking place. The social changes could be reversed; the ethnic movement among Mayans to promote language and culture maintenance may stem the tide of language shift, and Mayan attitudes towards their own languages may be changed. The social setting must at some point restabilize, and the language use situation will seek to re-establish equilibrium as well. The best attempt to predict the outcome is to take the pulse of K'iche' ethnolinguistic vitality by examining the factors identified by the sociology of language and social psychology, and by fitting that data into the framework of EIT.

Factors in the K'iche' setting which affect ethnolinguistic vitality include:

> impassable, but weakening group boundaries
> ascribed rather than achieved status
> the restriction of access to both roles and proficiency
> the role of industrialization, modernization, universal education and literacy in bringing about increased access to the full range of roles in society
> the acquisition of proficiency in the encroaching language
> the abandonment of traditional norms
> the early acquisition of the second language in the home and neighborhood domains (evidence of intergenerational code switching)
> the role of work and education in providing reinforcement and motivation for the acquisition of the second language
> the support of societal institutions is in favor of the encroaching language, and the rewards of society are in favor of those behaviors, including linguistic ones, which promote the acquisition of control of the economic means of production.

A complete profile of a language contact situation must include factors for measuring objective ethnolinguistic vitality such as demographic factors, institutional support factors, status factors, and subjective vitality factors. Though not exhaustive, these areas of concern can be an important first step in the description of K'iche' ethnolinguistic vitality.

## 2.13–2.15 The description of Guatemalan communities

As described in the preceding chapter, the *municipio* is the result of colonial policies which concentrated Mayan populations in and around town centers as a means of control and exploitation of the Mayan peoples. Rather than openly resisting this attempt at control, the *municipio* was taken over by the Mayans and became the locus of Mayan identity and social interaction. It is the most significant Mayan sociopolitical unit.

Anthropological and ethnographic studies of Mayan culture, have tended to be studies of individual communities.[8] This approach recognizes that ethnic identity for Mayans is based on their communal relations focused around the *municipio* as a social, political, religious, and ceremonial center.

Though similar in function, the isolation and separatism of the *municipios* distinguishes one from another in the following ways:

> Differing in birth and baptismal customs, in modes of courtship and marriage ceremonies, in types of family organization, in religious and magical beliefs, in the use of and the rituals of shamans and sorcerors—in almost every aspect of culture—the municipios differ from one another in greater or lesser detail. (Tax 1969:88)

In contrast to these differences, there are clearly many areas of similarity that exist within all Mayan communities in Guatemala. Even more so there are shared cultural norms in any set of communities that can be linked together under a cover term such as Quichean.[9] Those communities that can be grouped together for comparison are those which differ in "lesser detail".

In chapter 4 the demographic, institutional support, status, and subjective vitality factors identified by Giles and Johnson (1987) are considered in detail for each of seven K'iche' communities. As a summary orientation to the analysis of the seven communities in this study, I will survey in the rest of this chapter some of the differences between communities identified in the anthropological literature on Guatemala, followed by a

---

[8]Tax and Hinshaw (1969:70) provide ample evidence of this as of the date of their writing, by listing more than twenty-five such studies undertaken in the region of the midwestern highlands beginning in the 1920s.

[9]The definition of Quichean identity is fraught with the same difficulties that accompany the attempt to specify K'iche' as a separate language. Just as there are linguistic dialects so there are social and cultural dialects. Different observers will draw the boundaries at different points. In spite of these disagreements there still exists a generally accepted core of communities which are clearly K'iche' and which recognize themselves as being distinct from the Kaqchikel, the Tzutujil, the Ixil, and other Mayan groups.

discussion of the identity maintenance mechanisms named by Tax and Hinshaw (1969): (1) endogamy within the *municipio,* (2) economic specialization, (3) linguistic distinctiveness, and (4) a common worldview.

## 2.13 Distinctive community types

While the *municipio* is the most significant cultural unit and serves as the distinctive locus for the numerous Mayan ethnicities, not all *municipios* are identical in their organizational patterns. In his description of settlement patterns in the Guatemalan highlands deBorgheyi (1956/71:101) identified three major types of communities: (1) compound villages, (2) dispersed villages, and (3) concourse centers. He proposed that these three community types are remnants of preconquest settlement patterns and cannot be related to political, social, or economic factors operating in contemporary society.

The first of these, the compound village, is one where the Mayan inhabitants live close together. These communities tend to be the typical small town with central plaza and intersecting streets lined with houses and shops. The most imposing building in the community is the Roman Catholic church, which is often built in the town square and at the highest point so as to be visible (much like the Mayan temples at the ancient ceremonial centers) from every direction.

The second type, the dispersed village, is marked by a less concentrated settlement pattern and may not have a well-defined central plaza. Usually more rural, these types of communities have houses scattered over the countryside and located in and among the fields where crops are grown. Typically, in such communities there will be no Roman Catholic church or only a small chapel which is visited by an itinerant priest. In such a community the central plaza may serve as the soccer field and grazing land for cattle and may also be the site of a small open-air market on certain days of the week.

The third type of community is the concourse center. This is a community where the central plaza serves as an important market and ceremonial center, and unites residents from a large area including residents of communities of the other two types. In my observations it seems that both the compound village and dispersed village may also serve as a concourse center for important religious and social holidays.

Tax and Hinshaw (1969:72) identify the differences between communities as being of two types: (1) differences in the distribution of inhabitants between urban and rural settings, and (2) differences in the proportion of Mayans and ladinos resident in the community. The combination of these two factors provides a classificatory scheme which enables the communities to be categorized in different ways. Many *municipios* can be characterized in terms of two extreme types: the vacant town—a relatively urbanized town center which has very few full-time Mayan residents—or the town nucleus—a town center where the majority of the population live and from which they go out on a daily basis to work the surrounding land. Tax (1937) identified Chichicastenango, one of the communities included in this study, as a vacant town where many Mayans may own homes in the town center. Generally, however, those homes stand empty except on market days and during the yearly festivals. The Mayans more often reside in their homes near their fields and crops. This geographic duality is based on a weekly market cycle that interlocks with a yearly religious festival cycle and with a lifelong political and religious service system. The vacant town corresponds with the compound village described above although the town center may be a concourse center as well.

In contrast, the nucleated town is one where the majority of the population resides in the town center.[10] The men leave the town every morning to go to the fields and mountains to do their agricultural work, leaving the women to do their daily work without reference to the "outside" world. Some such communities have daily or even twice-daily markets. In these communities, the geographic duality characteristic of the vacant town is less pronounced since the cycle of activities is more focused on the daily routine than on the weekly and yearly pilgrimages between urban and rural homes. Significantly, in nucleated towns, community boundaries are less important while in the vacant towns "municipio boundaries are all-important" (Tax and Hinshaw 1969:75).

The second type of difference between communities is the proportion of ladinos to Mayans in the community. Chichicastenango is typical of the vacant town, where the proportion of Mayans to ladinos is high. Totonicapán, another community included in this study, is typical of the community where the number of ladinos is relatively high though still not the majority. It also is similar to the compound village described above. In this kind of town, the marketing opportunities, provided by the ladino population for pottery, weavings, and woodworking, have motivated relatively large numbers of Mayans to become full-time residents of the town

---

[10]Tax and Hinshaw are of the opinion that these nucleated towns are located primarily in the area of Lake Atitlán, an area not inhabited by K'iche' speakers and propose that this particular communal organizational pattern may be influenced by the peculiar geographic features of that regions: steep volcanic mountainsides with very little flat land found only on the shores of the lake. One K'iche' town which follows this pattern is Nahualá, located on the steep southern slopes of the mountains, and very much in the orbit of the lakeshore communities described by Tax and Hinshaw.

center though they still may have land and houses in the surrounding area.

## 2.14 Ethnic identity maintenance

The mechanisms of ethnic identity maintenance include *municipio* endogamy, economic specialization, linguistic distinctiveness, and shared world view. These function as boundary maintenance strategies which exemplify a posture of divergence from the out-group. The loss of any of these strategies might be indicative of a loss of ethnolinguistic vitality. While this study is confined to the maintenance of ethnic distinctiveness vis-à-vis the ladino out-group as evidenced by language use patterns in particular, I comment here in a general way on these identity maintenance mechanisms. They are discussed more fully in the description of each of the seven communities in chapters 4 and 5.

In general, the patterns of *municipio* endogamy seem to be breaking down based only on the anecdotal evidence we were able to gather. In Chichicastenango, for example, there were several reports of marriages taking place between residents of Chichicastenango and Tz'utujil or Kaqchikel speakers from neighboring communities in the department of Sololá. As might be expected, this seems to be the general pattern for less isolated communities. Improved roads, bus service, and telecommunications have brought about an influx of outsiders and the ability to reach the outside world and have been influential in breaking down the prohibitions against marrying outside of the local ethnicity. For the communities which are more difficult to reach (and to leave), patterns of *municipio* endogamy seem to be relatively intact. Marriage of Mayans to ladinos is rare and subject to social stigmatization from both groups.

Regarding the second mechanism of economic specialization, the general pattern is that *municipios,* taking advantage of local natural resources and climate, specialize in the production and marketing of specific goods and services. While almost all Mayans grow corn and beans which are the staple foods in the Mayan diet, some communities also maintain and develop skills in weaving, pottery, or woodwork. One result of encroaching modernization has been an increasing diversity in the economic activity of the communities. The introduction of the cultivation of fruits and vegetables as cash crops is particular evidence of this shift in the economic systems of the communities. The demands of tourists for Mayan "typical" items have also been influential in encouraging diversification in the production of textiles, particularly in Chichicastenango and Totonicapán. When tourism was frightened away by the civil strife in Guatemala, artisans and farmers alike began to diversify their crops as a means of obtaining cash.

The linguistic distinctiveness among K'iche's is apparent in that every *municipio* speaks its own variety and feels more-or-less strongly that its particular variety is the true K'iche'. Speakers from each community have diverged from the speakers of every other community, reinforcing and even exaggerating the differences between their varieties as a matter of ethnic pride. Such a high degree of variation between communities has led to several different analyses of how many "dialects" of K'iche' there are and where the boundaries should be drawn between languages. The finest grained analysis would posit that there are fifty-two varieties—one for each K'iche' community. Two thorough analyses by Kaufman (1974; 1976) and reported on in Cojtí Macario (1987) as well as the earlier work by Henne (1964), which are based entirely on lexical and phonological similarities, do not take into account the speakers' perceptions of ethnic identity.

The fourth mechanism, shared world view, is discussed in Lewis (1993) and describes how members of the same *municipio* develop their group identity through their shared world view. I summarize that discussion here very briefly. The Mayan cosmology is animistic and has easily absorbed features of Christianity introduced by the Spanish priests. Many of the symbols of Christianity were easily adaptable or already existed within the Mayan world view. For example, the Mayans had a cross, representing the four corners of the earth or the four cardinal directions. The Christian cross was easily adapted and reinterpreted. Similarly, the Mayans view the moon as their Mother and so the Virgin Mary, the quintessential mother, became for them another form for the same religious figure. In the same way, the Christian saints have been syncretistically adopted as the spirit owners of the town along with the other spirit beings associated with geographical locations such as mountains, caves, and rocks. Further, the spirit world is populated by the ancestors who remain present and watch over a family's maintenance of traditional ways and their stewardship of the ancestral lands. This general cosmology is universal among Mayan groups but in its distinctive forms is a mechanism of maintaining group solidarity in the present and continuity with the past. Hile (n.d.:4) states:

> Performance of these acts and participation in the system give an Indian his community identity, his sense of belonging, his hope for the future life, and his assurance of the good life here. Conversely, to forsake the customs of the ancestors is certain to incur not only their [the spirits' and ancestors'] wrath, but that of the community as well.

Typically, the local, distinctive world view is realized as an allegiance to a coterie of saints and one patron saint in particular who is the caretaker of the community. This saint is cared for and offered devotion, honor, and respect by the members of the community through their participation in the civil-religious system of service. Members of the community view the saints as local deities who are intimately tied to the historical as well as spiritual roots of the community. Residents of the town are generally named after one of the town saints, and frequently the ethnic group as a whole is referred to as "those who pertain to" the patron saint of the community. Legends about group origins are often related to the exploits of the town patron. The distinctive dress of each community further reinforces this sense of group identity and may have symbols relating to the town origin legends woven into the pattern of the clothing. The distinctive world view of each community serves both to unify and to distinguish the members of that community both at the family level (through obligations to the ancestral spirits and the land) and at the community level (through obligations to the town patron saint and the other associated saints of the community).

## 2.15 Summary

The anthropological literature on Mayan communities in Guatemala shows clearly that the *municipio* is the appropriate unit of analysis for the examination of ethnicity and language use patterns. It also demonstrates that many of the factors identified by ethnolinguistic identity theory can be related to the distinctive features of Guatemalan communities as well as to the shared mechanisms for the maintenance of ethnic identity. Boundary maintenance, in particular, is an area of investigation that should have ample data for examination. Another important factor to be examined is maintenance or shift of world view, since much of the focus of the Mayan world view is on the maintenance of the status quo. A shift in world view away from this heavy traditional focus is likely a prerequisite for any major shifts in cultural behaviors. Of interest, too, is whether the categorization of a community, as tending towards the vacant town or the nucleated town type, or in terms of the proportions and distribution of Mayans and ladinos, has any implications for the maintenance of identity and language in that community.

# 3
# Research Project Design and Methodology

## 3.1 General description

The argument of this study is that, as the result of changes in Guatemalan social relations, the longstanding compartmentalization of roles for K'iche' and Spanish based on race, sex, age, setting, and interlocutor has broken down as K'iche' communities have adopted a more modern identity. This general statement can be recast as two hypotheses. The first is:

*K'iche' and Spanish are not in a stable diglossic relationship.*

While there is considerable qualitative evidence that the stable diglossia which has characterized Guatemalan society since the Spanish conquest is now giving way to a period of bilingualism without diglossia, possibly leading to language shift or even the death of the Mayan languages, there has been little large-scale investigation based on quantitative methods. One goal of this study is to examine quantitative data regarding language use among the K'iche' in order to document the current state of affairs.

Ferguson (1959) identified stability as one of the defining characteristics of diglossia. Stability along with compartmentalization are the two most significant characteristics of diglossia according to Fishman (1967). Fasold (1984) notes that "Two characteristics of changing diglossia are: (1) *leakage* in function; and (2) *mixing* in form." This study confines itself primarily to an examination of the first of these two. While the data on language use which I analyze contain many observations of mixed forms, these were not transcribed, and therefore, I make no attempt to characterize the nature of such code mixing.

Evidence of "leaking diglossia" is seen when a number of domains are identified in which it is unclear which language is appropriate, or in which the language used is not the one traditionally expected for that domain. It is further expected in a diglossic situation that an implicational scale might be identifiable in terms of independent variables such as age, sex, race, and interlocutor (cf. Gal 1978) which would provide a certain amount of predictability of language use. If such scalability is not encountered in the data, it would indicate that diglossia is being lost. I examine language use data from the K'iche'-speaking area to see if there is evidence of leaking diglossia and/or a lack of scalability in the data. These data and the methods used to collect them are described below.

The second hypothesis has to do with the relationship between the patterns of language use and ethnic identity:

*There is a significant relationship between language use and degree of acceptance of modern (i.e., nontraditional) identity factors in K'iche' communities.*

In order to test this hypothesis I examine data from seven K'iche' communities and identify for each the degree to which it has accepted modern identity factors. In addition, I compare the language use patterns for these communities to see if a relationship between the degree of identity shift and language use can be determined.

This second hypothesis assumes that diglossia is breaking down, and therefore tests the assertion that there is a significant relationship between an identity shift towards an acceptance of nontraditional innovations and the loss of K'iche' use in at least some domains of use. Evidence of such an identity shift is derived from comprehensive ethnographic and sociological descriptions of the communities. These descriptions take the data that have been gathered and place them within the framework of current research on ethnicity, social identity, and ethnolinguistic vitality.

I examine the seven K'iche' communities in order to discover the relationship between the ethnolinguistic vitality factors summarized in chapter 2, and actual language use patterns in those same communities. I use both qualitative and quantitative data in order to gain a global perspective on the K'iche' situation. While the data-gathering methods were primarily qualitative, when possible I have quantified them within the framework of ethnolinguistic vitality theory so as to make the data comparable between communities.

## 3.2 Selection of the communities

The data for this study are the result of a large-scale study in the sociology of the K'iche' language in which I was the principal investigator, under the auspices of the Summer Institute of Linguistics in Central America. While the scope of that study was the entire K'iche'-speaking area of Guatemala (see map 1), it focused primarily on those communities which were identified as being both linguistic and demographic centers. The bulk of the data gathered come from seven communities, six of which were the home bases for investigators on the Quiché Survey Team (hereafter QST). Data were gathered in other communities as well, but the quantity and quality of the data for the secondary communities is insufficient to allow firm conclusions to be made and so are not included in this analysis. Map 2 shows the communities which were included in this study.

The following criteria were used for the selection of the primary communities to be studied.

1. Each community should be clearly within the K'iche' culture as determined by the fact that more than 75% of the population was classified as Mayan in the 1981 Census; and that the women wear the distinctive *traje*.[11]
2. Each community should be homogeneous enough to be treatable as a unit of analysis, as determined by the fact that the inhabitants of the community have a recognized attachment to their community as the focus of their ethnicity.
3. Each community should be representative of one of the linguistic varieties of K'iche' as identified by Henne (1964).
4. The communities as a group should represent as large a block of the K'iche' population as possible.

Based on these criteria the communities selected were: Chichicastenango, Cunén, Joyabaj, Sacapulas, San Andrés Sajcabajá, Santa Cruz del Quiché, and Totonicapán. These seven communities comprise a little less than one quarter of the K'iche' population according to the 1981 Guatemalan census. All are in the K'iche' highland area of the departments of El Quiché and Totonicapán which is the area of highest

---

[11]The term *traje* (Spanish "suit") is used to denote the distinctive style of clothing connected with most of the Mayan communities in Guatemala. While these styles traditionally were worn by both men and women, in many locations the men have abandoned the traditional dress for more Western clothing. The traditional clothing styles of both men and women for many Mayan communities are beautifully depicted in Pettersen (1976).

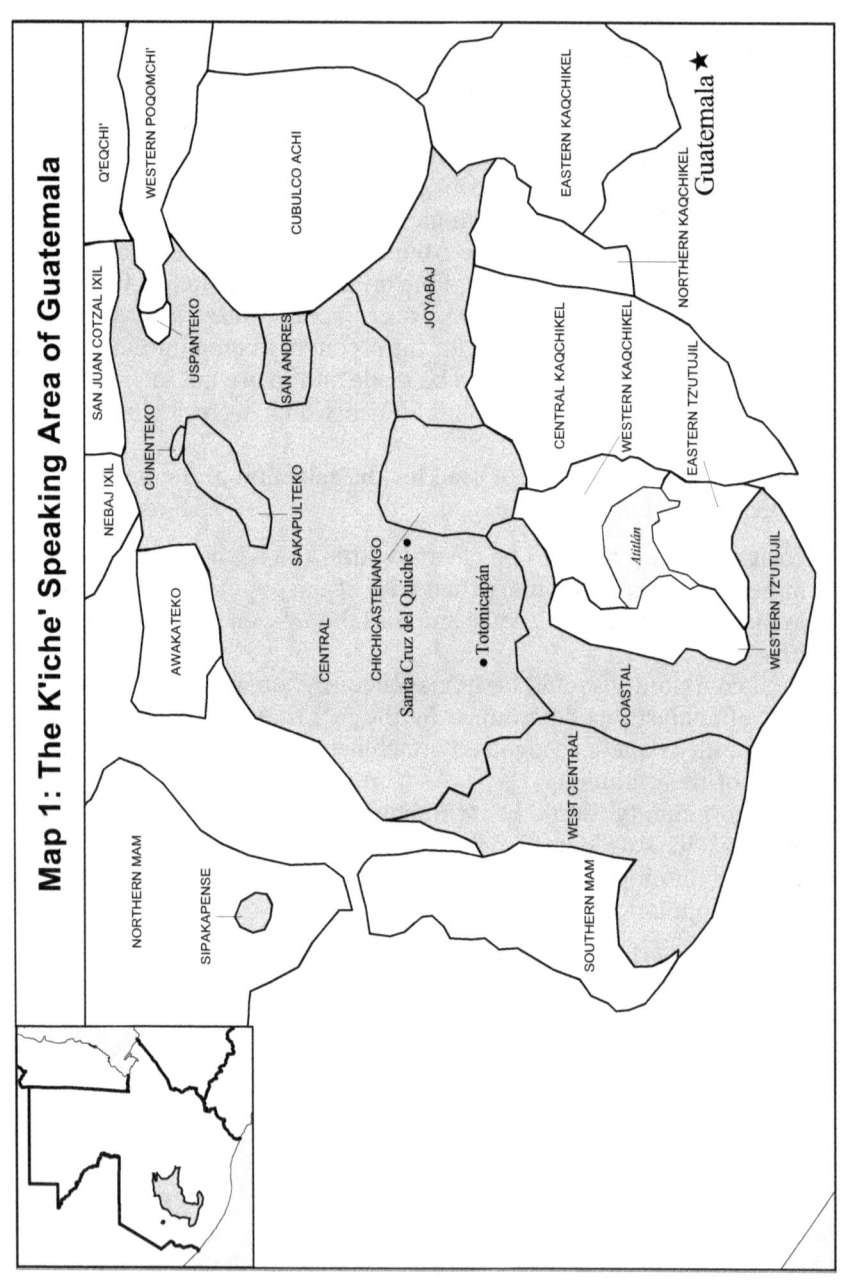

Map 1: The K'iche' Speaking Area of Guatemala

## 3.2 Selection of the communities

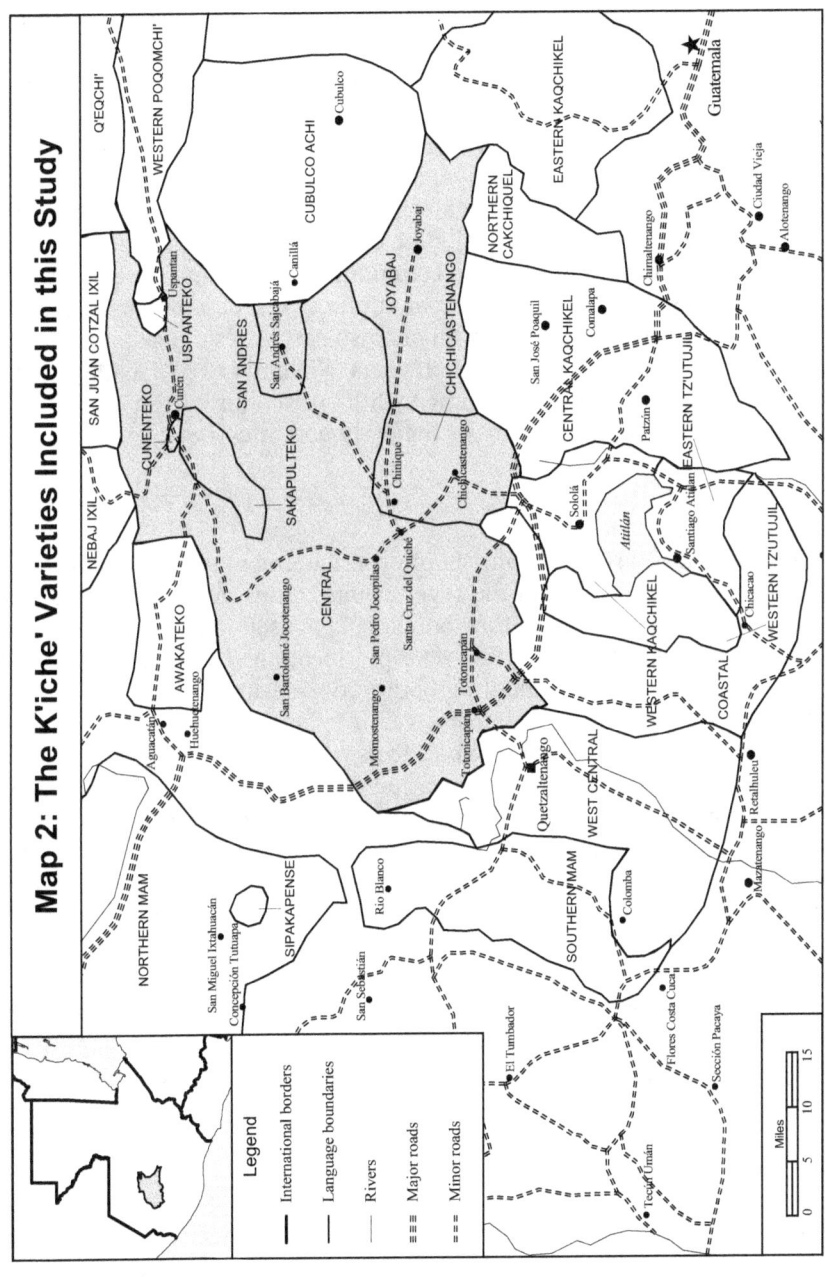

population density. At the same time they provide access to the major dialect groups of the K'iche' language complex. Each of the communities is also the center of a recognizable ethnicity within the larger K'iche' group, is more than 75% Mayan in its demographics according to the 1981 Guatemalan census, and is characterized by a distinctive *traje* (traditional clothing) which is still widely worn by the women. In six of these communities (all but Joyabaj), investigators were resident for a period of two years, attempted to learn the local variety of K'iche', and engaged in participant observations. In Joyabaj, data on language use were gathered by a K'iche'-speaking resident of the community at the same time as similar data were gathered in the other communities. The data on Joyabaj community resources are also based on my own earlier residence in that community for a period of two and a half years (November 1977 to May 1980) and on observations made by other SIL linguists during their brief residencies in the community during the early and mid-1980s.

## 3.3 Language use data

The language use data consists of observations of speech interactions among members of each of the seven communities. Age, sex, race of the speakers and their interlocutors, and language used were tallied. Speaker interactions were also classified by topic/location. The data consist of a convenience sample collected by both native-speakers of K'iche' and by the QST over a period of almost a year beginning in August 1987. The data were collected on observation sheets which were entered into a computer database. Each data observation sheet recorded a single speech transaction observed by the data collector. In the seven communities, 4,920 speech transactions were observed and reported on. Speech transactions, however, are complex events and might involve many participants engaged in multiple interchanges between themselves. Each interchange within a speech transaction consists of a combination of interlocutors making use of language. The data being analyzed consist of a combined total of 11,222 interlocutor interchanges from the seven communities. The details of these interchanges are the basis for the analysis of language use which follows. The language use observation forms and the data they elicited are described more fully below.

## 3.4 Data collection

The language use data collection phase of the project was designed to collect quantifiable data on "who speaks what language to whom and

## 3.4 Data collection

when" (Fishman 1965). The primary objective for this phase of the research project was to collect data on "natural" language use in order to minimizing the observer effect as much as possible by using participant observation techniques. Interviews, questionnaires, and self-report methodologies were rejected because of the strong possibility that the results would not truly represent the actual language use patterns of the target communities. Respondents (especially those who are illiterate) often have difficulty in dealing with the questionnaire as an instrument, and their responses to oral interview questions do not always coincide with observations of their behavior. While such disparity between observed behavior and response is revealing in itself, I felt that such an endeavor would add a level of complexity to the study of K'iche' language use that could not be adequately dealt with given the time and resources at hand.

### 3.5 Unit of observation

The unit of observation of this study, the "speech transaction", is defined as any instance of language use involving one or more participants in a particular social setting. This definition allows for the inclusion of such varied uses of language as posted signs, oral public announcements by loudspeaker, speaker-audience interactions in public meetings and church services, written uses of language (letters being read/written, books being read), casual exchanges on the street and in the market, and more formal exchanges in government offices. The data-gathering method required a fairly static view of what comprised a speech transaction. Observations of language use were generally made quickly and the characteristics of any single speech transaction were usually rapidly assessed and recorded. The methodology is not well-adapted for a thorough description of dynamic situations with participants coming and going nor does it provide adequate data for documenting the long-term interplay of changing roles and speech styles over the entire span of an extended conversation.

Over a period of almost a year beginning in August 1987, expatriate and Guatemalan (K'iche'-speaking) observers tallied data concerning speech transactions using predesigned observation record forms. These observers were residents of the communities where the observations were made. The expatriate observers had established themselves in the community through a year of residence prior to the beginning of this phase of the data collection.

## 3.6 Language use observation data forms

The observation form provided space for information about location, date and time of day, situation/location category, and observer's initials. There were blank lines for identification of up to nine participants by age, sex, and race (Mayan or ladino). There was also space for comments and written observations regarding actions, location (physical orientation of the participants), instruments used in the interaction, and for a written description of the language use in the speech event.

For the purposes of this analysis the data primarily in focus are those regarding participants' identity (age, sex, race) and language used, as well as the situation category and community. The secondary data on spatial orientation, instruments used, and other observer comments must remain for future studies more oriented toward the ethnography of speaking.

## 3.7 Sampling method

The method of collecting observations was unsystematic in that the observers were instructed to make observations as they went about their daily life as well as by going to specific situation/location categories with the express purpose of making observations. No attempt was made to observe a random or even a stratified sample. Observers were instructed not to repeatedly describe the same situation which occurred on a routine basis, though multiple observations of church services were admitted. However, a data-gatherer's observations of his or her own home were to be made once and not repeatedly over the six-month data-gathering period. This reduces the likelihood that the data represent repeated measures of the same sample group, though some repetition of participants may still exist in the data. I have classified a service held on Sunday morning to be a different event from a similar service held on a week night, even though most of the same individuals might be present in both cases. This decision is based on ethnographic data which provides evidence that the participants themselves see these as being two different kinds of events with different levels of formality required. While such insights were used in the classification of observations during the data collection phase, such a fine-grained classificatory scheme has not been maintained during the analysis phase. Rather, a number of separate categories have been conflated to simplify the analysis. Thus, the conclusions drawn here are simplifications and approximations which attempt to make generalizations about a complex situation.

## 3.7 Sampling method

In addition to the approximate nature of the conclusions because of the broadness of the analytical scheme, the limitations of the sampling method place some limitations on the generalizability of the conclusions that can be drawn from the data collected. Eighteen of the twenty-nine observers were native K'iche' speakers, making observations, for the most part, in their home communities. These eighteen observers also account for the majority of the observations that were collected. These facts, to some extent, ameliorate the skewing introduced by the nonrandom sampling method in that the domains observed are more likely to be authentic "loci of talk" than if the sample had been collected on a more mechanical basis and entirely by outsiders. The fact that observations were made during normal routines of the observers over a six-month period, a kind of language use diary, would tend to make the sample much more like a stratified sample of the possible speech situations (though not of the participants). In spite of these ameliorating factors, however, this skewing of the sample must be kept in mind as the data are analyzed.

Inevitably, the sample is skewed towards those domains where the observers themselves were apt to be and towards those domains selected as being in need of representation, a de facto kind of stratification of the sample. The sample is also, undoubtedly, skewed toward observations of K'iche' being used since the observers knew that the intent of the study was to observe how and for what purposes K'iche' is used. This, however, tends to make the sample more conservative, i.e., skewed towards showing a greater retention of K'iche' than may, in fact, be the case. Thus, while the conclusions may not be strongly generalizable because of these sampling problems, evidence of reduced K'iche' use in any domain can be taken seriously.

### 3.8 Sample size

The goal of the study was to obtain approximately 1,000 observations of speech transactions in each of the target communities during the six-month data-gathering period. In every case the actual number of observations obtained was less than the target figure and particularly so in the smaller communities (Sacapulas and San Andrés Sajcabajá) and in Joyabaj where data were gathered by a single observer over a much shorter period of time. Table 3.1 shows the tally of observations and number of participants (both speaking and nonspeaking) observed for each of the communities.

Table 3.1. Tally of observations by community

| Community | Oberservations | Participants |
|---|---|---|
| Chichicastenango | 898 | 2,329 |
| Cunén | 808 | 1,852 |
| Sacapulas | 631 | 1,257 |
| Joyabaj | 406 | 550 |
| San Andrés Sajcabajá | 418 | 1,033 |
| Santa Cruz del Quiché | 876 | 2,267 |
| Totonicapán | 883 | 1,941 |
| Total | 4,920 | 11,229 |

The language use study resulted in more than 11,229 participants being observed in the seven target communities. This relatively large sample size is another factor which ameliorates the skewing caused by the nonrandom sampling method. Since some of the participants consisted of groups of people (e.g., a church congregation, a group of students—each as a whole counted as a single participant), the actual sample of observed individuals is considerably larger. Generally, however, such groups were observed as nonspeaking participants or as speaking with one voice (e.g., singing a hymn, reciting a prayer). Evidence of such collective uses of one language or the other provide another margin of reliability to the data since unexpected language use in such cases is unlikely to be the purely idiosyncratic behavior of a marginal individual.

### 3.9 Data recording and analysis methods

Each observation was coded to indicate the topic/location category, and the participants' race, age, sex, and language used with each of the other participants. Nonspeaking participants were also identified for each of these categories. In the data collection and entry process, coding schemes were developed to indicate the various possibilities. The speech behavior of the participants is analyzed for the effect of each of these factors on the choice of language, i.e., language choice is the dependent variable and the other factors (race, sex, age, interlocutor(s), topic/location category, prestige, and formality) are independent variables.

**3.9.1 Race and sex.** The racial affiliation and sex data that were collected are two-level nominal variables. Since there are very few direct descendants of the Spanish conquerors, and since the process of ladinoization has been going on since the Conquest, the criterion for racial classification must be based more on cultural factors than on

## 3.9 Data recording and analysis methods

bloodlines. Thus, the term race as used here is actually a matter of social group classification in which dress, language, and social custom are the factors which are most significant.

No explicit instructions were given to the data gatherers, but their knowledge of the community norms regarding Mayan identity increased as they identified who was and who was not a Mayan. The primary factor seems to be dress as each community has its own distinctive *traje* which is used only by Mayans. Such clothing is universally worn by Mayan women and in a few communities by the Mayan men. However, even in those cases where the men have adopted more Western styles of clothing, a Mayan man can be identified by some rather subtle distinctive features of his dress.

The second feature which is connected with social group identification is that of language. Mayans speak Mayan languages, Ladinos rarely do. This, of course, introduces some circularity into the study. If we are interested in observing who speaks what to whom and when and base our identification of the "who" on "what they are speaking", we have made one of our independent variables dependent on the fluctuation of what is, in this case, the dependent variable. This dilemma touches the very core of the point of this study: the inevitabale connection between social identity and language use. This connection is not necessarily a direct one. K'iche's speak K'iche', but the observers also noted K'iche's speaking Spanish. Thus, while identity is in part tied to language, it is not entirely based on language use. What is of interest here is that there are K'iche's who are recognized as K'iche's by their peers and that these have been identified as such by the observers. While the language use data alone is not sufficient to draw firm conclusions concerning identity shift, it is sufficient to make at least some tentative conclusions regarding it. Furthermore, the language use data when combined with other data about the changes in the K'iche' communities can help to fill in the outlines of the picture of identity shift that might be occurring in the K'iche' communities.

**3.9.2 Age.** In many traditional societies age is an important social variable with greater respect being afforded those with greater age. This holds true for Mayan society as well. In Mayan communities, age correlates with rank and prestige and with the level of achievement in the civic-religious duty system (Cancian 1967; McArthur 1961, 1969). Ideally, we should attempt to use those age categories which are recognized by the community members themselves in our quantitative analysis. That, however, is not feasible for this study. Instead, arbitrary mid-decade cutoff points have been chosen. It is likely that the six age categories being used for this quantitative analysis represent a level of precision that exceeds that which is significant within the communities themselves.

In the data collection phase, the age of each participant was estimated by the observer. Since the observation process was designed to be as unobtrusive as possible, there was no attempt to interrogate participants as to their ages. Observers provided their own estimates of age based on their knowledge of the communities and experience with the population. On the data collection forms numerical figures for age were used. For the purposes of the analysis by age these have been converted into nominal categories consisting of six age groups:

> A01 - 1–12
> A02 - 13–24
> A03 - 25–34
> A04 - 35–44
> A05 - 45–54
> A06 over 55

These categories coincide, in part, with those used by Langan (1990) in her study of Chichicastenango. The population examined here, however, includes a greater range of ages and so the younger age categories have been added. For some participants (e.g., groups) no single age assignment was appropriate. These participants were not included in the analysis by age groups but were included, as appropriate, in the other analyses.

**3.9.3 Interlocutor.** Gal (1978) brought to the attention of sociologists of language the importance of the interlocutor in affecting language choice. Accordingly, participant characteristics (race, sex, age, topic/location category) were noted even for those participants present at a speech transaction who did not themselves speak during the period of observation. There is considerable likelihood that even nonspeaking participants can have a significant role in determining a speaker's choice of language.

**3.9.4 Topic and location category.** The social settings for speech events were initially defined using twenty-five situation/location categories. Soon after data collection was begun these categories were increased to twenty-eight. Near the end of the data collection phase a detailed analysis of the "residue" category was done and twelve more categories were identified. For the purposes of this analysis, this category scheme is too fine-grained and a number of these categories have been consolidated in order to arrive at a more manageable number of domains of use.

*3.9 Data recording and analysis methods* 61

In other studies of language use, various domains of use have been identified, such as home, work, religion, national institutions, local public life, and written uses of language (Dorian 1981:75). More recently, Fishman (1991) has identified a progression of disruption as language shift takes place from more peripheral domains to more central domains such as the home and hearth. He advises that any attempt to reverse language shift must work from the surviving inner domains and attempt to resecure successively more inclusive outer domains to "become the language of interfamily interaction, of interaction with playmates, neighbors, friends and acquaintances" (Fishman 1991:93). Beyond this network of local intimate affiliations, the language must also be used in even wider domains identified as literacy, work, education, mass media, and governmental services.

Based primarily on Fishman's broadest identification of domains of language use, I have taken the forty situation and topic categories identified in the data collection phase and have recategorized them. This recategorization does not precisely match either Fishman's nor Dorian's schemes but best fits the data that were collected in this case. In grouping the categories together into a manageable number of domains, there is a possible loss of precision in the description. In an attempt to ameliorate this loss, I supplement the domain analysis presented here with an analysis in terms of formality which is described in the next section. The ten domain categories described below are categorized in terms of sociocultural contexts.

**3.9.5 Hearth and home (D01).** The home domain includes all of the activities which take place in connection with the house and home, but excluding work which goes on outside of the home setting (e.g., fieldwork or gathering of firewood far from home). The K'iche' home is made up primarily of a sleeping area and a kitchen; much familial interaction takes place either in the kitchen area or in the outside patio where the family may sit and talk when resting from their work.

**3.9.6 Personal encounters (D02).** Personal encounters include meetings between individuals, generally in the street or in the market place (but not between vendors and customers or between customers in the marketplace engaged in a commercial transaction), and telephone conversations. A typical situation in this category would be the meeting of two acquaintances as they pass on the street, perhaps on a market day.

**3.9.7 Recreation (DO3).** This category includes all observations of both children and adults at play. It might be children playing tag, or chase-the-hoop in the street, or it could be something as well organized as a weekly soccer game on the town field. The speech transactions recorded are both those of the players and of those observing them, e.g., cheers and teasing. This category does not include the speech of a formal play-by-play announcer using a public address system. Such examples of speech would be classified under mass media.

**3.9.8 Market (DO4).** The public market is the high point of the weekly cycle in most Guatemalan towns. It is the meeting place, the gossip exchange, and is generally recognized as being a thoroughly Mayan activity. Nevertheless, both Mayans and ladinos go to the market since it is the primary source of fresh fruits and vegetables, meat, clothing, housewares, and other staples. Included in this domain are all areas of the weekly or bi-weekly public market including not only the fixed stalls which are set up and taken down each week, but also the numerous circulating salesmen who walk the streets on market days, and visit door-to-door between markets to sell their wares. Not included in this category are stores which operate all week long and are located in buildings.

**3.9.9 Work (DO5).** The work domain includes all activities of life for both men and women which are related to subsistence whether they be farming or commercial activity, or activities related to the maintenance of the home, e.g., home repairs, animal tending, and food production excluding cooking, except in a restaurant or cafeteria.

**3.9.10 Religious meetings (DO6).** This category includes religious meetings of all kinds: Roman Catholic and Protestant, formal and informal. It also includes a few observations which were made of practitioners of the traditional religion (shaman) engaged in their ceremonial duties, and a few observations of religious ceremonies which occur at funerals and on other occasions in the cemeteries (e.g., All Saints' Day).

**3.9.11 Stores (DO7).** Stores are permanent points-of-sale which generally, but not exclusively, are owned by ladinos and which operate all week long. Included in this category are *cantinas,* bars, which are established permanently in a building rather than in a pole-and-canvas market stall.

## 3.9 Data recording and analysis methods 63

**3.9.12 Mass media (DO8).** Mass media is used here in the most general sense of the term to include not only radio and television but also any other kind of public announcement or dissemination of information whether oral or written. It is customary in Guatemalan towns to make use of the local ambulance (if there is one) or a donated pick-up truck to circulate throughout town with a public address system to announce public events and entertainments. These events range from the public showing of a film or video as a fundraiser to the inauguration of a vaccination campaign by the public health service. Since most of the radio stations are not local and all the television stations are located in the national capital, this is the most efficient way to broadcast news about events of purely local interest. I have also included in this category public open-air meetings (excluding church services) where a public address system is used so that a large part of the community can hear what is going on whether they are actually in attendance at the meeting or not. This category also includes most written uses of language that were observed such as signs, billboards, books, magazines, and includes more personal kinds of written communication such as personal letters and notes.

**3.9.13 Formal education (DO9).** The category of formal education includes all activities in and around the school. This includes both elementary and secondary schools in both urban and rural settings. It also includes interactions between students and teachers, students and students, teachers and teachers, both inside and outside the classroom.

**3.9.14 Government offices (DO10).** This category includes the use of language in the town halls and other government related functions in the local community. Included here are the civil registry where births and deaths must be registered, the public government-run health center or hospital, and the telephone company (government-run at the time of our data collection).

**3.9.15 Formal versus informal domains.** This grouping of categories masks some distinctions that may be significant in terms of their effect on language use. For example, the formal education domain may be divided between elementary and secondary schools with a significantly different language use pattern being observed in each. Or, perhaps the urban/rural distinction between school settings is significant in its effect on language use. Similarly, religious meetings might exhibit different language use patterns based on whether the meeting is being held in a church building or in a private home. Fishman's strategy for reversing language shift not only involves a progression from home and hearth to wider, more inclusive domains but also is characterized by a progression from informal, intimate domains, to domains of increasing formality and public access. With this in mind, and based on my acquired knowledge of the communities, I have undertaken a second recategorization of the thirty-seven situation/topic categories identified on the language use observation forms in terms of formality.[12] Each category has been classified as being either a formal or an informal domain giving a total of eighteen formal categories and nineteen informal. This two-value nominal variable is also used as an independent variable in the statistical analysis of the data.

Table 3.2 lists each of the categories and indicates its classification as being either formal or informal. While still only an approximation—there may be more than two degrees of formality that are significant—this classificatory scheme can serve as a second window into the dynamics of language use among the K'iche'.

**3.9.16 Participant Role.** The role relations of the participants in a speech transaction are an important aspect which shapes a domain of use. Gal (1978) found that language choice could be predicted using only the role relations of the participants as the independent variable. In our data collection process, the observers provided a brief descriptive label for each participant. Usually, these descriptions were generic, e.g., man or woman. Frequently, however, they provided other important information about the social status or role of the participant. I, however, do not include that data in the analysis here because of the great diversity and imprecision of the descriptive labels which were used.

**3.9.17 Language use.** The dependent variable in this research is the language used in each speech transaction. In this data collection methodology the observers were asked to identify whether the participants used K'iche', Spanish, or both. No strict criteria were given for determining when an utterance was only K'iche' or was code mixing. K'iche', like many low-status languages in contact situations, has borrowed a considerable number of Spanish lexical items. There are also a number of examples of Mayan (hence K'iche') interference in the semantics and syntax of

---

[12]As mentioned above, two of the original situation/topic categories have been eliminated by my recategorization of the speech interactions according to their sociocultural contexts. A third problematic category is the miscellaneous category. I examined each speech transaction originally categorized as miscellaneous and reclassified it into one of the ten domain categories (D1–D10) identified above. Transactions which were originally categorized as miscellaneous have thus been reclassified and will be counted according to their new classification.

## 3.9 Data recording and analysis methods

Table 3.2. Formality level of situation/location categories

| Category | Formality |
|---|---|
| 1. Protestant church service—in church | F |
| 2. Protestant church service—in home | I |
| 3. Roman Catholic Mass—in church | F |
| 4. Roman Catholic home meeting | I |
| 5. Town Hall—civil registry | F |
| 6. Town Hall—Mayan "mayor's" office | F |
| 7. Market—vegetable sales | I |
| 8. Market—clothing sales | I |
| 9. Market—butcher | I |
| 10. Market—restaurant/cafeteria | I |
| 11. Stores | F |
| 12. Personal encounter (street) | I |
| 13. At home | I |
| 14. Primary school—urban, in classroom | F |
| 15. Primary school—urban, outside of class | I |
| 16. Primary school—rural, in classroom | F |
| 17. Primary school—rural, outside of class | I |
| 18. Secondary school—in classroom | F |
| 19. Secondary school—outside of classroom | I |
| 20. Public health center or hospital | F |
| 21. Pharmacy | F |
| 22. Work | I |
| 23. Sports | I |
| 24. Radio, television, tape recordings | F |
| 25. Public announcements | F |
| 26. Public transportation (buses, trucks, etc.) | I |
| 27. Written uses (signs, books, letters, etc.) | F |
| 28. Public (nonreligious) meetings | F |
| 29. Public events and ceremonies | F |
| 30. Public offices (other than town hall) | F |
| 31. General market (other than 7–10 above) | I |
| 32. Traveling salesman (in market or at door) | I |
| 33. Bar | I |
| 34. Telephone conversations | I |
| 36. Shaman/traditional religion | F |
| 37. Funerals, cemetery rites | F |
| 38. Children at play | I |

Guatemalan Spanish. To the degree that an analyst is aware of the lexicon and structure of the two languages, it becomes more and more difficult to determine when either language is being spoken in its pure form. Instead, the intuitions of the observers were used as a kind of emic criterion. If the observer considered a code-mixed utterance as being validly K'iche', it was thus recorded on the observation form. If a second code-mixed utterance was felt to be a code-switch involving the use of both languages it was recorded thus. Observers were not socialized to any norm nor was there any attempt to prejudice them in one direction or another. Since the majority of observations in each community were collected by observers who were members of that community, it allows the data from each community to be treated as representative of the norms of language use and identification which are prevalent in that community. On this basis, the observations made within each community are generally comparable with each other.

While this imprecision raises some reliability problems in the analysis, it was felt that the time spent in trying to identify which utterances constitute code-mixing versus code-switching would have side-tracked the project. Any attempt to arrive at precise criteria in this regard would have gone beyond the resources of the project. Furthermore, since the design of the project emphasized the observation of speech in natural situations with observers being as unobtrusive as possible, no audio recordings nor written transcriptions of the content of the speech transactions were made. Without such recordings for careful analysis, it would be impossible to accurately assign an utterance to more precise categories, even if they were developed. It was impractical to expect observers, many of whom were fledgling linguists, to make such decisions in the field.

A second, and much more difficult, issue is that of comparability of the data between communities. Given the description of data collection methods above, it cannot be assumed that observers from different communities would share the same emic conceptualization of what is and is not a code-mixed utterance. The difficulties arise in those interactions where a speaker used elements of both languages in a single utterance. The analysis must distinguish consistently between (1) those utterances which are essentially K'iche' or Spanish and which may be characterized by more-or-less assimilated loan words from the other language and (2) those utterances which begin as essentially K'iche' or Spanish but switch mid-utterance to the other language and perhaps back again. In the first case, the utterance should be classified as clearly K'iche' or Spanish, while in the second case the utterance should be classified as bilingual or code-switched. The study design established no criteria in advance. Thus,

## 3.9 Data recording and analysis methods

there can be no assurance that two observers from different communities would make the same decision about any given utterance. The varieties which one community would accept as being pure K'iche' could contain sufficient code-mixing that speakers from another community would consider them as examples of code-switching. This is, in fact, precisely the case with the data collected in Joyabaj where the K'iche' variety has assimilated a large number of Spanish forms and structures. As a result, an observer from another community might classify utterances from Joyabaj as code-mixed while residents of Joyabaj would classify those same utterances as being pure K'iche'. There is no easy solution to this dilemma if comparisons are to be made between the communities. While hardly ideal, intercommunity comparisons have been made as though a single standard of language identification had been used by all of the observers in all of the communities. The assumption is that the majority of the observations involve clear-cut cases where the language used was unambiguously identifiable. Since code-mixed utterances, the most problematic cases, constitute only a small part of the total sample, this level of unreliability is felt to be acceptable.

The language use data, then, are considered to have generally adequate categorizations of the language used by each participant. The data identify each participant's language use with each of the other participants in a particular speech transaction. Participants are identified as having spoken K'iche' or Spanish or as having code-mixed.

### 3.10 Community resource data

The second data set analyzed is the ethnographic descriptions of the seven K'iche' communities. This provides a qualitative perspective and places the target communities on a scale of identity shift or ethnolinguistic vitality.

An ethnographic and socioeconomic description of each community has been developed using the Community Resource Profile (CRP). The CRP is an instrument developed by the Central America Branch of the Summer Institute of Linguistics (SIL) to aid in the evaluation of communities in which local-language literacy programs are being contemplated. It consists of 115 probe questions regarding geographic, linguistic, sociolinguistic, political, economic, world view, and cultural factors. The QST used a version of the CRP during a two-year period (August 1986 to July 1988) to gather data on K'iche' communities.

Generally, qualitative research data are not amenable to quantitative analysis. Data collected using qualitative methods tends not to be reliably quantified unless the research design initially contemplated such a use of the data and provided operational definitions which guided the data-gathering process. The use of post hoc operational definitions which may not be those which were actually in focus for either subjects or researchers when the data were being gathered can lead to very misleading results. The ethnographic data which were gathered for the seven K'iche' communities were not guided by a research plan which contemplated a rigorous quantitative analysis and so are subject to this caveat. Though the ethnographic data are not subjected to a quantitative analysis, they can serve to provide a global perspective on the communities, and the data can be related to the theoretical frameworks described in the preceding chapter. I have classified the community profile questions in terms of the type of information they provide: status, boundary maintenance, and subjective vitality. Some questions relate to more than one of these categories so that the data provided by the question can be used in more than one area of description. This categorization allows us to use the data to establish a description of each community in terms of the three kinds of factors. It also allows us to arrive at a profile which meshes more usefully with the theory and thus enables us to test the usefulness of the theory more effectively. Appendix A lists the CRP questions and shows the ethnolinguistic vitality factors assigned to them. Because of this categorization of the questions, a simple tally of the answers to the questions could allow for a quantification of the community profile, but the characterization of the communities is not so straightforward. The decisions that are made regarding the degree of identity shift in each community are based on my analysis of the qualitative data and so are somewhat subjective.

The CRPs have been supplemented by a compilation of demographic data from census statistics and interviews as well as an on-the-ground inventory of community agencies such as churches, schools, hospitals, and development agencies. In many cases, those in charge of these organizations were interviewed. The more quantitative data gained from the language use investigation combined with the qualitative CRP data provides a comprehensive description of each of the communities.

The overall description is used to arrive at an estimate of the degree to which the community as a whole has adopted nontraditional ways and allows the communities to be ranked relative to each other in terms of their identity maintenance or shift. The resulting categories could be considered to be ordinal variables.

## 3.11 Statistical analysis procedures

The most obvious procedure available for the analysis of the language use data is the CHI SQUARE test. This test indicates whether the differences between frequency counts for nominal variables are significant. If the test does not indicate a significant difference, then the variance must be attributed to chance. If the test does indicate significance, then the variance can be taken as support for the hypothesis being tested. Both the independent and dependent variables in this study are nominal categories where frequencies of occurrence have been counted. There are, however, a number of independent variables, each of which may account for some amount of the variance which is noted in the dependent variable—language use. For such a multiplex analysis the chi-square test is limited in that it cannot adequately measure the combined effects of several independent variables. Neither can it tell us about the interaction of these variables nor which of the independent variables best predicts the actual distribution. In the design of this study, there are several independent variables that are being considered: age, sex, race of both speaker and interlocutor, and topic/location category (i.e., domain and formality level). A more sophisticated statistical method is needed which allows us to tease apart the interactions between these variables and to arrive at an analysis of the contribution of each to the total variance that is observed. The categorial models procedure available in the SAS statistics program is a statistical method which allows nominal variables to be subjected to an analysis similar to that of the ANOVA (which is only useful with measures, not frequency counts). Like the chi square, the categorial models procedure compares actual distributions of frequencies to expected distributions of frequencies. It does so by analyzing the probability of the effect of any single independent variable on the dependent variable. The procedure allows the analyst to construct any number of models which attempt to account for the relative effect of each of the independent variables. I use the procedure, however, to identify the significant effects of the independent variables of race and sex and their interactions using a saturated model, that is, a model in which all possible interactions are examined for statistical significance.

The analysis first looks at the language use data separately for each community with the goal of identifying the significant variables and interactions as described above. The data is also examined to identify the role of age and domain in affecting language use. For these analyses, a language maintenance index is calculated by using weighted values for the frequency counts for K'iche', Spanish, and code-mixed utterances. The formula used for this computation is described in chapter 6.

Once this community-by-community analysis is completed, the communities are then compared to each other, using both the qualitative and the quantitative data. For this comparison, a global language maintenance index for each community is calculated. It uses the same weightings as previously described but also includes all of the speech transactions in which the language used was unambiguously identified.

Both the qualitative and the quantitative data are used to rank the communities relative to each other in terms of language maintenance. The interconnection of the two sets of data is identified and alternative criteria for ranking the communities are examined.

# 4

# Community Resource Profile Data Analysis—the Towns

## 4.1 Analysis of community resource profile data

This chapter and the next are a summary of the data collected in the seven communities included in this study: Chichicastenango, Cunén, Joyabaj, Sacapulas, San Andrés Sajcabajá, Santa Cruz del Quiché, and Totonicapán. This chapter covers the first five communities which are smaller and more isolated which I have called towns. The last two, Santa Cruz del Quiché and Totonicapán, I have called "cities" because they are departmental capitals and are much larger and more complex. They are described in the next chapter.

For each community there is a description of the objective and subjective ethnolinguistic vitality factors to provide a basis for a categorization of each community in terms of its ethnolinguistic vitality. The first, Chichicastenango, is the town where I personally resided for the duration of the data gathering. This description is somewhat fuller than the descriptions of the other communities and can be used as a reference point with which to compare the data from the other communities.

The objective factors fall under three rubrics: demographic factors, institutional support factors, and status factors. Demographic factors include data regarding population both in terms of absolute numbers and in terms of proportions and trends regarding density, growth or decline, marriage patterns, and immigration and emigration.

Institutional support is defined by Giles and Johnson (1987:71) as "recognition of the group and its language in the media, education, government"; or more precisely, "Institutional support refers to the degree of formal and informal support a language receives in the various institutions of a nation, region or community" (Giles 1977:315).

Informal support is "the extent to which a minority has organized itself in terms of pressure groups." Formal institutional support refers to the presence of minority group members in the decision-making levels of government, business, and cultural affairs.

Status factors are categorized under four subcategories: (1) economic status, which refers to "the degree of control a language group has gained over the economic life of its nation, region or community"; (2) social status, which refers to "the degree of esteem a linguistic group affords itself"; (3) sociohistorical status, a group's view of its past and whether that past inspires individuals to bind together as group members in the present; and, (4) language status, the status of the language of a linguistic group within and without the boundaries of the linguistic community network.

Subjective ethnolinguistic vitality factors constitute the fourth major category which is focused not so much on the objective reality in terms of the first three sets of factors as on group members' perceptions of those objective indicators of vitality. The theory predicts that a group that views itself as successful will be one that is more likely to focus on its identity and work for the advancement of that identity. A group which has an essentially negative perception of itself will not be as motivated to work to maintain that negatively evaluated identity.

In the sections that follow, I treat each of these sets of factors as thoroughly as possible using the available data.

## 4.2–4.5 Chichicastenango

Santo Tomás Chichicastenango[13] is a *municipio* in the department of El Quiché in Guatemala's western highlands. The town center is located on a plateau between two deep ravines at an altitude of 6,650 feet above sea level and is seven miles south-southeast of Santa Cruz del Quiché, the departmental capital. It became the market center for the Quiché Mayans following the Spanish capture of Utatlan (the Quiché capital city located near the site of modern-day Santa Cruz del Quiché) and is much visited by tourists today. Its traditional economic specialization was the weaving of cotton

---

[13]The Quiché Survey Team members who gathered these data on Chichicastenango were JoAnn Munson, Mae Toedter, Adalee Lewis, and Paul Lewis.

and wool which continues to be a major cottage-industry but now has been eclipsed by the manufacture of clothing for the tourist trade. The cultivation of apples, peaches, pears, and plums for export is also a source of cash.

The town government follows a common pattern in having a mayor assisted by auxiliary mayors for the rural *cantones*[14] as well as a Mayan mayor and officials who are responsible for Mayan affairs but have very little real authority. The mayor is elected for a four-year term. The town has a military post, an office of the national police force manned by a chief and eight officers, a justice of the peace who is the local judicial authority, a post office which also houses the local telegraph service, and an office of the national telephone company from which calls can be made both nationally and internationally.

## 4.2 Demographic factors

Demographic data for Chichicastenango include group distribution, absolute population, growth trends, and some information on marriage patterns, immigration, and emigration.

**4.2.1 Group Distribution.** The *municipio* includes the town center and sixty-six *cantones* and covers an area of approximately 400 square kilometers. There is a tradition that Chichicastenango is the site where the conquered Quichés fled after the fall of Utatlán. As such, it has strong ties to the roots of the Quiché nation. Further links with the past and the great tradition of the Quiché-Maya kingdom are derived from the fact that the *Pop Wuj*, a compilation of the ancient Quiché creation legends and historical narratives, was "discovered" in Chichicastenango and transcribed by the Dominican friar Ximenez.

**4.2.2 Absolute population.** The 1981 Guatemalan government census[15] indicates the population of the *municipio* to be 56,615 with only

---

[14]The *canton,* as used in the descriptions of the communities in this study refers to a small settlement of households in a rural area of a *municipio* which are in control of their plots of land. An *aldea* is a population center which is dependent on the *municipio* government for its political administration. Thus, a more densely populated *canton* can simultaneously be an *aldea* since the two terms refer to different aspects of the community. The next smaller political unit is the *caserío* and indeed many *cantones* are politically classified as *caseríos* (Hill 1987:9–11; Hunt 1967).

[15]Guatemalan census figures have always been held to be unreliable and the 1981 census is particularly fraught with problems since it was during that period (1979–1982) that guerrilla/army violence reached its peak. Census-takers were unable to reach many rural communities. It may be assumed that some of the continuities shown in the census figures over the sixty-year period described here are due to the "smoothing" of the data in order to fill in for the gaps in the collected information.

3,199 residing in the town center. This follows the pattern of the "vacant town". The people reside on their traditional ancestral lands rather than being concentrated in the town center which results in the dispersion of the population over a fairly large and extremely mountainous area. Population density is 141.5 people per square kilometer. The only point of contact for residents of the different outlying areas is in the market held in the town center. Of the total population 97.5% (55,175) were identified by the census as being Mayans and 2.5% (1,426) as ladinos.[16] These group distribution numbers generally would militate towards a strong ethnolinguistic identity. The population is predominantly Mayan by an overwhelming margin. Though one might expect that a more dense concentration of the population in the urban center would strengthen group solidarity, this function is performed by the twice weekly ingathering of the population for the market; and by the annual cycle of religious festivals and participation of the rural residents in the hierarchical political-religious system of community service. The effect of such a consolidation of the population is not entirely predictable since it could either inhibit language shift, by providing solidity and security and many opportunities for use of the endangered code, or it could accelerate language shift, because there would be a lot of contact with innovations.

**4.2.3 Growth trends.** The absolute group numbers are also positive evidence of ethnolinguistic vitality for Chichicastenango. The Mayan population is one of the largest among the K'iche' communities exceeded only by that of Totonicapán. Population growth is also strong. The population of Chichicastenango in 1930 was estimated to be 25,000 Mayans and 628 ladinos. The earliest census data available is from the 1955 census which sets the total population at 27,718 but gives no data on numbers of Mayans and ladinos. This total represents an increase of 10.4% over the 1930 estimate. The 1964 census, however, indicates that 35,032 Mayans were resident in Chichicastenango out of a total population of 36,968 (94.8% Mayan). This represents a 33.4% increase in total population in the period from 1955 to 1964. The next census, that of 1973, shows the population of Chichicastenango to have reached 45,733 with a Mayan population of 44,675 (97.7%) and an increase of 23.7% in the total population. The growth from the 1973 census to 1981 has followed a similar pattern and represents a 23.8% increase during the eight-year period. The increase of population over the entire period, from 1955 to 1981, is 104.3% and an increase of 125.2% over estimates for the early

---

[16]If they were counted at all, presumably this group includes resident foreigners such as a few families related to development agencies, mission agencies, and the Peace Corps as well as a few long-term tourists—never a very large number at any point.

1930s. An even more recent, unofficial, figure for the population of Chichicastenango comes from a survey conducted by the local health center in the mid-1980s. This survey estimates the population to be 68,000 people which would represent an approximate growth of 20.1% over the 1981 population figure.

The proportion of Mayans in the community has remained relatively stable through the entire period which might be interpreted as a sign of stability (but see note 15). The Mayan segment of Chichicastenango is not decreasing over time. However, the surge in population over the period beginning with the 1964 census indicates that a major segment of the population in Chichicastenango is made up of young people. Indeed, the 1981 census data indicate that 58.6% of the population (33,190 individuals) are nineteen years old or younger.

**4.2.4 Marriage patterns.** As mentioned above we have only anecdotal data on the breakdown of endogamous marriage patterns. Indications are that residents of the *cantones* which are located along the high mountain ridge to the west and south of the town center, and which border with non-K'iche' speaking communities in the department of Sololá, are demonstrating an inclination to go to market in those neighboring communities. This is because of improved roads and transportation facilities. In an increasing number of cases social networks have been established which include Kaqchikel and Tzutujil speakers from the neighboring communities. Inevitably, the young people of these communities are meeting and marrying one another.

**4.2.5 Immigration and emigration.** Even less data are available on long-term immigration and emigration. Because Chichicastenango is a major market center, not only for the residents of the *municipio* but also for Guatemalan and foreign tourists, there is a great deal of temporary immigration as vendors from other communities arrive for the markets. Similarly, the popularity of the goods produced in Chichicastenango has led many Chichicastenango merchants to gravitate to other tourist centers where they may have more-or-less permanent points of sale. I was personally aware of several Chichicastenango families who had become permanent residents of Panajachel, a tourist mecca on the shores of Lake Atitlán in the department of Sololá. Other Chichicastenango natives have taken up residence in Guatemala City either to engage in tourism-based selling, or to find employment as a means of obtaining cash, or, in a few cases, to escape the guerrilla/army violence.

Another promoter of travel (though not permanent emigration, in most cases) is the increasing importance of fruit cultivation and exportation. Some Mayans who are representatives of the fruit growing cooperatives take extended trips to other parts of Guatemala and even into El Salvador and Mexico as part of their marketing efforts for their products.

Finally, there is the lure of the economic opportunities available in the United States which has influenced some, but proportionately few, of the Mayan residents of Chichicastenango to emigrate to the United States in search of economic gain. Most of the residents of Chichicastenango who manage to get to the United States are ladinos, but there are some Mayans who have followed this route as well.

For the same reasons that many Chichicastenango residents have left to go elsewhere, residents of several other communities, both K'iche' and non-K'iche', have taken up residence in Chichicastenango in order to take advantage of the market opportunities and, in a few cases, to flee the violence which made their former homes unsafe.

Another kind of migration based on economic motivation is the periodic migration to the coastal plantations for temporary employment in the harvesting of cotton, sugar cane, and coffee. This phenomenon has become institutionalized in Mayan communities and is discussed below as one of the components of institutional support.

### 4.3 Institutional support factors

Institutional support factors considered for Chichicastenango include the stance of government, church, formal education, business, and cultural entities towards the use and maintenance of K'iche'.

**4.3.1 Government.** The typical pattern in Guatemala Mayan *municipios* is the existence of two parallel power structures, one for ladinos and a separate, subsidiary system for Mayans. The municipal mayor outranks the Mayan mayor who is responsible only for resolving disputes between Mayans. The major center of power is in the office of the municipal mayor who is usually, but not always, a ladino. There is a typical pattern in the *municipios* wherein the day-to-day running of the community bureaucracy is handled by the town secretary who usually is a ladino but quite often one who speaks K'iche'.

In Chichicastenango, at the time that the data were collected, the mayor was a ladino who did not speak K'iche'. Our observations were that all parts of the town government with the exception of the *alcaldía indígena,* the Mayan mayoralty, were domains where Spanish was assumed to be the

## 4.3 Institutional support factors

language of business but where K'iche' could be used when necessary. Almost all of the town officials were ladinos. The mayor seemed resigned to the inevitable need to use K'iche' for some purposes in government and community life, but thought this was an indicator of the town's backwardness. Societal bilingualism was seen as an obstacle to development. Our language assistants also expressed strong feelings that the municipal officials were not supportive of the use of K'iche'. This seemed based, however, on the race of the current officials. They felt that if the mayor were a Mayan rather than a ladino, the negative feelings towards the use of K'iche' for governance would change.

The Mayan component of the municipal government, the *alcaldía indígena*, is the only portion of the government structure where K'iche' is commonly used and is seen as the expected language for that situation. This segment of the government is, however, largely seen by ladinos to be irrelevant to the "important" governmental functions. The Mayan mayors and the functionaries associated with them are part of the civil-religious hierarchy. This hierarchy operates in many Mayan towns where prestige and status are gained through acts of service and financial sacrifice on behalf of the community. Access to the highest positions of prestige and power (within the Mayan segment of the community) comes only after a lifetime of participation in this system. Thus, the Mayan officials are old men, who are viewed as wise advisors and trustworthy arbiters of disputes. Bunzel (1952:5) describes their functions on a typical weekday thus: "The Mayan *alcaldes* (the municipal officers) on benches in front of the courthouse, were busy with spinning and embroidery." In contrast to such idleness when the town is vacant, market days find these same officials "on duty in the courthouse. Today there is no time for spinning in the corridor, for all day long the courthouse is thronged with litigants and their witnesses" (1952:7).

Apart from the local municipal government there are also agencies of the national government operating in Chichicastenango. The national police force, the postal and telegraph service, the military, and the government-owned telephone company are all governmental institutions where Spanish is the assumed language of business. None of these institutions have any mechanisms in place to support the use of K'iche'. The National Police may hold literacy classes, but these generally use Spanish materials. The government policy states that telegrams sent in any language other than Spanish will be charged at double the normal rate. All of the employees at the telephone company were ladinos.

There are a number of government-related development agencies at work in Chichicastenango as well. DIGESA, a governmental agricultural development agency, is involved in projects related to agriculture, home economics, and nutrition. The staff assigned to Chichicastenango included an agronomist who worked part time as a teacher in the local schools as well as in programs with young people. The office receptionist, a young ladino woman, was responsible for classes with homemakers and young girls. The third staff member was a U.S. Peace Corps nutritionist. In addition, there were four agricultural "representatives", two men and two women, all K'iche' speakers, who interpret for the specialists and occasionally fill in for the specialist when he or she is out of town. The DIGESA receptionist recognized that at times the language differences presented a problem but felt that generally enough of the Mayan people could understand Spanish well enough to benefit from their programs. This program is on a relatively small scale, considering the size of Chichicastenango, and reaches approximately ten to fifteen of the rural *cantones* as well as the town center. Here again, the view of K'iche' is that it is an unfortunate but necessary fact of life. Communication would be more effective if Spanish only were needed. The use of translators is a grudging acceptance of this state of affairs and no written materials have been translated from Spanish to K'iche'.

The town Health Center, another government agency, is manned by a medical director, a ladino doctor, three health promoters, one registered nurse, four practical nurses, a secretary, a social worker, a lab technician, a driver, and a janitor. Two of the practical nurses speak K'iche', but all of the other professional staff speak only Spanish. There is also a trained midwife who is a K'iche' speaker who teaches prenatal care and attends to the delivery of babies. When one of the two staff members is not available to interpret for the medical staff, another patient is asked to assist as interpreter.

The health promoters work in the communities to promote preventative medicine and public health programs. None of the community health promoters speak K'iche', so all of the classes given in the *cantones* are conducted in Spanish. The medical director told us that it is the responsibility of the auxiliary mayor for that *canton* to ensure that the people understand what is being said.

The Public Health Department has also set up "Community Betterment Committees" in each of the *cantones*. These committees are chosen by the members of the community but are oriented by the health department.

The medical director felt that the use of written materials in K'iche' would be of little use since the illiteracy rate is so high among the Mayans. However, one of the K'iche'-speaking practical nurses felt that the use of

## 4.3 Institutional support factors

K'iche'-written materials would be valuable, albeit as a means of making the rural people more "civilized".

Three of the *cantones* have their own government health centers which are smaller than the "hospital" in the town center. These would have a doctor (usually a last-year medical student doing a required practicum) and a practical nurse, who is likely to be a resident of the local community and thus a speaker of K'iche'.

A third government agency with operations in Chichicastenango is the Office of National Development. This agency has its departmental office in Santa Cruz del Quiché, eleven miles away, from which it oversees development programs in agriculture and home economics throughout the department. The receptionist and secretary both speak K'iche', and the former stated that it is the policy of the agency to use the Mayan language of the community in which they are working. She also said that she got her job because of her ability to speak K'iche' and that the agency is actively recruiting Mayan bilinguals. The staff of the agency consists primarily of social workers (none of whom were we able to interview) and an agronomist working in the Ixil-speaking area of the department.

DIGESEPE is an agency of the national government which is concerned with veterinary care, training and development programs. Most of its workers speak K'iche' or have access to interpreters. Some of the workers even took classes in Ixil when they began to work in that part of the department. The programs of the agency include preventative veterinary medicine, training in small animal husbandry, and in cooperation with another agency, a program of evaluation for loans to small-scale farmers. Small animals are primarily raised by women, and so the programs in training for small animal husbandry are aimed at women which requires the use of K'iche' since fewer women than men speak Spanish. Our informant at DIGESEPE felt that literature in K'iche' about animal husbandry would be useful.

Finally, a quasi-governmental agency, COGAAT, is a cooperative food-for-work effort between the Guatemalan and German governments and local development-oriented groups. This group works in various parts of Guatemala, but of particular interest is their work in the southern part of the department of El Quiché. They have offices in both Santa Cruz del Quiché and Totonicapán. The cooperation with the Guatemalan government is channeled primarily through the National Development agency mentioned above. They have three main areas of interest: agriculture, infrastructure construction (schools, roads, bridges, latrines, community centers), and women's concerns (nutrition, childcare, preventative health and hygiene, vegetable production, small animal husbandry, weaving and other manual arts, and marketing of cottage-industry products). They work only in the rural areas yet their policy is that the liaison with the community must be a Spanish speaker. The coordinator whom we interviewed said that literacy is a value that they would like to reinforce, but they have no literacy promotion programs and see no particular value in promoting literacy in K'iche' since they feel the people must move into Spanish in order to be part of the productive segment of society.

All of the governmental institutions except DIGESEPE, the veterinary agency, expressed negative attitudes towards K'iche', and its existence was seen as an obstacle to progress and development. In one case, that of COGAAT, the German-funded agency, a community without at least one Spanish speaker who could act as liaison would be denied access to the agency's programs. Only DIGESEPE had accepted the existence of K'iche' and was actively pursuing a policy of using it in the implementation of development and training programs. One other notable exception is the peace corps worker who was assigned to DIGESA, the agricultural agency, and who was reported to have taken some K'iche' lessons. This was probably the result of a personal motivation, however, and not a matter of policy. It is safe to say that governmental institutional support of K'iche' in Chichicastenango is all but nonexistent.

**4.3.2 Church.** Guatemala is becoming increasingly divided along Roman Catholic and Protestant lines. Protestant evangelization efforts are making more and more inroads into both the practitioners of the Mayan traditional religion and the more orthodox Roman Catholic faithful, both of whom call themselves Roman Catholics. The division is reflected in language use and institutional support of K'iche'. In general, as a result of the decisions of the Second Vatican Council to celebrate the Mass in the vernacular language, the Roman Catholic church has positioned itself as the repository of traditional K'iche' identity and values. The Protestant churches to varying degrees have rejected not only what they perceive as Mayan paganism, but also Roman Catholic heresy and have acquired a much more contemporary and progressive image.

In Chichicastenango the most visible church is, of course, the Roman Catholic church on the town square. At the time of our survey, however, there were fifteen Protestant churches of various denominations within the town center and another fifty-three Protestant congregations in the *cantones*. The Roman Catholic church also had several other chapels in the *cantones* as well as a strong and active network of catechists, trained lay-leaders, who carried on a teaching ministry throughout the *municipio*.

## 4.3 Institutional support factors 81

Estimates at the time were that Chichicastenango was about 30% Protestant.

The Roman Catholic priest in Chichicastenango for most of the time of our residence was Father Felix,[17] a young K'iche' man who actively promoted the use of K'iche' in the church and in literature. He said that he had experienced years of study abroad using Spanish, French, Latin, and English and that he had almost forgotten his native K'iche'. When he returned to Chichicastenango, his hometown, he had to relearn his mother tongue. He had struggled to institute the use of K'iche' in the services of the church. He said that he had found more positive response to the use of K'iche' in the rural areas, but still there is some opposition even from Mayans who feel that the use of K'iche' for worship is inappropriate. Father Felix introduced a K'iche' mass every Saturday evening which was well attended. This mass used a K'iche' liturgy, had the Scripture lessons read in K'iche', and had a number of choral responses sung in K'iche'. The sermon was preached first in K'iche' and then repeated (sometimes in a slightly edited form) in Spanish. The Sunday morning Mass was offered as a bilingual Mass (both liturgy and sermon in Spanish and K'iche') and was mainly for the benefit of the few ladinos and tourists who attended. Some of the Mayans not otherwise occupied in the market also attended. A third Mass was offered on Sunday afternoons in Spanish only, but was attended by a fair number of Mayans. The Saturday evening Mass in K'iche' was designed to meet the needs of the rural Mayans who would come to town on Saturday in order to participate in the Sunday market. This service was discontinued when the priest was forced to leave town over a political dispute in which his life was threatened.

Father Felix noted that the Mayans are more religious than the ladinos. He estimated that only about 15% of those who attend the masses are ladinos. While the whole world of the Mayan is wrapped up in religion, the ladinos only attend for major festive occasions. Therefore, Father Felix felt that the three Masses offered by the church ought to more adequately meet the needs of all those who attend.

In designing the K'iche' liturgy, Father Felix said he worked hard to make the K'iche' used as "pure" as possible, avoiding Spanish loans, and attempting to find authentic K'iche' words for Biblical terms and concepts. He felt this was his obligation as a leader in the community in order to counteract the tendency of some K'iche's to use Spanish loans in order to appear to be of a higher status.

Father Felix said he had organized his ministry activities into six areas. He had teams of lay-leaders who offered classes to provide instruction on

---

[17]This and all other names attributed to language assistants are pseudonyms.

baptism and marriage, to produce a weekly radio program, to teach preventative health measures, to form a choir which was writing its own music using not only K'iche' words but musical styles as well, and a dance troupe to keep alive community identity. The music of the church is now focused around the marimba, Guatemala's national instrument and a symbol of Mayan identity. In many Protestant churches the marimba is considered to be a "pagan" instrument.

The radio program offered music, information about the Mayan calendar, poetry, and readings from the *Pop Wuj*. He reiterated that the purpose of these activities was to unify the Mayan people of Chichicastenango.

Interestingly, Father Felix had also made efforts to strengthen the links of the Roman Catholic church to the practitioners of the traditional religion. He told us that he had been studying the *costumbres* "customs, traditions" and had organized a meeting which was attended by 103 shamans from Chichicastenango. His strategy, he says, is to end the alienation from the church that these religious practitioners have felt and to "infiltrate" Christian teachings into their belief system.

Another group organized by Father Felix is a kind of K'iche' think tank which spends its time in "reflection", thinking through the problems of the community and dealing with issues such as the role of the woman in K'iche' society or missionary strategies for reaching the K'iche' people.

Protestant churches are also predominantly Mayan, though the ladinos who attend are likely to be in the positions of authority. These ladinos are likely to be more regular in their attendance and more active in their participation than the Roman Catholic ladinos. Thus, although the ratio of Mayans to ladinos in the Roman Catholic and Protestant churches is quite similar, the Roman Catholic church in Chichicastenango is clearly a Mayan institution while the Protestant churches are less clearly so.

While there are subdivisions and factions among the Roman Catholic population, the Roman Catholic church in Chichicastenango is more monolithic than the Protestant community. The sixty-eight Protestant congregations in Chichicastenango represent many different denominations each with its own organizational pattern, style, and attitudes towards the use of K'iche' in its services and ministries. One pastor we interviewed, Pastor Diego, felt that the leadership of his church was not interested in using or learning K'iche' because it was a difficult language to learn. He also noted, however, that he felt he had been invited to be the pastor of his church because he could speak K'iche' and thus could work more effectively with the K'iche' speakers who are the majority of his congregation. In spite of this felt need to use K'iche' in order to achieve adequate communication, Protestants are less likely to use K'iche' for the liturgy or the sermon. K'iche' is, however, used at the end of

## 4.3 Institutional support factors

the service when announcements are made regarding the times and locations of upcoming meetings and activities and would more likely be used at church meetings held in homes during the week.

Pastor Diego noted that even those K'iche's who were literate would not bring their K'iche' New Testaments to church. They expected the pastor to read from the Spanish Bible and "adapt" it to K'iche' so that the people could understand. Pastor Diego was particularly concerned that fully 98% of his congregation could not understand his Sunday sermon. Still, he felt that this is the way the congregation wanted it and if he were to start preaching in K'iche' there would be protests. In his church, a Thursday service[18] had been instituted which was ostensibly a K'iche' service, though still much of the singing was from the Spanish hymnal. Pastor Diego said that he often preached the same sermon in K'iche' on Thursday that he had preached on Sunday in Spanish, in order to make sure that the people understood it. Another service held on Tuesday evenings also was the venue for some use of K'iche' other than for the announcements.

His church also maintained a K'iche' Sunday School class which was attended by older women. Only infrequently would a K'iche' man attend. They had at one time had a K'iche' Sunday School class for children but could not find anyone willing to teach it and so had discontinued it. Pastor Diego felt that his congregation was interested in having their children learn Spanish so that they could be "part of the community", and could have the linguistic skills needed to defend themselves against injustices.

A second Protestant pastor, Pastor Julio, noted that in his church there is a division between those who would like more Spanish used and those who would like more K'iche'. In his efforts to sell K'iche' religious literature, he noted that people were interested when they heard K'iche' being read aloud because they could understand it, but still felt that they would rather learn to read in Spanish.

Both pastors felt that though there is interest in literacy, it is confined to the use of Spanish, and even then it is difficult for adults to find the time to study. The children are sent to the government schools where they are taught to read and write in Spanish.

**4.3.3 Education.** Although some K'iche's recognize that illiteracy hinders them, there is also a sizable segment of the population which places no value on the acquisition of literacy skills. These were characterized by our informants as older people who fear that schooling will have a deleterious effect on the character development of the children, i.e., children

---

[18]The two market days in Chichicastenango are Sunday and Thursday. So a service held on Thursday would make it convenient for rural people to attend since they would already be in the town center for the market.

who attend school will not learn how to do manual labor in the fields and therefore will grow up unable to feed their families. With this handicap they must turn to thievery to maintain themselves, and this accounts for the increase in crime in Chichicastenango since the introduction of formal schooling.

The general attitude seems to be that literacy is valuable, but it is not a skill that every individual needs. The illiterate can find a literate person who will read or write for him when needed. The local schoolteachers were seen as having this role in the society, and it was inexplicable to our language helper why some of the ladino schoolteachers were unwilling to provide this service to the community.

In the town center Chichicastenango has three primary schools, a middle school, and a high school. In addition there are thirty-three rural elementary schools located in the *cantones*. One of the *cantones,* Chicua, also has a junior high school.[19] Of these, none of the town schools are part of the national bilingual education program although thirty-one of the rural schools are part of that program which attempts to use K'iche' during the first four years of elementary education. The bilingual program is understaffed, however, and only twenty-nine of the schools have bilingual teachers. We interviewed the director of the bilingual education program in Chichicastenango and he observed that there is a high drop-out rate in the schools due to illness, the need for students to work, and the indifference of parents towards education in general. He felt, however, that most parents were happy with the program although in some cases there were complaints when a teacher was "too bilingual" in K'iche' so that the children did not learn Spanish. The director identified these people as those who had "problems with their own self-identity as Mayans".

Other sources informed us that some parents in the rural communities had decided to send their children into town for schooling since they did not want their children to participate in the K'iche'-based bilingual education schools. Their hope was that the schools would teach their children Spanish, and they were unhappy with the attempt to use K'iche' in the educational domain. One ladino school official told us that between 80–95% of the parents want their children to learn Spanish and see no need for schools to use K'iche' because "the children already know K'iche'".

Based on data provided by the bilingual education office in Chichicastenango, in 1988 there were 5,085 children enrolled in the preschool program but only 1,327 first graders. Of these first graders, 177 dropped out and 324 were not promoted to the second grade. Enrollment for each successive grade decreased until in the same year there were only

---

[19]The data are based on the previous school year's attendance figures.

143 sixth graders of whom only 130 were promoted. These data indicate that a large number of the school-age children are not attending school. The attrition rate represents a progression over time of less than three percent of those who start the preschool program continuing on to sixth grade.

**4.3.4 Business.** In Chichicastenango, as in other town centers, the most visible center of business is the town square where twice weekly markets, held on Sunday and Thursday, draw large crowds. The market is clearly a Mayan domain and is the locus of not only the exchange of goods and services but also of information and opinion. The market serves as a reinforcer of community values and mores. Participation in the market and the use of K'iche' in that domain is an important means of producing solidarity.

The market in Chichicastenango, however, also serves as an important point of contact between the Mayan and ladino cultures and between the Mayans and outsiders from many parts of the world who come as tourists. The ladino residents of Chichicastenango must buy their vegetables, meat, and other perishables from the market. This requires them to deal with Mayan merchants (not all of whom are from Chichicastenango). Some ladino women have acquired some K'iche' in order to engage in these transactions, although almost all of the merchants speak enough Spanish to be able to deal with these business matters.

The physical and spatial organization of the market is iconic of these social relations. The outer fringe of the market is devoted almost exclusively to the sale of tourist items, textiles, masks, and leather goods and is a lucrative source of cash. Almost every Mayan family that I met in Chichicastenango had some connection to one of these stalls. The Mayan merchants who man these stalls frequently have acquired some rudimentary skills in English, French, German, Italian, and Japanese as well as Spanish. The next most inner band of the market is the domain of Mayans and ladinos and a few of the more adventurous tourists. Here fruits and vegetables and some tourist items are also sold. Many of the merchants here are traveling vendors from other communities who speak K'iche' when necessary but also have considerable command of Spanish. The inner core of the market is the exclusive domain of the local Mayan population. Mayan clothing, coffee, beans, and corn are sold here, and open-air lunch counters are operated to feed those who have come from a distance. This part of the market is almost entirely monolingual in K'iche'.

The other segment of the business community in Chichicastenango is made up of those few stores and businesses that are open all week long and occupy buildings in the town center. While there are a few women who come to the market square even on non-market days to sell their produce, the stores are the only fixed places of business that can be found all week long. Many of these businesses are owned by ladinos. There are several pharmacies, a few general stores, a bakery, a bank, several restaurants and hotels targeting the tourist trade, a furniture/department store of sorts, and other small businesses of various types. The town center also has two gasoline stations. Generally, Spanish is used in these places of business, but some ladino merchants use K'iche' with their Mayan customers if communication becomes difficult. Though we did no testing, our impressions are that the level of K'iche' spoken by these merchants is quite rudimentary and is comparable to the level of Spanish spoken by the Mayan merchants in the market setting.

Another small, but important, segment of economic activity in Chichicastenango is centered around the hotels and restaurants which cater to the foreign tourists who arrive semi-weekly for the market. Chichicastenango has two large hotels which cater to tour groups brought in on modern buses. There are also three smaller hostelries which cater to Guatemalans and the hardier tourists who may be traveling on the public buses which pass through Chichicastenango several times a day. Chichicastenango has several restaurants besides those connected to the hotels. Mayans work in these establishments as waiters, cooks, maids, and in other menial services. Many of the waiters, in particular, are bilingual in at least English and perhaps in several other languages as well, at least in the vocabulary and structures required for the serving of a meal. Some of the waiters have also been able to get jobs in Guatemala City where the combination of their skills and their ethnicity provides them with an entré into some of the more tourist-oriented hotels. At least on the surface, this sector of town-based, nontraditional employment, serves as a reinforcement of the Chichicastenango identity. The waiters are dressed in the typical clothing of Chichicastenango, now normally worn only by the older men who are involved in the *cofradías* (discussed in the next section). They are the objects of admiration by the tourists and this lends some prestige and status to the identity.

Proportionately, very little business activity involving Mayans goes on in the stores. Except for the pharmacies, Mayans generally do most of their purchasing in the marketplace. The stores, even those owned by Mayans, generally serve the needs of the ladino and tourist community.

Another business institution which must be mentioned is the institutionalized system of migrant labor which is recruited in the highland communities for work on lowland coffee, sugar cane, and cotton plantations. This institution is decreasing in importance and influence in Chichicastenango because the tourist trade and the introduction of cash crops has lessened the need for the residents of Chichicastenango to go to the coastal areas to work for cash. Nevertheless, several hundred people, sometimes men only but frequently entire families, migrate each year to the coast for a period of from thirty to ninety days. This migration takes them away from their homes and their community networks and places them in contact with people from other communities and speakers of other languages. In that setting, Spanish becomes the lingua franca. This migration becomes then a primary means by which Mayans acquire their Spanish competence, albeit in a nonstandard variety.

**4.3.5 Culture.** It is difficult to make a sharp division between religious life and cultural life. Therefore, some of the observations about the role of the Church in providing institutional support or lack of it for language and identity maintenance are equally appropriate in the discussion of cultural institutional support.

The primary and most visible cultural institution in Chichicastenango is the system of *cofradías,* a civil-religious hierarchical system made up of religious brotherhoods which are charged with the care of the town saints. This system is hierarchical in nature in that the individuals enter at the lowest level, and through faithful discharge of their duties in service to the community (along with considerable economic sacrifice), rise through the ranks to fulfill greater and greater obligations and to gain status and prestige as well. Although these brotherhoods function within the Mayan cosmology and religious system, they are closely associated with the Roman Catholic church where the statues of the saints are kept. The *cofradías* are K'iche' institutions, however, and are one of the reinforcers of K'iche' ethnic identity for those who participate in the system. The *cofradías* are the organizers and main participants in the annual town festival in December to honor Saint Thomas. They are the primary actors in the preparations for Christmas, New Year's Eve, Holy Week, and the Day of the Dead (All Saints Day). One of our language helpers observed that these events used to be much more festive, but now there are so many Protestants in town who will not participate that the festivals are not as elaborate nor as colorful as they used to be. In spite of this perceived decline, the celebration of the Day of the Dead on November 1 begins a period which lasts through the annual fiesta for Saint Thomas in late December and on through New Year's Day. The town is alive with noise, music, fireworks, dancers, bands, colorful costumes, and an overflowing market which reaches out of the central square and up the side streets for several blocks. The celebration continues almost non-stop and there is much drunkenness and occasional fighting as the revelry reaches its peak.

Other non-native cultural institutions also exist in Chichicastenango, though many of these could be considered under the other categories already covered. There is, for example, a Canadian-backed nongovernmental development organization, REDH Integral, working in the *municipio*. They work in many of the same areas of concern as the governmental agencies described above, although generally they are more focused on health and welfare than agricultural or infrastructure development. They tend overall to be more aware of the need to use K'iche' in order to communicate successfully, though they do not use written materials in K'iche' because of the high illiteracy rate among the people with whom they work. Still, the thrust of their work is the introduction of new ideas: improved hygiene, improved growing methods, teaching widows how to care for and provide for their children, medical services, etc. These innovations can be seen as being nonsupportive of the traditional K'iche' way of doing things.

All of these well-intentioned efforts to "help", in parallel with the growing Protestant segment of the Mayan population who no longer participate in the *cofradías* and the fiestas, places the traditional expression of K'iche' culture under pressure. The traditional culture must fight to maintain itself against these institutional pressures to modernize.

### 4.4 Status factors

The attempt to evaluate the status of a group inevitably runs up against the dilemma that status and prestige must be measured against a standard that is based on a group's value system. Under normal conditions, low status behaviors would be avoided and high status behaviors would be emulated. When there are two competing value systems, however, it is more difficult to evaluate how the individual or group perceives different behaviors. This is, I propose, one of the indicators of an identity shift. Just as leaking domains are indicators of language shift, so the unpredictability of behavior because of competing systems of values used by the group members themselves are indicators of a loss of identity focus.

**4.4.1 Economic status.** In the traditional K'iche' value system the possession of wealth is not a high status behavior. Higher status in the community is achieved through the use of any acquired wealth in the service of the ancestors (and thereby the community). Thus, economic activity for traditional K'iche's has been primarily to sustain the family and to

## 4.4 Status factors

amass the needed surplus so that community service could be performed. Wealth is not to be ostentatiously displayed.

This world view is gradually changing, however, as the residents of Chichicastenango are faced twice a week with intense contact with a very materialistic outside world. Tourists with cameras, cars, and money to spend are one source of this contact. The ladinos and other resident non-Mayans in town are another. Their value system prizes comfortable homes, the possession of a car, electric lights, telephones, televisions, and other modern conveniences.

The third, and probably most important, source of contact with the materialistic world view, however, comes from those Mayans who have been successful in the production of cash crops or in the sale of goods to the tourist market. These Mayans, a good number of them prominent in the Protestant churches, have set an example of what a Spanish-based education and participation in the cash-market system can do. Increasing numbers of younger Mayans are becoming dissatisfied with the prospect of being subsistence farmers, obligated spiritually, culturally, and economically to their ancestors and the saints, and to a life of egalitarian poverty. Economic status cannot be found in that value system. All of the economic rewards are available through the maintenance of a Mayan identity, but a Mayan identity that sells.

**4.4.2 Social status.** The K'iche' identity is seen by many in Chichicastenango, and not just by ladinos, as symbolizing backwardness and lack of development. Most of the government institutions view the K'iche' identity as an obstacle to be overcome. The Roman Catholic church supports the identity, but not without internal opposition even from some of its Mayan members and in the face of a growing Protestant community which sees Spanish as the language of upward mobility.

Ladinos view K'iche's as little more than ignorant childlike savages who must be cared for and put up with. Several of our ladino neighbors expressed the opinion that Guatemala would be so much more progressive ("like the United States") if the Mayans did not present such a problem for development. One ladino merchant expressed the view that the situation is hopeless because the Mayans cannot learn, so there is no way to teach them to better themselves.

Though for a while there was a strong attitude among the Mayans which opposed the intrusion of innovations such as schooling, that attitude has gradually given way. Now there is a more general acceptance of the view that to maintain a traditional Mayan lifestyle is to aspire to backwardness. Though most Mayan residents of Chichicastenango feel proud to be Mayans, they do not want to be "backward Mayans", but rather up-and-coming progressive Mayans like those merchants who have education and cars and businesses. While there is still a general sentimental attachment to K'iche' and to being a Mayan, there is a strong instrumental pressure to participate in the ladino world on ladino terms.

**4.4.3 Sociohistorical status.** Chichicastenango is a center of K'iche' history. As mentioned earlier, the *Pop Wuj,* the sacred book of the K'iche's, was discovered here. It is traditionally held to be a site that was the refuge of those who fled Pedro de Alvarado and his conquering troops when Utatlán fell. Chichicastenango is advertised to tourists worldwide as one of Guatemala's most Mayan towns. There are several important sites for the practice of the traditional animistic rites in and around Chichicastenango. The existence of at least one hundred shaman as noted by the town priest is an indication that the historical-religious connection is still strong.

**4.4.4 Language status.** Spanish is clearly the language of power in Chichicastenango while K'iche' is the language of solidarity. While it cannot be stated with certainty until the empirical data on language use is analyzed, it seems that a number of K'iche's view power as being within their grasp and so are opting for the language of power. One grandfather told me that he was going to speak Spanish to his grandchildren until they were six years old, because he wanted them to be able to "better themselves". He was of the opinion that they could always learn K'iche' because it was all around them. Another young K'iche' couple, in spite of their activism in the promotion of K'iche' literature, spoke only Spanish to their children. As a result, the children were growing up as passive bilinguals in K'iche' with Spanish the only language they had productive competence in.

K'iche's were always amused and a bit surprised at my efforts to learn the language. I believe they were also a bit embarrassed by my efforts to use it in public, formal domains where they would have felt more comfortable using Spanish. Several of our younger language assistants told us of cases where high school students would deride others for using K'iche' on the street as they were walking to and from classes and teased them about acting like "hillbillies" (Spanish: *montés*).

## 4.5 Subjective factors

Much of the self-perception of the Mayan population of Chichicastenango has already been dealt with in the foregoing discussion. As with all of the objective vitality factors, the subjective perceptions are mixed. It is difficult to determine which particular self-perception will prevail. To a great extent these subjective perceptions are not consciously held and therefore are not explicitly expressed. While very few Mayans would clearly state that they feel that ladinos are better than Mayans, there seems to be a large number who share the perception that with the economic opportunities that are opening for Mayans in Chichicastenango, they now have a chance to compete with ladinos on the ladinos' terms. This is an implicit acceptance of ladino values and of the ladino evaluation of the Mayan culture. While not abandoning their Mayan identity totally—they do not want to give up their Mayan dress, their social organization, or even their language—they feel that they must be progressive enough to take advantage of the economic (and thereby social and political) opportunities that are available to them.

There are some voices being raised in opposition to this. One group is the older generation which now represents a minority of the population. These folk do not like the innovations because they are morally and spiritually bad. They will lead to the abandonment of the traditional world view which requires the maintenance of the status quo as much as possible in order to maintain the equilibrium of the cosmos. These older folk are also dismissed by many of the younger people as simply not understanding how the world has changed.

A third segment is much smaller. This group could be called Mayan nationalists. They are younger people, many of whom have succeeded in the ladino-dominated educational system and now are fighting for a new K'iche' identity which would encompass the whole range of social and cultural domains, not just those which have been relegated to the Mayans by the dominant society. There are very few spokespersons for this point of view in Chichicastenango. The bilingual education program personnel would be the most vocal of this type. The Roman Catholic priest, Father Felix, also shares some of these views. They feel confident that a person can be both modern and K'iche' without sacrificing all of the historical, sentimental, social, cultural, and linguistic heritage that is associated with that identity.

The first segment, the group which says that the K'iche' identity must change to take advantage of the opportunities, is the most numerous in the town center and in the more progressive *cantones,* such as Chicua. It is also predominantly made up of young people who comprise the largest segment of the population of Chichicastenango.

The second group, the older generation, is declining in numbers but is the generation of power and authority in a society which traditionally has used age as a marker of prestige. Still, as more and more young people reject the traditional Mayan world view, this influence is likely to decrease as well. The older generation's values are still influential and widespread, particularly in the rural areas. The core of town-based young people who are avidly pursuing their education and dreaming of economic success find themselves increasingly in conflict with this older group. Other young people, like the young couple cited above, find themselves living in cognitive dissonance where their expressed attitudes and their actions contradict one another.

The third group, the young Mayan nationalists, in 1987, lacked in numbers and credibility what they hoped to make up for in activism. They were few in numbers because few Mayans have had the opportunities they had had to complete university-level training and to obtain employment as professionals. They lacked credibility because many of them were no longer residents of their own *municipio*. In some cases they had adopted some ladino customs. They also lacked credibility because they were attempting to instruct their elders and peers without having achieved status through the traditional hierarchical system of status and prestige. As activists, however, they were working to marshal as much institutional support as they could in favor of their point of view. As a result, they should not be dismissed as a force in shaping the potential shift of K'iche' identity.

### 4.6–4.9 Cunén

Cunén[20] is located in the department of El Quiché about five miles north-northeast of Sacapulas. The town center is located near the eastern end of the Cuchumatanes mountain range at an altitude of 5,000 feet above sea level (Moore 1973:72). The *municipio* occupies an area of approximately 160 square kilometers. The town center and communities of Cunén are spread out along the main east-west road which crosses the *municipio* and runs up into the mountains surrounding the town center. There is also a road branching off of the main road which leads to the Ixil communities to the northwest. Another community to the west along this road, Chiul, is an *aldea* of Cunén.

---

[20]The Quiché Survey Team members who gathered these data on Cunén were Reg and Ivy Willems, JoAnn Munson, and Mae Toedter.

Cunén is known as a wheat-growing community, though the staple corn and beans are grown as well. The community has an abundance of water which is used for irrigation. The water also drives three stone mills which grind the wheat into flour. With flour easily available, the community is known as a town of bakers, and the traditional Cunén loaves, called *xecas* /'ʃekas/, are sold throughout the community and even carried to markets elsewhere. A second industry is the cutting of wood for lumber. The mountain forests around Cunén have an abundant supply of trees. Several carpenters keep busy in the town center. Some entrepreneurs have bought trucks in order to transport the flour, lumber, and garlic, a more recently introduced cash crop, to other areas of Guatemala.

### 4.6 Demographic factors

The 1981 Guatemalan census estimated the population of Cunén to be 12,732 of which 86.0% (10,953) are Mayan. This places Cunén in the middle range of the communities included in this study in terms of the proportion of Mayans to ladinos in the population. Of the total population 87.6% (11,155) live in the rural areas and 1,577 (12.4%) live in the town center. The population density is 79.6 persons per square kilometer.

The population of Cunén also shows a pattern of considerable expansion over the twenty-five year period beginning with the 1955 census. The 1955 census lists the total population of Cunén as 5,612 which rose to 8,291 by 1964, a 47.7% increase. In the period between the 1964 census and that of 1973 the total population rose to 9,762, a 17.7% increase. The increase from 1973 to 1981 represents a 30.4% increase. An unofficial estimate of the population made in 1988 by the local government health center placed the population at 16,382, a 28.7% increase in that seven-year period. As in Chichicastenango, there has been a very rapid expansion of the population. Cunén is also a predominantly young population with 7,498 individuals (58.9%) nineteen years old or younger.

The demographic profile of Cunén differs somewhat from that of Chichicastenango in that Cunén is not as much a vacant town. While the town center is the primary locus of ladino residency, there are also *aldeas* where ladinos are resident. While ladinos constitute a minority of the population in terms of numbers, they are spread more uniformly through the entire community than in other communities included in the study. Cunén thus demonstrates some of the characteristics of a nucleated town.

It should be noted that Cunén has twenty-five *aldeas* and twenty-one *caseríos*. The recognition of a rural community as an *aldea* provides it with slightly greater prestige than other rural localities. An *aldea* is somewhat in competition with the town center as a focus of identity and as a place where the social and economic needs of the people can be met. The elevation of a community by the government to the status of *aldea* is a response to the lobbying efforts of the members of that community. Thus, it is the change in focus of identity of the residents sociopsychologically which effects a change in the political status of their community.

Cunén presents a special problem for this analysis in that it is an ethnically complex community. Besides the ladino minority, representatives of three other K'iche' ethnicities reside within its boundaries as well as some Aguacatecos, speakers of a Mamean language, and a few Ixiles. The largest single group, estimated at 33% of the total population are the traditional residents of Cunén who speak a distinctive dialect called Cunenteco. While many of these people live in the town center, the *aldea* of Los Trigales is recognized as the place where the Cunentecos live.

A second K'iche' ethnic group present in the community are descendants of K'iche's who migrated into the area from San Francisco el Alto and Momostenango, two communities in the highlands of the department of Totonicapán. The *aldea* Chiul, mentioned above, is populated by speakers of the Momosteco variety of K'iche'.

The third ethnic group is made up of immigrants from Santa María Chiquimula, many of whom arrived in Cunén after more than a century of migration in search of grazing lands for their sheep. This migration first brought them to Sacapulas only five miles away at the foot of the mountains just below Cunén. The Chiquimultecos, perhaps because they are shepherds and because of their lower social prestige, tend to reside in the outlying, more rural, communities. The other K'iche's (the Momostecos) are spread more uniformly between the town center and the *aldeas*. According to the Health Center data, these two groups constitute 55% of the population. Ladinos make up the remaining 12%. The Health Center data indicate that 88.0% of the community is Mayan, a figure not too disparate from the national census figure of 86.0%. The Mayan groups, in spite of long years of contact and co-residence, have maintained their separate identities at least in terms of their linguistic varieties. Our observers in Cunén noted that the only men who still use the distinctive clothing of the community are those over 60 years of age. The women still wear either the distinctive Cunenteco *güipil* (blouse) or any other style of *güipil* that is sold in the market.

Although the three ethnic groups are separate from each other in many respects, they are treated without distinction in this study for the purposes of describing their collective ethnolinguistic vitality vis-à-vis the ladino segment of society. Our observations in Cunén revealed that while

## 4.6 Demographic factors

the three Mayan ethnic groups maintain a certain degree of separation, they interact with each other frequently and, in spite of the differences in their linguistic varieties, communicate with each other without major problems. Many individuals at least claimed to be able to speak Cunenteco along with their own native variety (Momosteco or Chiquimulteco), though when problems of understanding did arise, they were attributed to the fact that the offending utterance was Chiquimulteco.

We have no concrete data on marriage patterns in Cunén except for anecdotal references to individuals' backgrounds which indicate that there is at least some intermarriage between the Cunentecos and members of the other K'iche' groups. Here, as in Sacapulas, the Chiquimultecos are not well thought of and identification with that group is not prestigious.

There is not a great deal of emigration from the community on a permanent basis among the Mayan segment of the population. As evidenced by the complexity of the ethnic mix in Cunén, however, over the years there has been a noticeable amount of immigration by Momostecos, Chiquimultecos, and Aguacatecos. Of these, the first two groups have a longer history of residence in the community and a great deal of accommodation has taken place between the native Cunentecos and the others. It seems likely that the suitability of the land and climate for wheat growing and the availability of that land was the attraction that brought the Momostecos from their home communities of San Francisco el Alto and Momostenango, *municipios* in Totonicapán, where much wheat is grown. More recently, the Aguacatecos, who speak a Mayan language not closely related to K'iche', have arrived in search of land on which to grow garlic. The more prosperous Aguacatecos were willing to pay well and as a result they drove up the price of land in the area. There was a move by the residents of Cunén to have the Aguacatecos expelled from the community, but that was overruled by the departmental authorities. At best, the relations between the established residents of Cunén and the Aguacateco entrepeneurs is uneasy. More than the Momostecos and Chiquimultecos, the Aguacatecos are clearly seen as outsiders. However, they have introduced garlic as an additional cash crop which some residents of Cunén are accepting as an innovation. Another much smaller group of new residents consists of Ixil refugees who have fled their homelands because of the intense violence of the conflict between the government and guerrilla insurgents. Cunén provides a close and somewhat safer haven for them.

## 4.7 Institutional support factors

**4.7.1 Government.** The government structure in Cunén is the standard form of municipal government with a mayor, auxiliary mayors, and a town secretary. However, in Cunén there is no *alcalde indígena* (Mayan mayor) office. Cunén was, however, one of the communities where the town mayor was a Mayan. This was the first time in the town's history that a Mayan had attained such a position of power. It was anticipated that this change might also bring about a change in the use of language in the town hall, where the assumed language of business is Spanish, but at the time of our data gathering it was still too early to tell if that would happen. Of course, there is no way to know if such a change in language use would be more than a temporary one. Under the then current administration, the only ladino in the town hall hierarchy was the town secretary.

There are few government agencies working in Cunén. INACOP, an agency that works to promote the establishment of cooperatives, is a government-sponsored agency and has an office in Cunén where several agricultural cooperatives are thriving. DIGESA, the government agricultural service, also provides consultation but has no permanent presence in the community. The government health center is manned almost entirely by ladinos and is generally shunned by the Mayans except in dire emergencies. The doctors assigned to the health center are graduate medical students who often feel that their assignment to Cunén is a kind of forced exile from the capital city and "civilization". The telegraph office was also manned by ladinos, but the staff would provide help in writing out telegram messages for the illiterate.

**4.7.2 Church.** Cunén has a Roman Catholic church and several Protestant churches of various denominations. Mormon missionaries have also worked in Cunén over the years and there is an active Mormon group in the community. For several years, the resident priest in Cunén was a native of the community and used Cunenteco for the activities of the church. He was replaced temporarily by a K'iche'-speaking priest who was also transferred, and at the time these data were collected the church in Cunén was without a resident priest. It was reported to us that although the Mayans liked the Cunenteco priest, ladino attendance at the masses dropped during his tenure. The priest returns on Saturdays to teach catechism classes in Spanish.

The Roman Catholic church sponsors a small restaurant which is run by the Cunenteco priest's sister in a room adjacent to the church. There is also a church-sponsored general store and pharmacy. The restaurant is staffed by Cunentecos and the radio (turned up loud-enough for all the customers to hear) is tuned to the Roman Catholic K'iche'-language station broadcasting from Santa Cruz del Quiché.

There are five Protestant churches located in the town center and ten to twelve others located in the *aldeas*. Besides representing different denominations, these churches also seem to be divided along ethnic lines. One church is made up of Cunentecos and ladinos. Another has a mixed group of Cunentecos, Chiquimultecos, and Aguacatecos. A third is primarily made up of Momostecos. In spite of the fact that all of the churches have sizable Mayan components in their congregations, the churches predominantly use Spanish. The pastor of one church is a native Cunenteco, but he uses mostly Spanish, only occasionally making the effort to translate his sermon into Cunenteco. A second pastor preaches first in Spanish and then repeats the sermon in K'iche'. The church that uses K'iche' most still uses Spanish for Scripture readings and for singing. Though the New Testament is available in K'iche' (though not in the Cunenteco variety), none of the K'iche'-speaking pastors used it. One would attempt to translate extemporaneously Scripture verses in his sermon. All of the churches observed used K'iche' or Cunenteco for the announcements of important events. Our observation was that wherever there was a significant presence of ladinos in a church, Spanish was predominantly used, though no negative comments about K'iche' were ever expressed in our hearing.

Mormon missionaries had a fair amount of success in the past in making converts in Cunén and for a few years operated a medical and dental clinic in the town center. They also were involved in some other community development efforts and were instrumental in organizing a cooperative which established and continues to operate the middle school. Although a few families in Cunén still call themselves Mormons, there was no active congregation meeting at the time our observers were resident in the community.

**4.7.3 Education.** There are twenty-six primary schools in the *muncipio* and one middle school located in the town center. Two of the primary schools are located in the town center; all the rest are rural, and only three of these have grades one through six; most only include the first three grades. Some may go through fourth grade if there are enough teachers available. Twenty-three of the sixty teachers who work in Cunén speak K'iche' and many of these are natives of the community who have completed high school training and have returned as elementary schoolteachers. Students who wish to complete high school must go to the departmental capital, Santa Cruz del Quiché, or to Guatemala City. There are eleven teachers under the administrative direction of the bilingual education program. All of these were in Cunén before the bilingual education program began as part of the earlier program to teach Spanish to students in the lower grades. These teachers reported that they had not changed their teaching methods or activities in spite of the change in their place in the organizational structure of the Ministry of Education. They do, however, use K'iche' as the medium of instruction for teaching Spanish reading and writing in the first two grades.

The school director for Cunén reported that 96% to 97% of the town children will finish the school year but that the figure drops to around 85% in the rural areas. One of the teachers that we interviewed reported that he would lose six students out of his class of twenty. The only reason that these informants could provide for this attrition was that the Mayan families would migrate to the coastal plantations, thus removing their children from the school before the school year ended.

The school director, a ladino, reported that parental attitudes towards the use of K'iche' in school were generally negative. He said that parents felt that it was a "regression" to have to learn in a language that they already knew when what was needed was the opportunity to acquire Spanish. The director's own attitudes were quite negative towards the bilingual project and he felt that it was bound to fail. He saw no benefit to a child in using the mother tongue in the early grades. In contrast to this, the bilingual teacher reported that parental response to the program had been good.

The bilingual teachers in the community expressed interest in seeing reading materials produced in the Cunén variety of K'iche' and a few of them were at work on the production of some materials. Generally, they supported the use of K'iche' for educational purposes in contrast to the other teachers and school leadership who generally seemed to be against the use of K'iche'. Notably, one rural *aldea,* Xetsac, has a local educational committee which is made up entirely of Mayans.

**4.7.4 Business.** The primary industry in Cunén is agriculture. The community is rapidly shifting to a cash-based economy as it finds more and more agricultural products which can be grown for export to markets outside of the community itself. While all farmers grow some corn and beans for the feeding of their own families, wheat and garlic are important cash crops. Although migrant work on the coast in the past was an important source of cash, and remains so for poorer Mayan families, most Mayans who have land are now obtaining their cash through the sale of their own crops.

A garlic growers' cooperative, made up mostly of Aguacatecos, was formed to assist those who wish to take advantage of that cash crop. Another innovation was the formation of a cooperative to promote the cultivation of vegetables, particularly brussels sprouts. This cooperative was formed specifically to reduce the need for Mayans to leave their communities in search of sources of cash and thus to reinforce Mayan cultural maintenance. The cooperative was given technical and marketing assistance by a German company which contracted to buy the entire crop of brussels sprouts. The cooperatives had a mixed effect, however, in terms of their support of the use of K'iche'. The technicians and trainers who traveled to Cunén used Spanish for their training sessions, and many of the members of the cooperatives used K'iche' for discussions about cooperative business. The North American advisor and promoter of the cooperative, however, used words and phrases from a K'ichean-related language (Uspanteko) when he was addressing the members of the cooperative either individually or in a group. The only place in which K'iche' is regularly spoken by cooperative members is when they are working in the fields.

A third cooperative is one made up of widows and is given direction and instruction by a ladino woman from a neighboring *municipio*. This cooperative bakes bread, and members must go through a year-long program of training in hygiene and other technical matters before they can begin baking. All of this instruction is in Spanish.

**4.7.5 Culture.** Traditional cultural life in Cunén is less robust partly because of the smaller size of the community and partly, because of the diversity of cultural groups that exist within the community. The town festival takes place in February when the day of St. Mary Magdalene, the town patron, is celebrated. There are *cofradías,* but they are less prominent than in Chichicastenango though still important to the social and religious structure of the community. Our observers felt that the motivating force in Cunén was making money. If that is indeed the case, then the preservation of the cosmological equilibrium through devotion to the saints and ancestors might be seen as less important than economic advancement. Our informants, when asked about what people value and how people are evaluated, expressed their answers in economic terms. In many Mayan communities, for example, a good person is one who helps another—doing service is an important cultural metaphor—whether by means of advice, physical assistance in manual labor, or by giving or lending money. In Cunén, a good person was described as someone who would "do a favor for you if he had enough to be able to help".

The market in Cunén is the traditional gathering place for people of all ethnicities in the community. It has less overall importance to the community economically because most of the money in the community is generated through exports. Outsiders come into the market from nearby Ixil communities, from Sacapulas, and from some more distant K'iche'-speaking communities. Our observers heard K'iche' being spoken in the market by both Mayans and ladinos.

## 4.8 Status factors

As mentioned above, the primary status differential runs along racial lines between ladinos and Mayans, though relations between ladinos and Mayans are amicable. Ladinos and Mayans were known to cooperate on many projects and most of the ladinos also speak K'iche' to some extent.

There are also some differences in status among Mayans based on ethnic identity, with the Chiquimulteco ethnicity the least prestigious. The Cunenteco ethnicity seems to have the highest status though the difference between Cunentecos and Momostecos is not great. We observed that the various dialects of K'iche' were used everywhere that there were people who could speak them. Young people as well as old were observed to be speaking K'iche' in public places, and members of the different K'iche' ethnicities interacted freely with each other. Only two Mayan families in town were known to use Spanish at home.

In Cunén, use of the local language(s) is not associated closely with the notion of backwardness and lack of development. The agricultural cooperative, which is an engine of economic progress in Cunén, though advised and guided by outsiders, is clearly a Mayan institution. Interestingly, however, those elected to the governing board of the agricultural cooperative are all teachers from the bilingual program. It seems that some prestige is derived from being literate, a skill which until recently has been confined to those who have participated in the Spanish-based educational system.

Another indicator of the lack of apparent conflict between economic progress and Mayan identity is that Mayans have achieved fairly high status positions in the community and still retain the use of their mother tongue and their Mayan identity. The Mayan mayor is one such example. Another is a Mayan man who had run for the office of mayor, had served as vice-mayor, and was serving as the commander of the Civil Patrol, the military-sponsored civilian anti-insurgent militia. He was also a businessman, operating a pharmacy, and gave instruction in the use of modern fertilizers and pesticides, using K'iche' without embarrassment. In addition,

## 4.9 Subjective vitality factors

he owned a typewriter and would type letters for people for a fee acting as both scribe and translator.

We have very little subjective vitality data for Cunén. It seems, however, that at least for the segment of the Mayan population that is able to participate in the growing economic development of the community, there is a feeling of optimism about the likelihood of group success. The motivation of the community is not so much to shift identities as it is to take advantage of the economic opportunities. Because of its isolation in the mountains, Cunén has not received much outside assistance until recently. Missionaries and other outsiders have only been temporary residents of the community. As a result, the community is more focused on being self-sufficient than on depending on outsiders for assistance. Outsiders are seen as sources of knowledge and skills. Our language helpers told us that knowledge is valued only to the degree that it has a practical application. The farmers who grow the wheat and the garlic are more useful than the agronomists who can only talk about how to grow the crops. Independence is not encouraged in spite of the entrepreneurial nature of the community. The fact that the economic organization of the community is being reshaped in the form of cooperatives is telling. The general feeling seems to be that by working together, prosperity can be shared by the entire community. Innovations are welcomed only if they result in community good. Failure in a new endeavor results in the loss of reputation and credibility. As long as the Mayans of Cunén are experiencing economic success, it seems likely that their subjective evaluation of their group vitality will be high.

### 4.10–4.13 Joyabaj

Joyabaj[21] is located in the department of El Quiché and the town center is located on the southern slope of the Sierra de Chuacus, twenty-three miles east of Santa Cruz del Quiché at an altitude of 4,200 feet above sea level (Moore 1973:114). The *municipio* covers an area of approximately 304 square kilometers. When the road from Santa Cruz del Quiché to Joyabaj was widened and paved in the late 1970s, Joyabaj became much more accessible to the outside world. What had once been a six to eight

---

[21]These data, unless otherwise attributed, are based on my personal observations during my residence in Joyabaj from 1977 to 1980.

hour trip to Santa Cruz del Quiché, the departmental capital, was reduced to a one-hour excursion. The town center of Joyabaj is long and narrow. At its widest point it is only three or four blocks wide. It stretches out between deep ravines on either side for almost a mile. This geographic feature tends to separate those from the lower end of town from those who live at the upper end. The road which leaves town to the east is unpaved and passable only part of the year. Even though it goes on to the department of Baja Verapaz, Joyabaj is seen by most outsiders as being at the end of the road, both literally and figuratively. Bus service was poor with the buses destined for Guatemala City leaving in the predawn hours and not returning until late at night. Occasional truck traffic was the only other means of getting in and out of Joyabaj. In the early 1970s, there were only a few private vehicles to be found in Joyabaj. Because of its relative isolation for many years, Joyabaj maintained only tenuous links with other K'iche' communities. Its closest neighbor, Zacualpa, served as an alternate market site which was reached with some difficulty until the road improvements were completed. Though accessible directly only by mountainous foot trails, Cubulco, a *municipio* in Baja Verapaz, is seen as being ethnically related and linguistically similar by the Mayan residents of Joyabaj.[22]

For several years, the community was served by an airstrip which was built on land adjacent to the town soccer field. This access to the outside world was strategic when the major earthquake which struck Guatemala in 1976 leveled the town center. The airstrip proved to be the only viable link to the outside world. Supplies were brought in and the injured evacuated using military and private aircraft. Since the mid-1980s the airstrip has been converted to an additional soccer field for the recreation of the soldiers stationed at a newly built military post.

The earthquake brought about major changes in the community. Almost all of the houses in the town center were destroyed. The Roman Catholic church, which dominated the town square, collapsed leaving only the facade which was preserved in front of the new building built in the reconstruction of the community. Homes which were previously built of adobe and clay tile were rebuilt using concrete block and corrugated tin. Those who could not afford concrete block built half-wall bases of adobe, using lighter and safer wooden plank construction for the upper parts of the building. Housing patterns were also changed somewhat. The people who had lived close to the central town square moved towards the edges of town where land was available, increasing the division of the

---

[22]For a brief description of the legendary origins of these two communities, see Lewis 1993.

town into upper and lower sections. New neighborhoods of safer houses were built mostly by ladinos who had been displaced by the earthquake. Another neighborhood of occupant-built houses also arose around the edges of the town center on town-owned land, sold to and built by Mayans who had lost their housing and who had no land of their own.

The destruction caused by the earthquake was a major economic setback for both the Mayan and ladino population who resided in or around the town center. It also brought Joyabaj to the attention of national and departmental government authorities as well as private philanthropies. For a short time it became a showcase for development and reconstruction efforts. The Roman Catholic church and other public buildings around the town square were rebuilt by the owner of one of the major sugar refineries in Guatemala, a native of Joyabaj. The government pushed forward the road improvement projects, the major streets of the town center were paved, and a hospital was built and staffed. A telephone exchange was built with a microwave link to Santa Cruz del Quiché. In short, Joyabaj was destroyed and rebuilt with most of the modern innovations that many other K'iche' communities would not even consider possibilities.

Joyabaj has many of the characteristics of the vacant town. Before the earthquake it was much more characteristically so with fully one-third of the houses in town empty except on market days. The permanent residents of the town center are predominantly ladino. A few "poor ladinos" also live in the rural areas. Since the earthquake more Mayans reside permanently in the town center than before, but the majority of the population is still based in the rural communities. These folk appear in town for the twice weekly market and jam the streets wearing their colorful distinctive dress. Joyabaj is one of very few K'iche' communities where men of all ages still wear their red jackets, white pants, and colorfully embroidered apron held on by a bright red, flower-embroidered belt. The town has the reputation of being "very Mayan" although the linguistic variety spoken in Joyabaj is decidedly more larded with highly-assimilated Spanish loans than many other K'iche' varieties.

Sugar cane is the principal cash crop. It is processed in local small-scale refineries to produce cannon-ball sized lumps of hardened brown sugar or molasses which are sold locally and exported to other markets. A subsidiary industry is the raising of pigs that are fed on the discarded sugar cane pulp. This produces a very sweet pork which is sold in the local market.

## 4.10 Demographic factors

Joyabaj, as of the 1981 census, has a population of 35,719. The Mayan population constitutes 75.1% (26,841) of the population and 93.1% (33,261) of the population lives in the rural areas. The population density is 117.5 persons per square kilometer.

Population growth in Joyabaj has been much slower than in the other communities in this study. In part this may be due to the great loss of life in the earthquake in 1976. However, the slower growth rate is evident even prior to 1976 and it may be indicative of how the economic disadvantages of residence in Joyabaj have resulted in emigration and a higher mortality rate. Alternatively, it may simply be a symptom of the difficulty of gathering census data in this remote community. From a population of 21,381 reported in the 1955 census, there was a fairly large 32.9% increase to the 28,410 total population figure reported in 1964. From 1964 to 1973, however, the population grew only by 13.1% to 32,134. The figure reported in the 1981 census, 35,719, represents an increase of 11.2% from the 1973 census figure.

Like the other *municipios* described so far, Joyabaj has a predominantly young population with 59.0% (21,087 individuals) of the population nineteen years of age or younger.

## 4.11 Institutional support factors

**4.11.1 Government.** Joyabaj has a mayor, a town secretary, and auxiliary mayors for the *aldeas* and *cantones*. There is also an *alcalde indígena*. The town government operates a small hydroelectric plant which supplies electricity to the town center and maintains personnel and offices in the town center which deal with the administration of that utility.

Unlike some other *municipios*, most of the longstanding ladino population of Joyabaj can speak K'iche', and so, much of the business in the town hall is conducted in K'iche'. In spite of this proficiency in K'iche', however, official dealings with the Mayans are not always amicable but are generally characterized by a very strong paternalistic attitude.

The national police force is generally manned by police officers who rotate their assignments from place to place so few if any are native to the community. All of the police officers with whom I had contact during my residence in Joyabaj were ladinos and to my knowledge spoke only Spanish.

## 4.11 Institutional support factors

The staff of the post office and telegraph office were ladinos and were natives of the community and therefore presumably had some proficiency in K'iche' though I never observed them using it.

At the time of my residence in Joyabaj I was unaware of any activities by such governmental agencies as DIGESA or DIGESEPE. More of the focus was on reconstruction after the damage of the earthquake. INFOM, a national infrastructure development agency, was active in funding and administering the street paving project which provided some employment for the Mayan residents of the community.

The Public Health center in Joyabaj was, until after the earthquake, poorly equipped and staffed. K'iche' clients reported the doctors to be angry with them, quite often drunk, and frequently required them to pay for what were supposed to be free services. The post-earthquake reconstruction brought a large, new, hospital to the town. Reportedly, this hospital is staffed and better equipped, though the doctors are still advanced medical students who are doing their final practicum before graduation and licensing.

**4.11.2 Church.** The Roman Catholic church in Joyabaj has had a varied history in terms of its support of the use of K'iche' for religious purposes depending on the attitude of the current priest. The Church did support the catechist movement, a training program for laity, which used K'iche' for many of its teaching functions. One faction of the catechist movement became especially interested in the use of K'iche' and eventually split from the Roman Catholic church. It formed its own non-Protestant, non-Catholic hybrid congregation. This group uses a form of the Roman Catholic liturgy in K'iche', the K'iche' translation of the New Testament, and K'iche' songs and choruses in their worship services. In the late 1980s the priest in Joyabaj was a comrade of the priest in Chichicastenango and was active in promoting the use of K'iche' for worship.

At the time of our survey, there were four Protestant churches in the town center and an unknown number of congregations meeting in the rural areas. The town churches were dominated by ladinos who held the important positions of leadership. One, however, was a faction of K'iche's who had split off from one of the ladino-dominated churches but was led by a ladino pastor.

In spite of the fact that most of the ladinos in Joyabaj could speak K'iche' with some proficiency, they were very much opposed to the use of K'iche' in the church services. One church did try to have a separate K'iche' service on Sundays, immediately preceding the Spanish service, but it was discontinued after a few years.

**4.11.3 Education.** Our data on the schools in Joyabaj is incomplete. The town center had two elementary schools and a middle school. Students wishing to complete high school were required to leave town. Data from the regional office of the bilingual education program shows only two rural schools in Joyabaj. These may be the only two schools connected to the bilingual education program and not the total number of schools in the *municipio*.

I have no data on enrollment nor on student attrition rates. Interviewees, however, commented on the fact that it was difficult for K'iche' children to attend school because the ladino teachers were so angry and so often punished them.[23] This cultural insensitivity may well be ameliorated in those schools where the bilingual education program is active now.

**4.11.4 Business.** As in the other communities, the market is the central place of business in Joyabaj and is a Mayan domain. Here, K'iche' is heard almost exclusively. Ladinos who come to the market use K'iche' in their dealings. The Sunday and Thursday markets are also the times for much of the social interaction between Mayans from outlying rural *aldeas*. The market is clearly a reinforcer of Mayan identity.

Joyabaj has a few permanent businesses which are owned and operated by ladinos. Two of these were the two competing general stores, one of which closed after the earthquake. The owner of the remaining store operated several other businesses including a winery and a gas station. This particular man was known among the K'iche' population as being a good man who dealt politely, though paternalistically, with his K'iche' customers. Similarly, his wife treated K'iche' customers graciously and politely but always with the air of a kindly aunt dealing with a youngster. In part, I suspect this good reputation was derived from a willingness to lend money (at interest) to customers in need. Other businesses in town included various small shops, a pharmacy or two, and a blacksmith. At least one of the bus lines was locally-owned and there were several trucks owned by ladino residents of the community. Although these businesses were owned by ladinos, in any of them one could speak K'iche' and expect to be understood.

---

[23]I feel quite certain that much of this perception by Mayans that ladinos are "angry" comes from a difference in rhetorical style in which ladino teachers and others use what I call "pseudo-questions" as a teaching device but which are interpreted by Mayans as anger. It is true, however, that in the past Mayan children were punished if they spoke K'iche' in school. Since many of the children were monolinguals, they would find themselves punished frequently at the beginning of their first year of school. With reason, they would not want to return and would drop out.

Since most of the Mayan residents of Joyabaj are subsistence farmers and can barely produce enough food to feed their families from their small plots of land, they have no means of earning cash except as migrant laborers on the coastal plantations. An estimate of the number of Mayans from Joyabaj who engage in migrant labor might be as high as one-third of the Mayan population. Sometimes only the men of the family go to the coast, but frequently entire families will leave for as long as three months at a time. If they are careful and fortunate, they will return with enough cash to enable them to buy corn and beans to supplement their own crops. Many, however, spend their earnings on alcohol, or fall into debt to the plantation owners, or fall ill with malaria or tuberculosis and return with nothing but chronic illness.

**4.11.5 Culture.** Joyabaj has eight *cofradías* providing care and devotion to the town saints. The *cofradías* are important Mayan institutions which provide coherence to the social and cultural structure of the community. They serve as the primary means among Mayans of establishing status and prestige. Joyabaj is one of the few communities where both men and women wear the clothing distinctive to the town and their group identity. Prestige cannot be determined by looking at the way one is dressed. Similarly, until the earthquake, housing size or style could not generally be used as a means of determining one's wealth nor one's standing in the community. Mayans in Joyabaj know where they stand socially in relation to each other by means of the number and rank of service positions they have held in the *cofradía* system.

I have no verifiable data on the number of Mayans who have left the traditional religious system to embrace either a more orthodox Roman Catholicism or evangelical Protestantism. My sense is that the number is small relative to the overall population. The sites for traditional religious practice, though somewhat altered by the destruction of the earthquake, are still well-used. The central cemetery just off the town square was much damaged and partially bulldozed away in the reconstruction. However, it is still the location for the activities of the shamans who perform their rites on almost any day of the week, but particularly so on market days.

Along with the government and private reconstruction aid that entered Joyabaj after the earthquake, several human development agencies either began or augmented their efforts in Joyabaj. The United States Peace Corps continued to work with school children in gardening projects. Save The Children Foundation began work with widows and orphans providing housing, food, clothing, and training in marketable skills. They had an expatriate staff resident in the community for several years as well as a number of Guatemalan employees.

SIL International had literacy and translation workers resident in the community beginning in the 1960s until shortly after the earthquake and then again for short periods of time in the 1980s. Their staff provided medical services along with classes in K'iche' literacy.

The Methodist mission also had staff resident in the community for many years until 1981.

All of these agencies used K'iche' to some extent. The SIL staff and the Methodist missionaries were most clearly committed to the use of K'iche' and to the promotion of its maintenance and wider use (e.g., in literacy). The two groups collaborated on the translation of the New Testament into the Joyabaj dialect of K'iche'.

Perhaps the force most hostile to Mayan culture in Joyabaj has been the longstanding practice of forced military conscription. Army trucks from Santa Cruz del Quiché arrive in town, often on a market day, and every young man in sight is summarily marched at gunpoint to the waiting truck to be carried off for several years of military service. Generally, ladinos find a way to pay their way out of the army after only a day or two of discomfort. Mayans are not so fortunate and many families have no idea what happened to their son or father for many weeks or months. Because of the isolation of Joyabaj, it has been a preferred site for this practice.

While there are some benefits for the conscriptees—many learn to read and write while in the army—the dangers of military service in the 1980s far outweighed the few benefits. Besides the constant psychological stress of loneliness, and verbal and emotional, if not physical, abuse, many Mayan men from Joyabaj have been killed in the civil strife where they have had to fight against guerrilla insurgents.

Beginning in the 1980s there was a permanent military presence in Joyabaj which led to tension and fear. The soldiers were not trusted by the K'iche's, and there were rumors that numerous K'iche' women and girls had been raped by the soldiers. Army units are generally poorly disciplined and are often commanded by young ladino officers who have little respect for the civilian Mayan population and hence are apt to ignore their troops' activities. The resulting negative perception of the army presence is, of course, fueled by the already strong antipathy towards the army's conscription practices.

## 4.12 Status factors

In spite of the fact that most ladinos in Joyabaj learn K'iche' and use it regularly when dealing with K'iche's, ladinos are clearly the higher status group in Joyabaj. While face-to-face contacts between K'iche's and ladinos are polite, there is a long history of distrust between the two groups. Mayans have been the victims of a great deal of ladino mistreatment and have very few positive feelings towards most of the ladino population. Ladinos see the Mayans as simple children of low intelligence who must be led by the hand in most practical matters. Mayans can be used as laborers, as beasts of burden, and should not be expected to reason or think for themselves. Mayans, on the other hand, see the ladinos as an untrustworthy and angry group but find them useful as consumers of their labor or their products. Boundary lines are hard and closed. In spite of the fact that the ladinos address them in K'iche', K'iche's do not accept them as being speakers of the language. The SIL workers and Methodist missionaries were recognized as being able to speak K'iche', however, and were admired when they wore the native clothing and attempted to identify with the K'iche' culture. Ladinos, who would never consider dressing like a K'iche', found this embarrassing and shameful.

## 4.13 Subjective factors

Mayan attitudes towards themselves have changed since the earthquake. Generally, Mayans in Joyabaj have a fairly positive evaluation of themselves and their identity. There is, however, a pervading sadness among the Joyabaj Mayans. This may be because of the terrible loss of life they experienced in the earthquake and because of the continuing loss of life as their men are carried off to military service. More generally, however, the sadness seems to be traceable to an awareness that at one time their race was great and powerful and now it is dominated and subservient. Helen Passwater (personal communication) has observed that Mayan self-esteem was higher before the earthquake than it is now. My observations during the town fiesta in 1978 led me to believe that there was a strong undercurrent of rage and despair which was only allowed to be released during the drunken revelry surrounding this celebration of the local ethnic identity.

Passwater also reports that the most important Mayan families were actively working to see that their children acquired Spanish, and they saw great importance in having their children attend Spanish school. This expressed attitude among the *important* families is a possible indicator of an incipient identity shift.

### 4.14–4.17 Sacapulas

Sacapulas[24] is located in the department of El Quiché, and the town center is located on the banks of the upper Chixoy River (also called the Río Negro at that point). The town is located about twenty miles north-northeast of Santa Cruz del Quiché and about five miles west-southwest of Cunén at an altitude of 4,035 feet above sea level (Moore 1973:179). The *municipio* is approximately 213 square kilometers in area. The community lies in the river valley at the foot of the Cuchumatanes mountains. It is at a major crossroads where the road from Santa Cruz del Quiché joins the extremely tortuous east-west route which runs through Cunén, connecting the departmental capitals of Huehuetenango and Cobán. Because of its location at this junction, Sacapulas is well-served by bus transportation. A thriving local business community caters to meeting the needs of travelers with food vendors, refreshment and fruit stands, restaurants of various types, and bars. Neighboring, but not directly accessible by road, are the K'iche' communities of San Bartolomé Jocotenango to the south and San Andrés Sajcabajá to the southeast. Each of these communities is connected to Sacapulas and to each other by a good system of foot trails.

Sacapulas, like Cunén, has more than one K'iche'-speaking ethnic group resident in the community. The largest group is made up of those who are the descendants of the original Mayan residents of the region. These Sakapultekos have their own distinctive clothing, are relatively endogamous, and speak a linguistically distinct variety called Sakapulteko. This variety is sufficiently distinct that some have maintained that it should be considered a separate language from K'iche' (Kaufman 1976; Dubois 1981). The second ethnic group present in the community are the K'iche' speakers from Santa María Chiquimula. These sheep herders began to settle in Sacapulas around the end of the nineteenth century when they were given the use of unoccupied lands. They continue to pay rent, either monetary or by community service, to the *municipio* for that privilege. The third ethnic group present in the community are the ladinos who are concentrated in the town center and in one small community in the western part of the *municipio*. DuBois (1981:9–11) estimates that there are approximately

---

[24]The Quiché Survey Team members who collected the community data for Sacapulas were Paul and Anne Stevenson. Some earlier data were also collected by Merieta Johnson and Jill Paulus, also members of SIL International.

7,500 Sakapultekos and a roughly equal number of Chiquimultecos present in the community. In terms of relationships between the groups, the Chiquimultecos are at the bottom of the social ladder. The term *chiquimulteco* is used throughout the K'iche' area as a general term of derision. While this represents a more complicated state of affairs than that found in other locations examined in this study (with the exception of Cunén), I will treat both Mayan groups as a single K'iche' group. This inevitably ignores some of the important dynamics of the situation in Sacapulas and warrants a fuller investigation. The bulk of our observations of the community and of language use were made among the Sakapulteko segment, but there are also observations of Chiquimultecos and of interactions between members of each group.

Sacapulas is comprised of the town center and nine *aldeas* and forty-five *caseríos*. The town center is also divided into five barrios. The entire *municipio* is divided into five *cantones* which are territorial divisions, rather than communal subdivisions like *caseríos*.

The major economic specialization of the community has traditionally been salt making. The river which runs alongside the town center has numerous volcanic hot springs flowing into it and concentrations of black salt which are mined and purified. This salt was traditionally sold to Nebaj, Chajul, and Cotzal, Ixil communities, high in the mountains to the north of Sacapulas. With the advent of roads and vehicular transportation, the salt is now exported to a much wider area. Irrigation, using the river water, has also brought about an increase in fruit and vegetable production.

## 4.14 Demographic factors

The 1981 census figure for the total population of Sacapulas is 20,744. Of these, 19,044 (91.8%) live in the rural areas. The population is predominantly Mayan with 19,576 or 94.4% of the total identified by the census as being Mayans. The population density is 97.4 persons per square kilometer.

Population growth in Sacapulas has also been high since 1955. The 1955 census shows a total population of 10,849 which by 1964 had grown to 13,884, an increase of 28.0%. In the period between 1964 and 1973, the population increased by 15.6% to a total of 16,458. The increase from the 1973 figure to the 1981 figure of 20,744 represents a 20.7% increase in the population over that period of time. The aggregate population change since the 1955 census is an increase of 91.2%.

I have no data on marriage patterns between ethnic groups in Sacapulas. The low status of the Chiquimultecos, however, would tend to make intermarriage of Sakapultekos with Chiquimultecos unlikely. As in the other communities, intermarriage between ladinos and Mayans is rare and stigmatized.

When the roads to Sacapulas became passable in the 1930s under Ubico's regime, many Sacapulas residents began to travel widely for trade. Some traders (frequently women) traveled as far as the market in Sololá and to many other *municipios* in the department of El Quiché to sell their produce.

DuBois (1981:10) estimates that as many as 2,500 Sakapultekos left in 1977 to go to Guatemala City to find employment. These "exiles", however, have maintained their identity in the capital by organizing a community organization which promotes solidarity and keeps alive ties with the *municipio*. Many of these displaced Sacapulas natives have gained employment as maids, and among the men, as officers in the national police force. The purpose of this emigration for employment is primarily to acquire funds with which to return to Sacapulas upon retirement or as soon as it is economically practical. Many Sacapultecos have an excellent knowledge of Spanish because of these outside contacts and experiences.

### 4.15 Institutional support factors

**4.15.1 Government.** Sacapulas has a mayor, vice-mayor, auxiliary mayors for the *cantones,* a town secretary, and an *alcalde indígena*. Spanish is the predominant language in the town hall, although at times the mayor and/or vice-mayor could speak K'iche' and would use the language with townspeople who called on them for assistance. The town secretary is ladino.

Other governmental agencies operating in Sacapulas are DIGESA (see under Chichicastenango), and the Ministry of Development which operates a vocational school which teaches tailoring. Sacapulas also has a small public health center, a post office and telegraph office, and a national police post. Because there is a strategic bridge across the river at Sacapulas, there have been military units stationed in the town from time to time.

**4.15.2 Church.** The Roman Catholic church in Sacapulas is located on the town square and occupies a central place in the town social structure. It is a predominantly Spanish institution, and uses Spanish in most services. Our language assistant, who is not a Roman Catholic, told us that the visiting priest, a K'iche' speaker, used mostly Spanish, although sometimes he would

## 4.15 Institutional support factors

translate what he has said into K'iche'. When the priest is not present, more K'iche' is used. Some of the groups associated with the Church, particularly the catechists, regularly use both K'iche' and Spanish.

Sacapulas also has a strong Protestant community which is predominantly made up of Mayans though positions of leadership are generally in the hands of ladinos. Our estimate is that about 25% of the population is Protestant. There are five separate Protestant church groups in the town center and at least two others in the rural areas. A Protestant missionary was resident in Sacapulas for almost fifteen years and did his work using Sakapulteko. He translated parts of the New Testament and made a start on the compilation of a Sakapulteko dictionary and produced some other reading material in the language.

Two of the Protestant churches have ladino pastors who use Spanish exclusively in their services. In the other churches, K'iche' is used for most activities though the Scriptures are always read in Spanish and most hymns and choruses are sung in Spanish. Some individuals will pray only in Spanish.

**4.15.3 Education.** Sacapulas has twenty-six elementary schools administered by the Ministry of Education. There is no middle school and no high school. Not all of the schools offer all of the elementary grades, and students who wish to go beyond sixth grade must go to Santa Cruz del Quiché, twenty miles away. A private typing school also operates in the town center. Of the twenty-six schools, twelve are related to the national bilingual education program. In these schools the bilingual teacher is a Mayan and speaks either Sakapulteko or some variety of K'iche'. Many of these teachers were trained by and continue to use the methods of the now-defunct *castellanización* program. We interviewed one of the bilingual teachers who informed us that there were approximately 4,500 school-aged children in the *municipio,* of which 3,700 successfully complete the school year. He made it clear, however, that even though the school year runs from January to November, most of the students leave for the coast with their families in mid-September. Teachers regularly make a determination about who will pass or fail by September. Our interviewees reported that parents in Sacapulas are quite opposed to the use of K'iche' in school. They say they want their children to learn Spanish.

**4.15.4 Business.** The principal means of income for the community is salt making, though the number of people who have access to the salt is fairly limited. It is seen, however, as being a lucrative business. Other sources of income are the sale of produce, fruits and vegetables which flourish in the hot dry climate of Sacapulas. Vegetables are grown along the river banks and in some of the higher elevations where water is available. Irrigation projects have increased the amount of arable land. Sales to travelers supplement income, and there are numerous small stores lining the main street through town.

The town market, held on Thursday and Sunday, is well-attended by the rural folk who bring their produce to sell and buy from others what they need. Residents of the rural communities bring vegetables, chickens, and eggs for sale. Other vendors, selling insecticide, hardware, plastic goods, soap, and ready-made clothing, come from other K'iche' towns both near and far.

Vendors from Sacapulas travel to other towns to sell vegetables and candied fruit and, of course, salt. Mangoes and papayas grow well in Sacapulas and are exported for sale in other markets. In Cunén, the vendors from Sacapulas sell *güipiles*, women's blouses.

Many students leave school early each year to go with their families to the coast as migrant agricultural workers. Our interviewees estimated that as many as 40% of the families in the *municipio* would leave and stay on the coast for from one to three months.

**4.15.5 Culture.** We have very little firsthand information on the activities of the *cofradías* in Sacapulas. They are active and functioning, however, though it would be expected that the inroads of Protestantism in the community will have lessened their influence somewhat. Hill and Monaghan (1987) provide a detailed description of the activities of the *cofradías* and their interrelationship with the *alcaldía indígena* to form the civil-religious hierarchy in Sacapulas. "Through a series of interdependent and annually circulating service obligations, the *Alcaldía Indígena* has the effect of integrating the various *cantones* into one organization" (Hill 1987:17).

In Sacapulas there is a major difference between rural Mayans and the urban Mayans. The urban families are actively promoting the use of Spanish among their children while the rural families are not. Our observers found that most town-based families reported that they used Spanish in the home and particularly with their children. Though the children could understand K'iche' they found it humorous to be addressed in K'iche' and would respond in K'iche' only when pressed to do so. One man had requested his mother to use only Sakapulteko with her grandchildren because he was becoming aware of the fact that they could not speak the language. Others of his generation, however, use only Spanish in the home.

## 4.16 Status factors

Though the ladinos are relatively few, they are obviously of higher status. The Sakapulteko speakers have traditionally looked down on Chiquimultecos, though our language assistant told us that this was no longer the case. Still, most of the Chiquimultecos, who live outside of the town center, are obviously poorer than their urban Sakapulteko neighbors. This ethnic division may account for the differences between urban and rural Mayans mentioned above. The urban Sakapultekos are more focused on economic gain through cash-based production and selling and on the acquisition of Spanish as a means to that end. The rural Chiquimultecos are more agriculturally-based, with sheep herding as their primary activity, and thus have fewer opportunities and less felt need to acquire Spanish and to participate in the more cash-based economic system.

Generally, illiteracy is connected with backwardness and ignorance. Since literacy is available only in Spanish, progress and education must be achieved through the acquisition of Spanish. Our interviewee told us that people feel "dead" or "sad" because they cannot read and write. At the very least people would like to be able to sign their names.

## 4.17 Subjective factors

As in Cunén, the perception of what is good and what makes a person good is no longer expressed simply in terms of character but rather in economic terms. Although a good person is one who is humble, sharing, and friendly, a person of power and prestige is a person who has plenty of money and who dresses well. The traditional hard-working farmer is pitied as much as respected because, although he works hard, he is not paid well. Knowledge is valued because it will help the individual become prosperous. The individual is, of course, expected to share his or her prosperity with the community by providing a service. Gain which is not shared with the community provokes jealousy.

This perspective reflects a subjective vitality which is focused on achievement in the ladino economic world rather than in the more traditional terms of economic sacrifice. The emphasis is still on service to the community, but that service is seen more in terms of shared gains rather than sacrifice. One example given to us of how a person might share their good fortune is by opening a store to provide goods for the community (as well as profit to the individual). This contrasts sharply with the *cofradía* system where prestige is gained through temporary impoverishment which might take years to recover from.

Our language assistant told us that ethnic identity was connected with the clothing and the language of Sacapulas. Yet, most of the Mayans in the town center are giving up the language quite readily. It seems that ethnic identity is focused more around the town itself than any single feature such as language or clothing.

### 4.18–4.21 San Andrés Sajcabajá

San Andrés Sajcabajá[25] is located in the department of El Quiché and the town center is located in the central part of the department at an altitude of 5,971 feet above sea level (Moore 1973:184). The *municipio* occupies a territory of approximately 230 square kilometers.[26]

While probably one of the least known *municipios* in Guatemala, its sociopolitical history has been exhaustively documented in a socio-historical study by Piel (1989) which traces the history of the community from 1500 to 1970 primarily by means of documentary evidence.[27]

San Andrés Sajcabajá, along with Joyabaj, is located in what was the eastern section of the ancient K'iche' kingdom and so shares some linguistic features with Joyabaj.

San Andrés Sajcabajá is located near the end of a difficult road that joins the community with Santa Cruz del Quiché, the departmental capital. Although at a somewhat higher elevation, San Andrés Sajcabajá, like Sacapulas, is located in the rain shadow of the mountains and is drier and warmer than many other communities at similar elevations to the south and west. The road was improved in 1964 and declared to be *"transitable"* (Piel 1989:360), but during the rainy season it becomes impassable for most vehicles. Bus service becomes intermittent at best, and only

---

[25]The data on San Andrés Sajcabajá were collected by Ed and Mary Fox.

[26]This number is uncertain but is the more likely of two proposed figures. The Guatemalan government statistics claim that San Andrés covers an area of 476 square kilometers. A French scientific mission sets the area of San Andrés at 230 square kilometers. The second seems more probable especially since the *aldea* of Canillá was granted separate status as a *municipio*.

[27]Piel's work, while more thorough than almost any other study I have seen of a single community, takes a very negative and disdainful stance towards the community. Apparently, the author had difficulty gaining access to town records because of local suspicions towards strangers and seems at pains to repay the community for this inconvenience by emphasizing the poverty, backwardness, and ignorance of the community. I and my colleagues found San Andrés Sajcabajá to be isolated and struggling with a number of serious problems but a delightful community made up of warm and friendly people.

four-wheel drive vehicles and heavy trucks make the trip between San Andrés Sajcabajá and Santa Cruz del Quiché carrying passengers and goods. Those hardy folk who travel by foot or beast take a somewhat shorter route over the mountains to the *municipios* of Chinique or Chiché, both located on the road between Santa Cruz del Quiché and Joyabaj. There they can trade in the market or obtain transportation to other marketplaces. Few residents of San Andrés Sajcabajá, however, go beyond these neighboring communities very often.

Piel (1989:371) provides other information about the modernization of San Andrés Sajcabajá: in 1926 the first steps were taken to provide potable water for the community, in 1945 a telegraph line was installed linking San Andrés Sajcabajá with Chinique, and in 1949 postal service was begun on a regular basis between San Andrés Sajcabajá and Santa Cruz del Quiché.

Piel also notes that although San Andrés Sajcabajá was recognized as a *municipio* from the colonial period onward, it has gone through various transformations over the years. In 1951 one of the major ladino *aldeas*, Canillá, was separated from San Andrés Sajcabajá and made a separate *municipio*. In 1957 San Andrés Sajcabajá was upgraded to the rank of *municipio* of the third category.

San Andrés Sajcabajá is both a Mayan and a ladino town. As in all *municipios*, political and economic advantage is primarily in the hands of the ladinos. The separation of Mayan and ladino cultures is less predictable though just as sharp. San Andrés Sajcabajá has four *aldeas* and forty-six *caseríos*. Some of these are primarily ladino, and unlike most other communities, some are mixed with K'iche's and ladinos living very similar lifestyles side by side. The town center is inhabited by both groups, and the cultural life of the town center is maintained by the ladinos (e.g., the rodeo) as much as it is by the K'iche's (e.g., saints' processions).

## 4.18 Demographic factors

The 1981 census lists the total population of San Andrés Sajcabajá as 11,602, with 861 residents of the town center (7.4%) and 10,741 resident in the rural areas (92.6%). Of the seven *municipios* included in this study, San Andrés Sajcabajá is one of the communities with the lowest proportion of Mayans, 9,771 individuals (84.2%). The population density of San Andrés Sajcabajá is 50.4 individuals per square kilometer.

While the population of San Andrés Sajcabajá has grown from the 9,855 individuals listed in the 1955 census, San Andrés Sajcabajá is the only community included in the study which at one point in its history actually showed a decrease in its population. The 1964 census shows a total population for the *municipio* of 8,079, a decrease of 18.0% in that period of time. Even by 1973, when the census shows the total population at 9,524, the community had not grown back to its 1955 size. The 1973 figure represents an increase of 17.9% from the 1964 levels, but a net decrease in population of 3.4% from the 1955 population level. In the period from 1973 to 1981 the population increased by 21.9%. Overall, the population has shown an aggregate increase of 17.7%, one of the lowest overall increases of any of the communities under study.

## 4.19 Institutional support factors

**4.19.1 Government.** San Andrés Sajcabajá like the other communities described so far has the typical municipal government structure. The mayor of San Andrés Sajcabajá at the time of our investigations was a K'iche', although the town secretary, as per the usual pattern, was a ladino. Although many of the transactions in the town hall take place in Spanish, there are enough personnel in the government who speak K'iche' that any item of business can be dealt with in that language through an interpreter. It was reported that most of the government jobs are held by ladinos yet many of them speak K'iche'.

The political and governmental leadership of San Andrés Sajcabajá views the use of K'iche' as a necessity given the linguistic makeup of the community, but would prefer that Spanish be the language of government.

DIGESA (see under Chichicastenango) has staff who visit the rural areas of San Andrés Sajcabajá using interpreters to communicate their instructions.

The government also sponsors a national literacy campaign and has a coordinator assigned to San Andrés Sajcabajá. Literacy instruction in this program is only in Spanish.

San Andrés Sajcabajá has a small public health center, staffed as in the other communities by advanced medical students. The national police have a presence in the community. There is also a telegraph and post office.

**4.19.2 Church.** The Roman Catholic church in San Andrés Sajcabajá is the Mayan church. Although many ladinos claim to be Roman Catholics they participate in no religious activities. The San Andrés Sajcabajá dialect is used frequently in the church services and in teaching. The liturgy, however, is more often read in Spanish which is also the language of singing and of Scripture reading. The church had some resident North

American nuns for a few years who promoted the use of K'iche'. A group called Catholic Action was active in the church for a while and aimed at purifying the church of the influence of Christopaganism. Many of its members were killed, however, in the guerrilla violence, and the group is no longer active.

There are five Protestant churches in the town center and at least three others in the rural communities. All of the churches in the town center are made up of ladinos. Only one Protestant church in the rural areas was known to be primarily made up of Mayans. This church used K'iche' primarily for preaching, but singing and Scripture reading were in Spanish. All of the Protestant congregations in the town center are small, fewer than thirty members each. The rural Mayan congregation, however, numbered more than one hundred and seemed to be growing.

Few missionaries have been resident in San Andrés Sajcabajá on more than a temporary basis. The two Roman Catholic nuns are the first to have maintained a long-term presence in the community and to have seriously taken on work with the Mayan peoples. Most other religious groups have worked in Spanish.

**4.19.3 Education.** San Andrés Sajcabajá has one school in the town center and thirty rural schools. The town school has both elementary and middle school grades. Most of the rural schools have been built and opened in the last ten years and most offer only grades one through three. Only the town center school has a teacher trained by the national bilingual education program, although perhaps as many as ten of the teachers in the rural area may be speakers of K'iche'. To our knowledge only three of these were native speakers of K'iche'.

Data provided to us by the school director for the *municipio* indicate that there were 311 first graders in 1986, forty-seven in the town school and 264 in the rural schools. Of these, only 172 students were promoted to the second grade, thirty-one from the town school and 141 from the rural schools.

Of total school enrollment of 743 students in grades one through six, only 153 students were in grades four, five, or six. More than half of the students were in grades one and two. These figures indicate that not only is the attrition rate high over the course of a single school year, but also that few students get beyond third grade. The attrition rate is even higher in the rural areas.

The primary reason for this dropout rate was that so many of the students' families went to the coast as migrant workers that they were unable to attend for a complete school year. A second reason was that many

Mayan families were unable to afford the inscription fees and the cost of books and school supplies. In some cases, the poor attendance of the teachers was given as the reason, demotivating the students who would give up and not come to school. Some parents would remove their students from the schools if they were not doing well, or if they needed them at home to work. In a few cases the students' poor achievement was blamed on their low proficiency in Spanish. In spite of this, it was reported that most parents who send their children to school do so because they want their children to learn Spanish.

The bilingual teacher assigned to the town school was not a native-speaker of the San Andrés Sajcabajá dialect of K'iche' but a native of Sacapulas and a speaker of Sakapulteko. None of the bilingual teachers who have been assigned to San Andrés Sajcabajá have ever been natives of the community. Teachers from the outside do not like to be assigned to San Andrés Sajcabajá and do not stay long because of its remote location and isolation.

Formal education is a relatively new phenomenon in most of the rural areas. It may still be viewed with suspicion and is somewhat ineffective because of the lack of bilingual teachers. Nevertheless, it serves as the means of introducing access to Spanish to the many rural communities which have had no means of acquiring Spanish until this time. The introduction of the school as an institution to these communities is an important, perhaps crucial, social change.

**4.19.4 Business.** The principal source of income in the community is agriculture—the production of corn and beans in particular. San Andrés Sajcabajá is a lowland area and therefore is warmer than many of the surrounding areas. As a result, the crops mature earlier and can be sold in the colder markets where the crops are not yet in. Sugar cane is also grown in the river valleys where there is water available.

San Andrés Sajcabajá is also a producer of cattle though not in large numbers. The warm, arid climate, as well as the topography of the area, is ideal for cattle. It is known, too, for its production of *petates,* woven straw or reed mats used by Mayans as a sleeping mat. The grass used for making *petates* grows in the area. San Andrés Sajcabajá is the only *municipio* that I have visited in Guatemala that has a large corral in the central market area of the town center where an annual rodeo is one of the highlights of community life. Cattle raising is more an activity of the ladinos who can afford to buy the animals, while *petate* weaving is a K'iche' activity which supplements cash income.

The isolation of San Andrés Sajcabajá makes its market more of a local institution than in many other communities. There are not many visiting vendors. A few come over the mountain ridge from Chiché and Chinique, and some from more distant locations come by truck from Santa Cruz del Quiché. These vendors bring in vegetables and other food items as well as clothing, plastic items, and sundries. The ladinos have more money to spend and are the better customers for these merchants, but the K'iche's also buy their wares from time to time. The language of the market is K'iche'. One ladino woman who moved into the community reported that she wished she could learn K'iche' because she was at a disadvantage in the market without it.

Some merchants from San Andrés Sajcabajá travel out to other markets, mostly carrying *petates* and other woven reed items. Guatemala City is one of their primary points of sale. Sugar cane and early corn may also be exported to some neighboring *municipios*.

There are only a few permanent stores in the community including a pharmacy or two and several small general stores. These are generally owned by ladinos who speak K'iche' with their K'iche' customers as needed.

**4.19.5 Culture.** The traditional civil-religious structure in San Andrés Sajcabajá is strong and active. There are a large number of shamans who practice their rites in and around the community. Neither Catholicism nor Protestantism have made many inroads into the belief systems of the Mayan community. The town and the town fiestas are important to the Mayans and are the primary source of ethnic identity. Distinctive dress is maintained by both men and women, and linguistic distinctiveness is maintained as well.

The Mayan and ladino cultures have remained quite separate from each other in San Andrés Sajcabajá. Most of the Mayan bilinguals are older men who have had more opportunity to be exposed to Spanish when they leave the community to go to the coast or to Guatemala City. Mayan children rarely know any Spanish and only acquire it slowly over the years. Ladinos, on the other hand, acquire K'iche' as youngsters in their contacts with their Mayan neighbors. Although their proficiency remains limited, they retain this facility in K'iche' throughout their adult years.

There have been very few innovations brought into San Andrés Sajcabajá, and opportunities for exposure to outside values are quite limited. The most recent is the rural school building program. Less than half of the Mayan parents in the town center send their children to school. Few Mayans have enough money to even buy a radio.

A few outside organizations have worked in the community either in providing literacy classes (in Spanish) or in providing help for widows and orphans. Most of these have used Spanish as their medium of communication.

## 4.20 Status factors

Mayans in San Andrés Sajcabajá are quite clearly of low status in the community in spite of their numerical and even cultural and linguistic dominance. The ladinos of the community, though not wealthy by any standard, have an aristocratic bearing and present themselves as being of a much higher level of society than might be expected in such a remote and isolated community. The few ladino families have gained a monopoly on the land and have thus become accustomed to having economic control.

In spite of this, few K'iche's have adopted the ladino system of values, though this will likely change under the onslaught of schools and other modernization factors. The Roman Catholic church is perhaps the most suitable symbol of Mayan identity in San Andrés Sajcabajá and, as such, shows a satisfaction with the use of K'iche' but not a devotion to its maintenance.

## 4.21 Subjective factors

Expressed attitudes towards San Andrés Sajcabajá Mayan identity are not negative but neither are they warmly positive. The acquisition of Spanish is seen as necessary if one wishes to raise one's standard of living and compete with the ladinos economically. Young people who have attended school generally favor the use of Spanish over K'iche'. This group is still a minority but as schools affect both the rural communities and the town center, it can be expected that this feeling will spread. The acquisition of literacy skills is seen as a need, but few Mayans have even considered the possibility that their own language could be written. People feel at a disadvantage because they cannot read and write, but most Mayans have access to someone else who can read or write for them. Thus, for most the need is not acute.

The overwhelming sense one gets from the Mayan people of San Andrés Sajcabajá is the sense of competition with the ladinos who have had all of the advantages. For many years the response to this has been a stoic resignation. A few younger Mayans, however, are gaining a sense of empowerment and are looking at ways to gain control of their own destinies. This feeling is not yet widespread in the community, but it is a growing one. San Andrés Sajcabajá is on the brink.

# 5

# Community Resource Profile Data Analysis—the Cities

### 5.1–5.5 Santa Cruz del Quiché

Santa Cruz del Quiché[28] is the capital of the department of El Quiché, and the town center is located about 50 miles northwest of Guatemala City in the western highlands at an altitude of 6,250 feet above sea level. The *municipio* covers an area of approximately 128 square kilometers. The town was built two miles to the east of the ruins of the ancient K'iche' capital stronghold, Utatlán. Tradition has it that the stones used to build the Roman Catholic cathedral and other public buildings were taken from the destroyed K'iche' temples and palaces at Utatlán. As departmental capital, it is not only a government center but a hub for transportation, education, commerce, and telecommunications. The town center is distinct in many ways from the rural areas. Because of this, I deal with the town center first under the rubrics that I have used for all of the towns described in chapter 4 and then provide summary descriptions of several of the rural communities based on the observations made by my colleagues.

---

[28]The data for Santa Cruz del Quiché were collected by Marty and Diane Quigley.

## 5.1 Demographic factors

The 1981 census lists the total population of Santa Cruz del Quiché as 35,301. Of this total, 28,046 (79.5%) are Mayans and 26,335 (74.6%) are residents of the rural area. This makes Santa Cruz del Quiché the *municipio* with the highest concentration of residents in the urban town center. It also has one of the lowest proportions of Mayan residents (only slightly greater than Joyabaj) of the communities included in this study. The population density of Santa Cruz del Quiché is 275.8 individuals per square kilometer.

Santa Cruz del Quiché is also characterized by a fairly slow rate of growth. The earliest census data available is from the 1964 census which shows a total population of 30,584. By 1973, the population had grown to 34,147, an increase of 11.7% over the nine-year period. The increase from the 1973 level (34,147) to the 1981 level (35,301) represents an increase of only 3.4%. Over the nineteen-year period from 1964 to 1981, the aggregate increase is only 15.4%.

The population of Santa Cruz del Quiché is comparable to that of the other communities in terms of its age with 19,440 (55.1%) under the age of 20.

Many Mayans and ladinos from Santa Cruz del Quiché have migrated to the United States to seek employment, mostly concentrated in Houston, Texas. Almost every family we had contact with had a close male relative living and working in the United States. There they work in textile manufacturing and other low-paying jobs. Some make regular trips back to Santa Cruz del Quiché to bring money to their families and vehicles for resale. There was a report that the plans for a large wooden loom had been taken to the United States by some of the people from Santa Cruz del Quiché so that they could begin weaving typical Guatemalan material there.

## 5.2 Institutional support factors

### 5.2.1 Government.
Santa Cruz del Quiché, as capital of the department, has several layers of government and the regional or departmental offices of many national government agencies. The governor's office is located in the large government building on the town square along with the tax department and the offices of DIGESEPE, the veterinary extension service. Other departmental main offices located there are those of DIGESA, Public Health, INAFOR (an infrastructure development agency), INTA (an agrarian reform agency), a child welfare agency, the program for potable

## 5.2 Institutional support factors

water and latrines, INACOP (the agency for development of cooperatives), INDE (the national electric company), the post office and telegraph service, the customs police, the electoral commission, the national reconstruction committee, and the national police.

With such a heavy overlay of departmental government, the municipal government is less visible but still present. The *municipio* follows the same patterns as the others with the mayor, vice-mayor, and secretary structure paralleled by the subsidiary, though much less visible, *alcaldía indígena*.

The town center of Santa Cruz del Quiché, though heavily populated by Mayans, is a ladino domain. Departmental and national offices, with few exceptions, carry on their work in Spanish and little provision is made for Mayans whether K'iche's, Ixiles, Uspantekos, or Sakapultekos, who do not speak Spanish.

Santa Cruz del Quiché has a public health center as well as two hospitals—one operated by the Ministry of Health, the other by the Social Security administration. These hospitals are notoriously understaffed and under-supplied and are known for their callous and indifferent treatment of Mayans who comprise the majority of their patients. Wealthier people either travel to Guatemala City or to Chichicastenango, 11 kilometers away, where there are private hospitals. The national hospitals in Santa Cruz del Quiché are free, though most Mayans wait until they are on the point of death before allowing themselves to be taken to the hospital.

An important governmental influence on Santa Cruz del Quiché is the presence of a major army base on the outskirts of the town. At one time, the army base was smaller and occupied a fortress-like building near the central market. As guerrilla activity in the department increased, however, the army base was moved to the land outside of town around the airstrip. It is now a large complex and serves as a major staging area for troops and supplies being airlifted by small troop carriers and helicopters to the areas of conflict. The commander of this army base controls a large number of troops and, acting with the commanders of similar bases in the other departments of Guatemala, has considerable influence on the political direction of the nation. Civilian authorities are considered to be subsidiary to the military authorities in matters where their interests may conflict. Most of the rank and file soldiers are Mayans conscripted from the various *municipios*. They are brought to Santa Cruz del Quiché, trained, armed, and sent out to their assignments. Military officers are almost exclusively ladinos, though a few Mayans have succeeded in entering and graduating from the military academy.

**5.2.2 Church.** There are three Roman Catholic churches in Santa Cruz del Quiché but the main focus of Roman Catholic worship is the cathedral on the town square. One of the smaller churches, however, bears the name of the patron saint of the community, Santa Elena de la Cruz. Just as Santa Cruz del Quiché is the capital of the political administration, it also serves as the diocesan center. The archbishop of El Quiché has his residence and offices in the town center. The Catholic services are in Spanish though there may be other meetings outside of the church buildings where K'iche' is used. One of our interviewees told us that the people of the town would never accept a Mayan priest. The lay training group, Catholic Action, is also active in Santa Cruz del Quiché, but during our observations of their public activities they used only Spanish. One of our observers also attended the wedding of two Mayans in the Catholic church and heard no K'iche' used.

There are numerous Protestant churches in Santa Cruz del Quiché. Our tally counted twenty-three in the town center alone. There was also a Mormon church located on the outskirts of the town center and many churches located in the *aldeas* as well. Each of these churches has a different profile in terms of its support of the Mayan identity. Some of the churches are predominantly ladino. Others have mixed congregations. One of the churches uses K'iche' for all parts of the service except singing and the Bible readings.

**5.2.3 Education.** As the departmental capital, Santa Cruz del Quiché is also the hub of the regional educational system. The regional supervisory offices are located here. In the town center, there are five public elementary schools, two middle schools, and the only public high school in the department. In addition, there are three private elementary schools, two private middle schools, and a private high school. The army also operates a middle and high school as preparation for entrance to the national military academy. In the rural areas, seven *aldeas* have public elementary schools.

The national bilingual education program is active in six of the rural schools. The program was initially met with opposition from the parents, but gradually parents in some of the communities are coming to believe that the program has value. The administrators and teachers of the program have been very active in doing public relations to convince the rural people of the benefits of bilingual education.

**5.2.4 Business.** Wealth in Santa Cruz del Quiché is not confined to the ladino segment of the population, and the usual stereotypes of what kinds of jobs are held by which race do not apply. There are several large stores and other businesses owned by ladinos with ladino clerks who have to hold second jobs in order to support their families. At the same time, one of the important bus companies is owned by a Mayan.

The town is an important hub for commerce and transportation. Trucks bring goods into it from Guatemala City. The merchants act as wholesalers for the smaller stores in the outlying *municipios*. Everything from clothing to construction supplies can be obtained here, but at a slightly higher price than in Guatemala City. Since transportation to the capital is relatively easy, many ladinos travel to the capital to make their purchases. As a result, although Santa Cruz del Quiché supports several businesses, it could not be classified as a thriving economy. There are two banks in the town but these do not seem as busy as the single bank in nearby Chichicastenango.

The central market is partially enclosed in a building, but on market days may spill out into the streets. There are vendors, both Mayan and ladino, in the market every day of the week and some have permanent stands. The market supplies not only the immediate community but also customers from all of the outlying *municipios*. Mayans from these communities may travel to Santa Cruz del Quiché to take care of other business but almost always go through the market to buy those things that simply are not available in their hometowns. Since the main bus terminal for the department is located here, residents of faraway towns who are making connections with buses to the capital or to another town may pass the time strolling through the market. K'iche' will as often as not be used in the market but since not all of the *municipios* in the department are K'iche'-speaking, Mayans who speak other languages may be seen and heard in the market as well. All of the merchants in the market speak Spanish well.

Rural residents of Santa Cruz del Quiché participate in the yearly migrations to the coast to provide labor for the plantations. Busloads of men, women, and children leave for from one to three months in order to earn cash. Land is not readily available in the *municipio* so crops are not always adequate. Cash is needed in order to buy corn and beans to supplement their limited harvests.

Hatmaking is one of the local industries that provides cash for many Mayans. The palm leaves are brought from the coast and bought by the bundle. Women pass their time braiding the palm leaves into narrow ribbons which are then sold to the hat makers who sew them together into hats. The hats are then sold in the local market or exported for sale elsewhere.

**5.2.5 Culture.** Santa Cruz del Quiché quite clearly displays a dichotomy between urban and rural societies. The town center is ladino-dominated and Spanish-oriented. Even though most of the residents of the town center are Mayans, there are no clearly identifiable Mayan neighborhoods. Mayans and ladinos live next to each other, all speaking Spanish for most activities of daily life. Some of the Mayans have a plot of land in one of the rural *aldeas* that they tend, but their primary residence is in the town center. This is not a vacant town by any means. Mayan women still maintain their typical dress, but have a slightly more sophisticated style of clothing than most rural women would feel comfortable with. Some of the Mayan women do not speak K'iche'. Our observers had the impression that the use of K'iche' was not integral to the urban Mayans' sense of identity. In the rural communities K'iche' is predominant but slowly giving way to Spanish under pressure from the economic demands of life. The urban Mayans are demonstrating that education and hard work can provide opportunities for advancement, and given this example, some of the younger rural K'iche's are finding this nontraditional world view to be alluring.

At the same time there is an effort among the urban, more educated, younger K'iche's to maintain and restore the Mayan culture. A K'iche' Authentic Cultural Association has been formed and sponsors such events as the coronation of a Miss Mayan Santa Cruz del Quiché. Tellingly, the contestants at the competition that my colleagues observed spoke Spanish to reply to the questions put to them. One young lady when asked whether there should be separate contests for Miss Santa Cruz del Quiché for Mayans and ladinos, as there currently are, replied that there should not be because it divides the community unnecessarily. On another occasion, of a similar sort, the contestants did use K'iche' but then translated their responses into Spanish.

Some of the organizers of this association are also bilingual education teachers who are beginning to write poetry and short stories in K'iche'. Some of them have expressed the desire to hold K'iche' classes for those who would like to learn (or relearn) the language. One motivation for this is that better paying teaching jobs are available to bilinguals under the national bilingual education program. According to one report given to us, most of the students studying to be teachers at the local public high school are Mayans.

We have no data on the activities of the *cofradías* in Santa Cruz del Quiché. They do exist and are functioning but are almost lost in all of the urban bustle of the town center.

Santa Cruz del Quiché has two radio stations, one operated by the Roman Catholic church, the other privately owned. The Roman Catholic station has quite a bit of K'iche' programming and is listened to throughout the department. It is the station used by the Roman Catholic priest in Chichicastenango to broadcast his weekly cultural program. The privately owned station broadcasts mostly music but does sell time for programming of various sorts. A number of Protestant churches buy time and broadcast their church services over this station. Some of these programs make use of K'iche' but most of the broadcasting is in Spanish. Santa Cruz del Quiché also has a cable television system which provides five U.S. channels to its subscribers.

## 5.3 Status factors

While the differences between ladino and Mayan that exist in other communities are equally strong in Santa Cruz del Quiché, the sharpest division seems to be between the urban and rural residents of the *municipio*. The urban residents are more sophisticated and upwardly mobile and perhaps a bit embarrassed by their country cousins. No ladino was ever observed to speak K'iche', and it was reported that there was no need to speak K'iche' in the town center because all of the Mayans there speak Spanish sufficiently well. One K'iche' woman reported that those K'iche's who lived in the town center no longer spoke pure K'iche'. Another young K'iche' professional stated that the use of K'iche' would only get you a job working in a cornfield. His parents only spoke K'iche' to their first child. Another woman reported that her five children understand K'iche' but do not speak it and that her daughter has typical K'iche' clothing that she keeps stored away but does not wear.

One interviewee told us that in some of the *aldeas* the *cofradías* have ceased to function, and that the shamans are ridiculed by the younger members of the Catholic Action group. As a result, they only perform their rites at night.

## 5.4 Subjective factors

As mentioned above, urban Mayans seem to feel embarrassment at the "backward" features of the Mayan identity including the use of the language. While women continue to wear a kind of distinctive dress, they have abandoned the use of K'iche' at least in public domains. The focus of the urban Mayans is on upward mobility and on obtaining education for themselves and their children. With the exposure of many of the citizens to the culture of the United States, both through migration to the U.S. and cable television, many feel that Santa Cruz del Quiché, and Mayan life in particular, are inferior to the many economic and social advantages that they have discovered.

## 5.5 Two rural communities

Since there is such a contrast between the town-dwelling Mayans and the rural Mayans of Santa Cruz del Quiché, this section describes some of the features of La Estancia and San José Lemoa, two of the rural *aldeas* of Santa Cruz del Quiché. Though geographically not very far from the town center, they are sociologically distant from the urban center although the effects of urban values are apparent.

**5.5.1 La Estancia.** Located about 3 miles from the town center, La Estancia is on the road that passes the ruins of Utatlán, the ancient fortress city of the Quiché. There is no bus service to La Estancia so transportation is primarily by foot. Occasionally, trucks reach the *aldea* if goods need to be delivered or carried out. There are no ladinos resident in the community. The community has no electricity though the high tension distribution lines pass close by. The community would like to have running water connected to each house and has begun working on a cooperative effort to bring that about. Currently water is only available from a few public faucets scattered throughout the community. One local resident opined that, once there is running water, the residents would probably petition for connection to the electric lines.

Entrance to the *aldea* is controlled by the Civil Patrol, a semi-voluntary militia, organized and supported by the army. All strangers entering the area must state their business and who they plan to visit.

The local school serves as a community meeting hall where community matters such as the water project are discussed. All such community meetings are conducted in K'iche'.

The *aldea* has three Protestant churches and two Roman Catholic chapels. The Methodist congregation uses K'iche' in their services but some of the singing is in Spanish. The Bible reading is done first in Spanish and then translated and commented on extemporaneously in K'iche'. Frequently, there is a ladino pastor who comes from the town center to provide a Spanish sermon.

The two Roman Catholic chapels are within sight of each other and no activity was observed at either one.

It was reported to us by an elderly native of the community that few people leave La Estancia to go to the coast. Some of the people reside in the town center but maintain their fields in the *aldea*. Many of the men are weavers or hatmakers and so have sources of income besides their fields.

We estimated enrollment in the school to be about sixty children. The teachers do not speak K'iche', and the parents of the community have opposed the introduction of bilingual education. Although Spanish is used by the teachers in the classroom, the children use K'iche' outside of the classroom setting without penalty. One of the parents in the community reported that, while Spanish is used in school, the children speak K'iche' in all other settings.

At least one of the community residents has a radio and listens to it regularly. One of the homes has a television antenna connected to a battery-powered television. There is also a gas-powered mill where the women can pay to have their corn ground for the making of tortillas. There is one very small store where soft drinks, snack foods, and salt are for sale.

**5.5.2 San José Lemoa.** Lemoa is a larger community than La Estancia and sits astride the paved road that leads from Chichicastenango to Santa Cruz del Quiché. The population of the community was estimated to be 1,000 people of which 350 are men and 650 are women and children. K'iche' was used in public by all those who were observed, and one of the residents of the community told our investigators that everyone in the community speaks K'iche'. A few of the men appeared to have very limited proficiency in Spanish.

Of the men, approximately three hundred go to the coast each year and an interviewee told my colleagues that most would prefer to go to the coast rather than learn a new skill which would enable them to earn cash at home. A few have expressed interest, however, in obtaining an apprenticeship to learn tailoring or carpentry, but the cost is very high and opportunities are limited.

This community, like La Estancia, is involved in a project to bring running water to the community. The citizens collected enough money to gain the rights to a water source nearly twenty miles away near the boundary with the department of Totonicapán. They have purchased the plastic pipe needed to bring the water to the community. This water source will not be sufficient for the entire community but is a help. There is another water source available which is closer but it would require a diesel-powered pump, and the men of the community were afraid that they would not be able to deal with the technology. The man we interviewed concerning this project was the treasurer for the project, but admitted that he could not read or write.

The community has a Roman Catholic chapel and three Protestant churches, a Public Health Center, and a primary school.

## 5.6–5.9 Totonicapán

Totonicapán[29] is a *municipio* in the department of Totonicapán and serves as the departmental capital. The department of Totonicapán encompasses an area along the crest of the mountains and is Guatemala's highest department. The town center is located twelve miles from Quezaltenango, Guatemala's second major city, at an altitude of 8,215 feet above sea level. The *municipio* covers an area of 328 square kilometers.

The *municipio* of Totonicapán is a market and textile center, known for its use of the locally-raised wool to produce thread which is in turn used for weaving. Cotton is also imported from the southern coastal plains for use in weaving. Other industries include pottery, furniture construction, and the production of leather goods.

### 5.6 Demographic factors

As of the 1981 census, Totonicapán had a total population of 62,407 making it the most populous *municipio* in this study. Of this total, 59,356 (95.1%) are Mayans and 54,929 (88.0%) are residents of the rural area. These numbers reflect the characteristics of a nucleated town which is predominantly Mayan. In this case, however, there is a greater concentration of the population resident in the town center. The population density of Totonicapán is 190.3 persons per square kilometer.

Population growth in Totonicapán in the period since the 1955 census was at its strongest between 1955 and 1964. The 1955 census figure for total population for the *municipio* was 32,751 and increased to 43,473 by the 1964 census—an increase of 32.3%. Growth was slower in the period between 1964 and 1973, when the total population reached 52,688, an increase of 21.2%. The growth rate decreased again in the period between 1973 and 1981 where it represents an 18.5% increase over the period. The aggregate increase in population since 1955 is 90.6% of the total population. Because of the high population, Totonicapán is one of the most densely populated *municipios* in the country—ninety-four persons per square kilometer. This density of population has resulted in the division and subdivision of the cultivable lands with land parcels that are

---

[29]The data for Totonicapán were collected by Charissa Crossley and Nancy Suiter.

extremely small and accounts for the need to find non-farming sources of income. The result is a pattern of residency in the town center in order to find employment in textile, wood, pottery, and leather production.

The population of Totonicapán is also generally young with 33,981 (54.5%) of the total population 19 years of age or younger.

## 5.7 Institutional support factors

Since Totonicapán, like Santa Cruz del Quiché, is a departmental capital, it shares some of the features of Santa Cruz del Quiché. There are both departmental and local (municipal) government functions operating within the town center. Some national level agencies have their regional offices in the town center. Unlike Santa Cruz del Quiché, however, Totonicapán is quite close to a major city, Quezaltenango, the capital of its own department. Some of the national government development agencies have established their regional centers of operations in the larger city from which they administer their programs in both departments. Like Santa Cruz del Quiché, there is a dichotomy between the urban center and the rural communities.

**5.7.1 Government.** Spanish is the language of government at every level in Totonicapán. Spanish use is assumed in the town hall, the governor's offices, the national police, and in most, if not all, governmental offices in town. Since most men in the town center of Totonicapán and its surrounding communities have reasonable proficiency in Spanish, there is less need for interpreters in the town hall, though they can be found if necessary. Generally, only the residents of the most remote *cantones* have difficulty with Spanish.

**5.7.2 Church.** The Roman Catholic church in Totonicapán uses Spanish predominantly in its masses and other services in the town center. Catechists and other lay leaders who hold meetings in the rural areas use Spanish materials for their teaching. The liturgy, the Ten Commandments, and doctrines of the church are all memorized in Spanish. Class discussions and the preaching may be done in K'iche'. Some singing is done in K'iche' and while prayers from the written liturgy will be said in Spanish, personal prayers and intercessions for the sick may be said in K'iche'.

There are at least two Protestant churches in the town center and both use Spanish exclusively. There are also a large number of Protestant churches in the rural communities where K'iche' is used for some functions including prayer, announcements, the singing of some songs, and for preaching. Spanish, however, is used in the sermon for biblical and doctrinal terms. Only a few of the Protestant churches read the K'iche' New Testament. In general, Spanish dominates singing and Scripture reading and heavily infiltrates the preaching. Conservative estimates place the Protestant segment of the population at 30% of the total.[30]

**5.7.3 Education.** The town center has two primary schools which are attended by girls in the mornings and boys in the afternoons. There are also three private elementary schools, one Roman Catholic- and two Protestant-run. There are three public middle schools, two located in the town center and one located in a rural *cantón*. One of the urban public middle schools offers its classes for adults in the evenings. The other public middle school offers three years of high school-level training for the preparation of elementary schoolteachers. One of the private schools also offers a complete middle school, and a second private school offers the first two grades of the middle school cycle.

There are forty-six rural primary schools in Totonicapán. Thirty-four of these schools serve as Castilianization Centers, where K'iche' preschoolers are taught Spanish in order to make them ready to start school.

The regional office of the bilingual education project is located in the town center and coordinates the bilingual education program in the entire department. This office is staffed by a regional coordinator and four area supervisors, one of whom is responsible for the *municipio* of Totonicapán. The other three are responsible for other *municipios* in the department of Totonicapán. There are about forty schools with bilingual education programs in the entire department, seven of which are in Totonicapán. All seven of these are elementary schools with grades one through six. The bilingual education program is functioning in the first two grades in most of the schools and in first grade in all of the others. The program employs a staff of ten teachers. All seven of the bilingual education program schools are located in the rural *cantones*.

The class size is large, about forty to fifty students, but the drop-out rate is high, unofficially estimated at about 25%. The statistics provided by the school officials, though incomplete, showed a drop-out rate of only 7%.[31] Reasons given for this attrition were sickness, economic needs, and

---

[30]Crossley (1989) reports that one of the officials of the Catholic church in Totonicapán estimated that only 60% of the urban population and only 45% of the rural population is Roman Catholic. It is unclear, however, if this source included practitioners of Christopaganism among those outside the Church.

[31]Of 4,802 students enrolled in the *municipio* of Totonicapán, 4,484 were reported to have completed the year.

migration. Some individuals (not school officials) also told us that in the rural areas in particular there was a lack of confidence in ladino schoolteachers, and that there were cases of verbal and physical abuse of the Mayan students by these teachers.

Many parents are opposed to the use of K'iche' in school because they want their children to learn Spanish. Most parents are not fully aware of the goals of the bilingual education program nor of the goals of the schools in general. A few parents, however, have expressed positive attitudes towards having their children learn to read and write in K'iche'.

Many of the ladino schoolteachers and some Mayan teachers who are not part of the bilingual program are also opposed to the bilingual education program. It was reported that they have tried to turn the parents of the communities against the program. They feel that bilingual education is an attempt to hold Mayan children back by forcing them to retain K'iche' rather than to learn Spanish. A few communities who invited a bilingual teacher to come to their school have refused to support the program after the teacher began to work.

The bilingual education program has also been hampered by a scarcity of materials and poor quality materials. This has given the impression that the bilingual program is not as good as the regular curriculum. There is a considerable need for public relations efforts in the local communities. Some of the employees of the bilingual program feel that there is a general lack of support from local and national authorities which makes it even more difficult to "sell" the program to the residents of the communities.

**5.7.4 Business.** As the departmental capital, Totonicapán might be expected to be a hub of commerce, but this is not so. The proximity of Quezaltenango, only 12 miles away by good paved road and the ready availability of buses, taxis, and vans to transport goods and people, all contribute to the more local nature of commerce in Totonicapán. The lines of commerce more readily lead to Quezatltenango as a regional center, than to Totonicapán. Still, the market in Totonicapán is large and active on market days, and there are a lot of outsiders who come to sell to the residents of Totonicapán. Vendors from at least seventeen other *municipios* were observed selling in the market. K'iche' is used by the residents of Totonicapán in dealing with many of these since they are recognized (by their clothing) as being from other K'iche'-speaking towns. If the vendor is from a non-K'iche'-speaking town, however, the transaction will be carried out using Spanish. Ladinos also generally use Spanish in the market although some ladino women have been heard to use a word or two of K'iche' when dealing with a Mayan vendor. One of our interviewees, a Mayan, remarked on this to make the point that they were just doing this for "fun" and did not intend any insult by it.

While the market is Mayan in its ethnicity, it is a mixed domain linguistically. Both Spanish and K'iche' are used as needed. The market is not a source where a great deal of cash is generated. It is primarily a place where agricultural products are traded, though cloth, ready-made clothing, plastic items, etc. are sold there as well. But agriculture is primarily done to raise food crops for the family. Cash is earned through the practice of a trade, several of which are flourishing in Totonicapán.

Weaving is the primary trade in Totonicapán and is the source of a great deal of wealth. Weaving is done in many parts of the *municipio,* but there are specific *cantones* which are centers of the weaving trade. The cloth is woven for use in women's skirts according to the distinctive patterns of the communities and for other uses as well. Much of the cloth woven in Totonicapán is exported to other communities for sale.

Furniture making is also an important trade. Specific *cantones* seem to have high numbers of carpenters and furniture makers. Beside making furniture to order for local customers, some of the carpenters carry their goods to other markets.

Leather goods and ceramics also are important sources of cash income. The latter requires access to land which has a lot of clay and so is not as lucrative a business as the others mentioned. The potters in the rural communities specialize in making clay cookware and roof tiles while those located in the town center make more decorative and ornamental items.

Because there are sources of cash readily available locally, most of the residents of Totonicapán do not migrate to the coast. Because of the altitude, the harvest in Totonicapán is later than in other areas, usually occurring in November, which is the primary time for harvesting on the coast. This also contributes to the relative stability of the population in Totonicapán. It was estimated that at most two or three busloads of people will go to the coast, mostly men, or families with few children.

Totonicapán has a number of stores and other permanent businesses but these generally are in competition with the more well-stocked stores of Quezaltenango. As a result, they are not thriving but mainly serve as conveniences for the residents of the town center or of the rural communities who cannot or will not make the longer trip to the bigger city. These are Spanish domains. Two pharmacies were remarked on by our interviewee because they have staff who can and will speak K'iche' to the older Mayan women. Generally, it was felt that only older ladinos might know some K'iche'. Younger people of either race in the town center were expected to speak Spanish.

**5.7.5 Culture.** In comparison with Santa Cruz del Quiché, Totonicapán is a much more Mayan community. Though more developed in terms of infrastructure (roads, water, electricity), Totonicapán retains more of a predominantly Mayan flavor. Most of the population would identify itself as Roman Catholic, but there is a large segment of the population which maintains the practice of the traditional rites and customs which are administered by the shamans. A number of Roman Catholics reject these practices, however, and the sizable Protestant segment also rejects the traditional beliefs and practices.

The Mayan people of Totonicapán seem to mark their identity by their clothing, their linguistic variety, of which they are very aware, their town (the saints, sacred places, etc.), and their work. Our observers overheard comments regarding whether a person was "from here" or not and found this to be an important feature in characterizing a person. The identification was based on both clothing and language. The people were able to identify quite accurately a person's provenance using only these two means of identification.

Work is probably not as important as other factors in making the contrast between those who are "from here" and those who are not, but it is an important symbol of pride and achievement which is connected with the *municipio*. The residents of Totonicapán take a great deal of pride in the fact that their community is the predominant center for weaving in Guatemala. They scorn certain other kinds of work which are associated with less prestigious places and ethnic identities.[32]

## 5.8 Status factors

Of the various K'iche' ethnicities, the residents of Totonicapán have high prestige. In part, this is because of the historical background of the community. Totonicapán is connected with the great battle against the Spanish where the Quiché-Mayan chieftain, Tecum Uman, gave his life. It was also the site of an unsuccessful Mayan rebellion in the nineteenth century. While Santa Cruz del Quiché is connected with Utatlán and the great defeat of the Quichés at Utatlán, Totonicapán is connected with battle and

---

[32]Among these is the gathering of *ocote* 'pitch pine', used to start fires. This work is done by the men of Santa María Chiquimula. It is hard to know whether the Chiquimultecos are less prestigious because they do the less prestigious work, or if the work has come to be scorned because of who does it.

resistance against the Conquerors. The community also became an important administrative center under Spanish colonial rule.

The residents of Totonicapán are well-off financially because of their weaving and other marketable skills. The Mayans of Totonicapán seem to suffer less from the sense of inferiority connected with being Mayan than the residents of the other communities described earlier. Though still not equal to the ladino, and still with a number of strongly-felt needs for betterment and development, generally the residents of Totonicapán are fairly well satisfied with their lot in life and see opportunities as being available to them.

## 5.9 Subjective factors

In spite of this general sense of economic well-being, and a pervasive Mayan ambience in the *municipio,* the Mayans of Totonicapán seem to connect success and opportunity with the acquisition of Spanish. As a subsidiary project, one of our investigators undertook a study of intergenerational language transmission in one of the rural *cantones* that is within easy walking distance of the town center of Totonicapán. This study (Crossley 1989) used formal interviews based on a questionnaire which were conducted with a sample of thirty-eight of the approximately 287 families living in the *cantón* Chuixchimal. Each of the families in the study had at least one child under fifteen years of age. The data that were gathered were analyzed in terms of the age of the parents, the first language of their children, and any difference in the amount of K'iche' and Spanish spoken by their children. The parents were divided into two age groups, those thirty-five years of age and younger and those over thirty-five. The results show that there has been a statistically significant increase in the number of homes in Chuixchimal where Spanish is being taught as the first language. Furthermore, this change began at about the same time that Protestantism began to gain ground in the rural communities of Totonicapán.

Crossley makes several other important observations about Totonicapán. First, she argues that her study based on self-report data shows that the home domain is a leaking domain, and that Spanish is rapidly gaining ground. Second, she says that K'iche' is of low prestige because it is not useful beyond the narrow confines of the K'iche'-speaking region. Third, education is available in Spanish. Schools participating in the bilingual education program are few and are not highly valued by parents who are teaching their children Spanish as their first language. Fourth, the social networks of Chuixchimal are dense and multiplex but are weakening under the influence of increased commercial contacts externally and religious diversity internally. Fifth, the broadcast media are having a strong influence on the younger people in particular, making them aware of lifestyles and opportunities that were never available to their parents and grandparents. Sixth, the mindset of Totonicapán is progressive, and changes are accepted quickly and easily if the people believe they will facilitate a better life. The widespread acceptance of education (in Spanish) for their children is an example. Finally, the area is becoming increasingly influenced by Protestantism. Crossley's analysis is that the presence of even one Protestant church in a rural community is an influence towards the increased use of Spanish.

Given these factors, the subjective vitality of Totonicapán can be characterized as one where economic development is paramount, and the acquisition and use of Spanish is seen as the key to economic advantages. While K'iche' is sentimentally valued, it is not seen to be instrumentally beneficial. Crossley's study showed that among the younger parents (those thirty-five and younger) more than 50% of them were teaching K'iche' to their children. Parents want their children to speak both languages, but if a choice must be made, increasingly they will choose Spanish first.

# 6

# Language Use in the Seven Communities

In this chapter I present the language use data for each community which was collected over a six-month period using the observation techniques described in chapter 3. I also present a statistical analysis of the data in an attempt to show the effect of the independent variables on the dependent variable of language use. In addition, the analysis in this chapter attempts to support the first hypothesis of this study, that K'iche' and Spanish are no longer in a stable diglossic relationship, by showing that some of the domains of use in these communities are leaking.

The analysis examines the effect of the independent variables of race, sex, age, and domain on the dependent variable of language choice in search of evidence that the compartmentalization of functions and roles for the two languages is breaking down. Such a loss of compartmentalization can be taken as an indication of a destabilization of a diglossic situation.

As described in chapter 3, the observers categorized participants by race as either K'iche', ladino, or as mixed-race groups. The speech transactions were classified as produced either by males, by females, or by mixed-gender groups. The language varieties were classified as either K'iche' only, Spanish only, or code-mixed. For the analysis of the effect of race and sex, I have excluded mixed-race and mixed-gender group participants and have considered only the language use patterns of K'iche' and ladino males and females. Speech transactions produced by K'iche's are considered in the analysis only by age and domain.

The primary measure of statistical significance used in this community-by-community analysis is chi-square. This measure is appropriate when the data consist of frequency counts of items or people in particular classifications or cross-classifications. The data considered consist of counts of speech transactions produced by different classes of participants according to the research design described in chapter 3. Chi-square, however, is limited when the classificatory scheme of the frequencies to be compared forms a matrix that is larger than four cells. The use of chi-square with data which is divided among many categories can only indicate whether the differences in frequencies are those expected in a normal distribution (i.e., are not significant) or if they are unexpected differences (i.e., are statistically significant). A chi-square analysis by itself cannot indicate precisely which of the categories is the source of the difference. Nevertheless, the cell chi-square value, i.e., the amount that each cell in the matrix contributes to the total chi-square value, can provide some indication of the degree to which that cell differs from the expected distribution.

Another difficulty with the standard chi-square analysis is that it does not account for any interactions in the effects of the variables being compared. This difficulty can be overcome by using categorical models statistical procedures which provide a means of arriving at a measure of the effect of nominal independent variables and of the interactions between variables and expresses that significance as a chi-square value. The variables and the interactions between variables that have a significant effect on language use are those with significant chi-square values as calculated by the categorical models procedure.

For the analysis of the effect of race and sex of participants on language use, I have used categorical modeling to examine a saturated model as a kind of analysis of variance (ANOVA) to indicate the share of the variance contributed by each of the independent variables and their interactions. Unlike ANOVA, however, the categorical models procedures do not assume that the data have been collected in a balanced research design and, therefore, are more suitable for this analysis of unbalanced frequency counts of nominal variables.

I have also analyzed the data to determine the role of age and domain on language used, using the age and domain categories described in chapter 3. I have characterized each grouping in terms of its level of K'iche' language maintenance by computing a language maintenance index (LMI). This index is arrived at by assigning a weighting factor to each of the language varieties used and multiplying the frequency count for each variety by that weighting. Since I have chosen to express this index in terms of K'iche' maintenance, I have assigned a weighting factor of 2 for K'iche' usage, a weighting factor of 1 for speech transactions identified by the observers as code-mixed, and a factor of 0 for Spanish utterances. The total of the weighted frequency counts for each of these three varieties divided by the total number of observations results in an index number which lies between 0 and 2. A higher index number indicates greater K'iche' language maintenance. A lower index number indicates less language maintenance. In the analysis of the effect of age on language use, an index number has been calculated for each age group. In the analysis of the effect of domain on language use, I have calculated an index number for each domain grouping. The collection of these indices for each of the groups produces a profile of language maintenance for each community. In addition, I have used a global count of all speech transactions produced by K'iche' participants, in which the language used was unambiguously identified, to calculate a global language maintenance index for each community.

The mean index number of all of the age groups and domains from all of the towns is 1.45 and the standard deviation is 0.33. For the purposes of categorization, all of the indices that fall within a range of one-half standard deviation of the mean index number (1.28–1.65) can be categorized as indicating moderate language maintenance. This range approximates the range between the 30th and 70th percentiles of the index numbers. Those index numbers which are above this range, from 1.66–2.00, will be taken as indicating strong language maintenance, and those below the moderate range, from 0–1.27, will be classified as indicative of weak maintenance.

As defined in chapter 3, a speech transaction is an instance of a participant speaking in a particular language to another participant in the situation. Thus, the same participant speaking once in Spanish and a second time in K'iche' is counted here as two separate speech transactions. The speech transactions are analyzed separately for each town. In some cases there were participants present who were not observed to speak. These were counted among the interlocutors in each observation where they were present. I have not, however, isolated non-speaking interlocutors as a separate class in order to examine the potential effect they might have on the speech situation.

### 6.1 Language use in Chichicastenango

The language use data for Chichicastenango consist of 898 observations of 2,329 participants producing 3,095 speech transactions. These speech transactions do not include those produced by participants which were either mixed-race or mixed-gender groups. The data were classified and cross-tabulated according to the independent variables identified in chapter 3. The analysis of each of these follows.

**6.1.1 Race and sex.** Each speech transaction was tabulated according to the race and sex of both speaker and interlocutor. Table 6.1 shows the counts of the speech transactions by language used according to the RACE (race of the speaker), SEX (sex of the speaker), IRACE (race of the interlocutor), and ISEX (sex of the interlocutor). Categorical models analysis was used to examine a saturated model of the interactions between these variables and produced the analysis of variance statistics shown in table 6.2. The results indicate that the three-way interaction between sex of the speaker, race of the speaker, and race of the interlocutor has a significant effect on language use. In addition, the two-way interactions between RACE and ISEX, and between SEX and ISEX are also significant. The two-way interaction between ISEX and IRACE is also just barely significant at the confidence level that I have set for this study ($p < .001$).

The interactions can best be understood if the frequency counts for the speech transactions are converted to a percentage and plotted on a line graph. Since the cells of the data contingency table are unbalanced, with far more observations of K'iche' participants than of ladinos, there is a considerable difference in the raw numbers of observations. Conversion to a percentage removes the differences in scale by representing each cell as the percentage of speech transactions for each combination of speaker and interlocutor variables. In this way, the effects of the independent variables are more easily seen. Table 6.3 shows the percentages calculated for the speech transactions included in the interaction between SEX, RACE, and IRACE.

Table 6.1 Speech transactions in Chichicastenango by race and sex of speaker and interlocutor

| Speakers | Interlocutor | | | | | | | | | | | | | | | | |
|---|---|---|---|---|---|---|---|---|---|---|---|---|---|---|---|---|---|
| | K'iche' | | | | | | | | Ladino | | | | | | | | Total Spkrs |
| | Females | | | | Males | | | | Females | | | | Males | | | | |
| Race Sex | CM | S | K | Total K/F | CM | S | K | Total K/M | CM | S | K | Total L/F | CM | S | K | Total L/M | |
| K'iche' Females | 65 | 166 | 433 | 664 | 60 | 79 | 276 | 415 | 6 | 22 | 13 | 41 | 9 | 31 | 19 | 59 | 1179 |
| K'iche' Males | 69 | 73 | 255 | 397 | 107 | 196 | 690 | 993 | 2 | 23 | 14 | 39 | 11 | 53 | 18 | 82 | 1511 |
| K'iche' Subtotal | 134 | 239 | 688 | 1061 | 167 | 275 | 966 | 1408 | 8 | 45 | 27 | 80 | 20 | 84 | 37 | 141 | 2690 |
| Ladino Females | 5 | 36 | 12 | 53 | 2 | 38 | 5 | 45 | 3 | 24 | 13 | 40 | 2 | 41 | 7 | 50 | 188 |
| Ladino Males | 3 | 50 | 5 | 58 | 0 | 88 | 2 | 90 | 2 | 12 | 12 | 26 | 3 | 26 | 14 | 43 | 217 |
| Ladino Subtotal | 8 | 86 | 17 | 111 | 2 | 126 | 7 | 135 | 5 | 36 | 25 | 66 | 5 | 67 | 21 | 93 | 405 |
| Grand Total | 142 | 325 | 705 | 1172 | 169 | 401 | 973 | 1543 | 13 | 81 | 52 | 146 | 25 | 151 | 58 | 234 | 3095 |

Speech transactions are either code-mixed (CM), Spanish (S), or K'iche' (K).

Table 6.2 Maximum likelihood analysis-of-variance
Race and sex data from Chichicastenango

| Source | DF | Chi-Square | Prob |
|---|---|---|---|
| SEX | 2 | 3.33 | 0.1888 |
| RACE | 2 | 78.31 | 0.0000 |
| SEX*RACE | 2 | 6.69 | 0.0352 |
| ISEX | 2 | 36.61 | 0.0000 |
| SEX*ISEX | 2 | 15.28 | 0.0005 |
| RACE*ISEX | 2 | 16.97 | 0.0002 |
| SEX*RACE*ISEX | 2 | 2.61 | 0.2710 |
| IRACE | 2 | 48.15 | 0.0000 |
| SEX*IRACE | 2 | 19.93 | 0.0000 |
| RACE*IRACE | 2 | 84.12 | 0.0000 |
| SEX*RACE*IRACE | 2 | 38.76 | 0.0000 |
| ISEX*IRACE | 2 | 16.07 | 0.0003 |
| SEX*ISEX*IRACE | 2 | 2.42 | 0.2983 |
| RACE*ISEX*IRACE | 2 | 3.55 | 0.1699 |
| SEX*RACE*ISEX*IRACE | 2 | 6.95 | 0.0309 |
| Likelihood ratio | 2 | 334.38 | 0.0000 |

Table 6.3 Tally of language use for SEX*RACE*IRACE in Chichicastenango

| Speaker/Interlocutor | Code-Mixed | | Spanish | | K'iche' | |
|---|---|---|---|---|---|---|
| | Count | % | Count | % | Count | % |
| Female K'iche'/K'iche' | 125 | 11.6 | 245 | 22.7 | 709 | 65.7 |
| Female K'iche'/Ladino | 15 | 15.0 | 53 | 53.0 | 32 | 32.0 |
| Female Ladino/K'iche' | 7 | 7.1 | 74 | 75.5 | 17 | 17.3 |
| Female Ladino/Ladino | 5 | 5.6 | 65 | 72.2 | 20 | 22.2 |
| Male K'iche'/K'iche' | 176 | 12.7 | 269 | 19.4 | 945 | 68.0 |
| Male K'iche'/Ladino | 13 | 10.7 | 76 | 62.8 | 32 | 26.4 |
| Male Ladino/K'iche' | 3 | 2.0 | 138 | 93.2 | 7 | 4.7 |
| Male Ladino/Ladino | 5 | 7.2 | 38 | 55.1 | 26 | 37.7 |

Figure 6.1 shows the plot of the percentages of the three-way interaction between RACE, SEX, and IRACE.

## 6.1 Language use in Chichicastenango

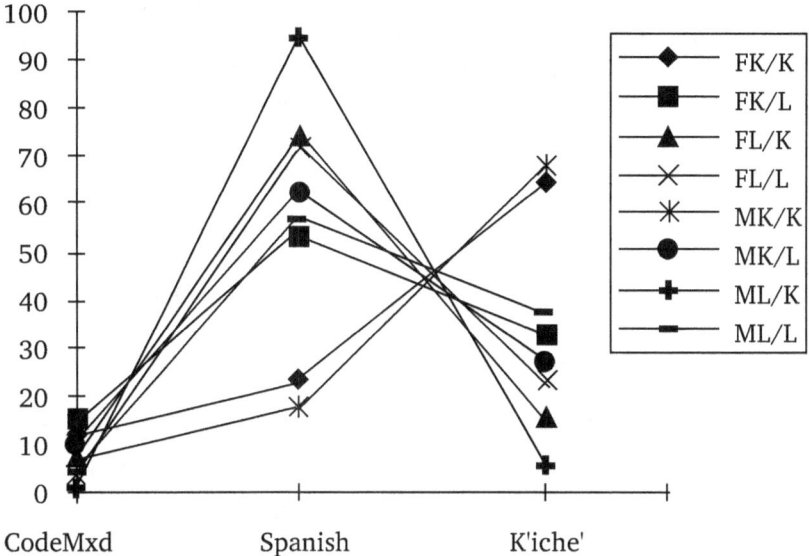

Figure 6.1 Interaction of RACE*SEX*IRACE in Chichicastenango

The language variety used in any given situation is dynamically determined by the combinations of the race and gender identities of the participants. One fact made apparent by the graph is the differential in conversational interaction between the races. While ladino speakers converse with ladino as well as with K'iche' interlocutors, most K'iche' speech transactions are with other K'iche's. This parallels the general sociology of race relations in Guatemala. Ladinos are both socially and conversationally mobile, the initiators of talk, while K'iche's are generally more restricted, confined to the passive role of hearer, not speaking unless spoken to. This state of affairs also highlights the K'iche''s lack of access to the means of acquiring and using Spanish.

Among K'iche' speakers, IRACE, the race of the interlocutor, is seen to be the most significant factor influencing language choice. Both female and male K'iche' speakers will use K'iche' predominantly with K'iche' interlocutors but will use relatively little K'iche' when addressing ladinos. The graph also shows that male and female K'iche's have virtually identical patterns of language use in Chichicastenango.

Ladino speakers, however, while showing a predominant use of Spanish with interlocutors of either race, show a difference between males and females in the levels of Spanish use. Female ladino speakers use Spanish about equally with K'iche' and ladino interlocutors and use about as much

K'iche' as do their male counterparts. Male ladinos, however, show a higher level of Spanish use when addressing K'iche's. This constitutes a point in interracial relations where K'iche's are under heightened pressure to use Spanish and are likely to feel strongly their lack of Spanish proficiency.

The two-way interaction between RACE and ISEX provides an alternative view of the role of the variables by bringing into focus the sex of the interlocutor in addition to the race of the interlocutor. Table 6.4 shows the tally of the speech transactions produced by speakers of each race in conversation with interlocutors of each sex. The percentages which are plotted in figure 6.2 are calculated in terms of the total number of speech transactions produced for each combination of speaker and interlocutor.

Table 6.4 Tally of language use for RACE*ISEX in Chichicastenango

| Speaker/Interlocutor | Code-Mixed | | Spanish | | K'iche' | |
|---|---|---|---|---|---|---|
| | Count | % | Count | % | Count | % |
| K'iche'/Female | 142 | 12.4 | 284 | 24.9 | 715 | 62.7 |
| K'iche'/Male | 187 | 12.1 | 359 | 23.2 | 1003 | 64.8 |
| Ladino/Female | 13 | 7.3 | 122 | 68.9 | 42 | 23.7 |
| Ladino/Male | 7 | 3.1 | 193 | 84.6 | 28 | 12.3 |

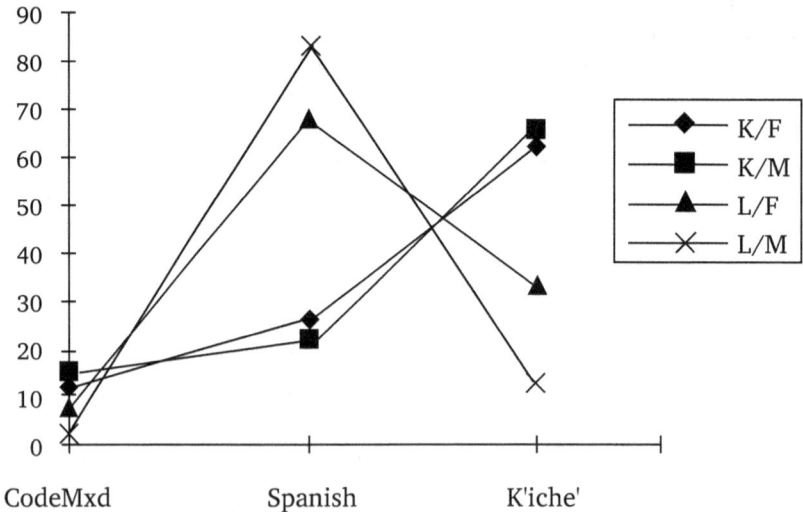

Figure 6.2 Interaction of RACE*ISEX in Chichicastenango

## 6.1 Language use in Chichicastenango

Again, while there are some differences in use based on whether the interlocutor is a male or a female, the primary line of demarcation is the race of the speaker.

K'iche' speakers show almost identical patterns of language use with interlocutors of either sex. Ladinos, however, show a greater propensity to use K'iche' with female interlocutors than with males. This parallels the pattern observed above and demonstrates that the heightened social pressure to use Spanish is particularly acute for K'iche' males.

In addition to the interactions described above, the interaction between SEX and ISEX is also significant. The frequency counts for this interaction and their percentage of the total number of speech transactions produced by speakers of the same sex are shown in table 6.5.

Table 6.5 Tally of language use for SEX*ISEX in Chichicastenango

| Speaker/Interlocutor | Code-Mixed | | Spanish | | K'iche' | |
|---|---|---|---|---|---|---|
| | Count | % | Count | % | Count | % |
| Female/Female | 79 | 9.9 | 248 | 31.1 | 471 | 59.0 |
| Female/Male | 73 | 12.8 | 189 | 33.2 | 307 | 54.0 |
| Male/Female | 76 | 14.6 | 158 | 30.4 | 286 | 55.0 |
| Male/Male | 121 | 10.0 | 363 | 30.0 | 724 | 59.9 |

The plot of the percentages shows some divergence based on whether the speech transaction is between same-sex participants or different-sex participants. This difference in language use between the sexes, however, is not as striking as that produced by the RACE and IRACE variables. The plot of the frequencies is shown in figure 6.3. The data include all participants of either race. The sharpest division in language use is between same-sex and different-sex speech transactions. There is a generally higher use of K'iche' when the speaker and interlocutor are of the same sex. Males speaking to males, and females speaking to females use almost the same amount of K'iche' in their speech transactions.

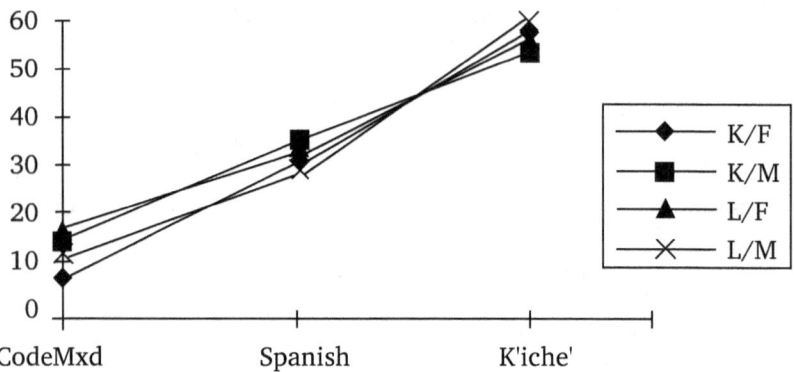

Figure 6.3 Interaction of SEX*ISEX in Chichicastenango

When the participants are not of the same sex, however, there are generally lower levels of K'iche' use, and the difference between male and female speakers is greater, with females using more K'iche' than males. This may be a reflection of the greater social mobility of men which provides them with more opportunity to interact with ladinos. It is another demonstration of the societal expectation that men will speak Spanish.

The final interaction that is significant is that between ISEX and IRACE. In the analysis of the variable interactions above, it has been seen that the race of the interlocutor and the sex of the interlocutor interact with the speaker variables to produce a significant effect on language use. The significance of this interaction between the interlocutor variables further demonstrates the importance of the identity of the interlocutor in the speaker's choice of language in each speech situation. Table 6.6 shows the frequency counts and percentages tabulated for the speech transactions according to these two variables.

Table 6.6 Tally of language use for ISEX*IRACE in Chichicastenango

| IRACE/ISEX | Code-Mixed | | Spanish | | K'iche' | |
|---|---|---|---|---|---|---|
| | Count | % | Count | % | Count | % |
| K'iche'/Female | 142 | 12.1 | 325 | 27.7 | 705 | 60.2 |
| K'iche'/Male | 169 | 11.0 | 401 | 26.0 | 973 | 63.0 |
| Ladino/Female | 13 | 8.9 | 81 | 55.5 | 52 | 35.6 |
| Ladino/Male | 25 | 10.7 | 151 | 64.5 | 58 | 24.8 |

The percentages are plotted in figure 6.4 and show the characteristic sharp division based on race. As in the other analyses, speech transactions involving ladino interlocutors demonstrate lower levels of K'iche' use generally but

## 6.1 Language use in Chichicastenango

also show the now familiar tendency for males to be addressed by ladinos more often in Spanish. For K'iche' speakers there is virtually no difference in language use in this analysis based on the sex of the interlocutor.

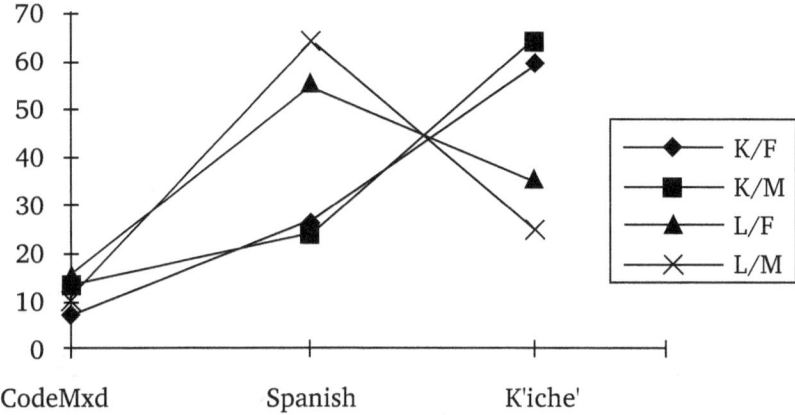

Figure 6.4 Interaction of ISEX*IRACE in Chichicastenango

The age and sex data from Chichicastenango provide evidence that the compartmentalization of the functional roles of Spanish and K'iche' is strong when viewed from the perspective of the race of the participants. There is also some evidence that there are significant differences in language use based on the sex of the participants. The data show as well the significant effect that the identity of the interlocutor has on language use.

**6.1.2 Age.** There were 2,606 speech transactions analyzed for Chichicastenango. Of these, 64.4% (1,679) were produced in K'iche', 25.1% (653) were produced in Spanish, and 10.5% (274) were classified as code-mixed. Table 6.7 shows the frequency counts of the speech transactions in the age groups by language used.

The chi-square analysis indicates that there is a significant difference in the language use patterns between the age groups. Table 6.7 also shows the language maintenance index (LMI) computed for each age group using the method described above. The levels of these indices are shown graphically in figure 6.5.

Table 6.7 K'iche' language use by age group in Chichicastenango

| Age | 1–12 | 13–24 | 25–34 | 35–44 | 45–54 | 55+ | Total |
|---|---|---|---|---|---|---|---|
| K'iche' | | | | | | | |
| Frequency | 260 | 373 | 421 | 364 | 186 | 75 | 1679 |
| Expected | 226.79 | 388.5 | 432.31 | 387.21 | 160.43 | 83.757 | |
| Cell chi-square | 4.8639 | 0.6186 | 0.2961 | 1.3917 | 4.0767 | 0.9155 | |
| Spanish | | | | | | | |
| Frequency | 71 | 147 | 183 | 173 | 43 | 36 | 653 |
| Expected | 88.203 | 151.1 | 168.14 | 150.6 | 62.393 | 32.575 | |
| Cell chi-square | 3.3551 | 0.1111 | 1.314 | 3.333 | 6.0279 | 0.3601 | |
| Code-Mixed | | | | | | | |
| Frequency | 21 | 83 | 67 | 64 | 20 | 19 | 274 |
| Expected | 37.01 | 63.401 | 70.55 | 63.19 | 26.18 | 13.668 | |
| Cell chi-square | 6.9257 | 6.0589 | 0.1787 | 0.0104 | 1.459 | 2.0796 | |
| Total | 352 | 603 | 671 | 601 | 249 | 130 | 2606 |
| LMI | 1.54 | 1.37 | 1.35 | 1.31 | 1.57 | 1.30 | |

($X^2 = 43.376$ p<.001, df=10)

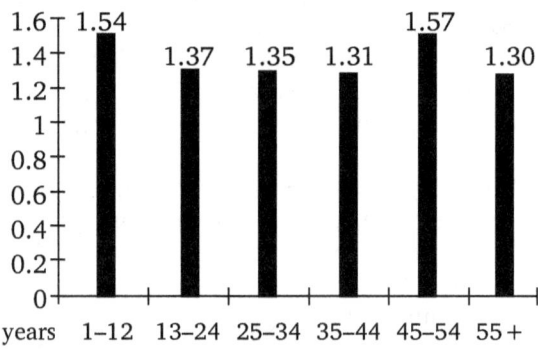

Figure 6.5 Language use by age group in Chichicastenango

An examination of the data reveals that all of the age groups in Chichicastenango fall within the moderate maintenance range. The distribution of the indices among the age groups, however, shows a pattern of weakening language maintenance in some of the younger age groups and an unexpectedly high level of language maintenance in the next to the oldest age group.

The younger age groups, which show lower levels of language maintenance, are the school-aged and young adult groups, 13 to 24-year-olds, 25 to 34-year-olds, and 35 to 44-year-olds. In these groups, maintenance decreases with age. Commensurate with this increase in Spanish usage is a slight decrease in code-mixing. The 13 to 24-year-old age group has the largest percentage share of the code-mixing in the sample with 30.3%. The 25 to 34-year-old age group accounts for 24.5% of the code-mixing in the sample while the 35 to 44-year-old age group accounts for 23.4%. This may represent a pattern of Spanish acquisition which at its earliest stages requires the production of code-mixed utterances followed by decreasing reliance on code-mixing as Spanish proficiency increases.

The 1 to 12 year and the 45 to 54 year age groups have LMIs that are very nearly identical (1.54 and 1.57, respectively) and that demonstrate higher levels of K'iche' maintenance than any of the other age groups in Chichicastenango. The cell chi-square values for these groups indicate that they are the two that depart most from the expected distribution. A possible explanation of this pattern is that the 45 to 54 age group represents those adults in the community who were born and raised before there was widespread acceptance of formal education and therefore avoided the influence of the government schools on language use. This group would have been born around the time that government language policy was in transition to the policy of *indigenismo*. They may have either avoided formal schooling altogether, or may have gotten through their schooling before the educational outworkings of *indigenismo* were fully implemented. There is not enough evidence here to confirm this explanation, but an investigation focused on these two age groups might reveal a link between their language behavior and events in the larger society during their developmental years.

Similarly, the 1 to 12-year-old group is made up of the youngest children and those in the early elementary grades who have not yet been strongly influenced by school attendance. The strength of the language maintenance index in this age group provides evidence that K'iche' is still being transmitted from one generation to another.

The proposals presented above, however, show a pattern of generally weak language maintenance in the majority of the age groups with only two age groups departing significantly from that pattern. The relatively low maintenance level of the oldest age group is representative of the overall pattern of increasing Spanish acquisition and the 45 to 54-year-old age group with its higher levels of K'iche' maintenance is, in fact, anomalous, perhaps representing a short-lived resurgence in K'iche' use.

This evidence and the evidence provided by the analysis of race and sex paints a picture of an increasing level of bilingualism with the general maintenance of the diglossic relationship between K'iche' and Spanish. If the hypothesis that diglossia is weakening is to be taken to be true in

Chichicastenango, we should look for evidence of leakage in the domains of use.

**6.1.3 Domain.** The domain data analyzed for Chichicastenango consist of 3,113 speech transactions produced by K'iche's divided between the ten domain categories as described in chapter 3. These domains consist of the following:

>D01 Home and hearth
>D02 Personal encounters (street)
>D03 Recreation (play)
>D04 Market
>D05 Work
>D06 Religious meetings
>D07 Stores
>D08 Mass media
>D09 Formal education (school)
>D10 Government offices

Of the total K'iche'-produced speech transactions, 61.4% (1,910) were produced in K'iche', 25.0% (779) were produced in Spanish, and 13.6% (424) were classified as code-mixed. Table 6.8 shows the distribution of the speech transactions among the domain groups by language used as well as the computed language maintenance index for each domain. (See table 6.8.)

The chi-square analysis of these data indicates that there is a significant difference in language use among the domains. This difference can be taken as evidence that at least some of the domains are clearly associated with one language variety or the other. The chi-square analysis, however, does not locate the source domains of language maintenance.

The language maintenance indices for each domain are shown as a bar graph in figure 6.6.

## 6.1 Language use in Chichicastenango

Table 6.8 K'iche' language use by domain in Chichicastenango

| Domain | Home | Street | Play | Market | Work | Religion | Stores | Media | School | Govt | Total |
|---|---|---|---|---|---|---|---|---|---|---|---|
| | | | | | K'iche' | | | | | | |
| Frequency | 284 | 347 | 13 | 226 | 173 | 318 | 81 | 215 | 136 | 117 | 1910 |
| Expected | 246.04 | 281.01 | 14.725 | 200.63 | 123.94 | 469.98 | 85.284 | 180.39 | 166.27 | 141.73 | |
| Cell chi-square | 5.858 | 15.497 | 0.2022 | 3.2073 | 19.421 | 49.149 | 0.2152 | 6.6422 | 5.512 | 4.3155 | |
| | | | | | Spanish | | | | | | |
| Frequency | 72 | 99 | 8 | 47 | 20 | 212 | 52 | 66 | 100 | 103 | 779 |
| Expected | 100.35 | 114.61 | 6.0058 | 81.829 | 50.549 | 191.68 | 34.783 | 73.571 | 67.815 | 57.806 | |
| Cell chi-square | 8.0075 | 2.1262 | 0.6622 | 14.824 | 18.462 | 2.1531 | 8.5215 | 0.7791 | 15.275 | 35.334 | |
| | | | | | Code-Mixed | | | | | | |
| Frequency | 45 | 12 | 3 | 54 | 9 | 236 | 6 | 13 | 35 | 11 | 424 |
| Expected | 54.617 | 62.381 | 3.2689 | 44.538 | 27.513 | 104.33 | 18.932 | 40.044 | 36.911 | 31.463 | |
| Cell chi-square | 1.6935 | 40.689 | 0.0221 | 2.01 | 12.457 | 166.17 | 8.8337 | 18.264 | 0.0989 | 13.309 | |
| Total | 401 | 458 | 24 | 327 | 202 | 766 | 139 | 294 | 271 | 231 | 3113 |
| LMI | 1.53 | 1.54 | 1.21 | 1.55 | 1.76 | 1.13 | 1.21 | 1.51 | 1.13 | 1.06 | |

($X^2 = 479.710$ $p < .001$, $df = 18$)

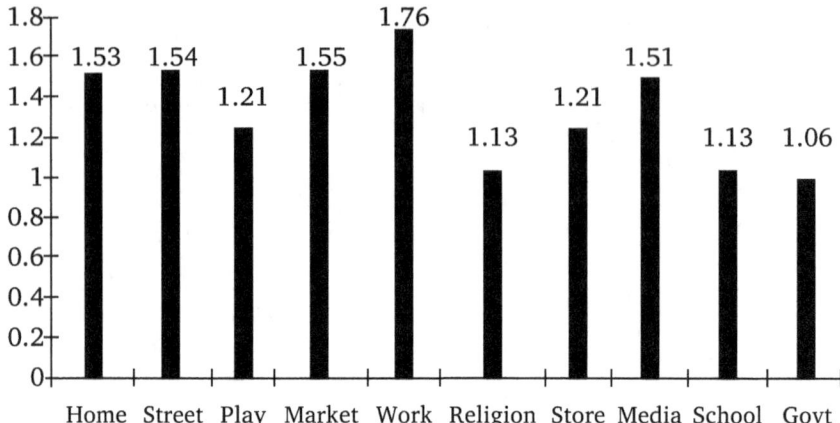

Figure 6.6 Language use by domain in Chichicastenango

The pattern of K'iche' maintenance which emerges shows a general, but not perfect, tendency for the more intimate, solidarity-related domains (those on the left side of figure 6.6) to have higher maintenance indices. The more formal, power-oriented domains (those on the right side of figure 6.6) tend to be more associated with Spanish use, and therefore to have lower LMI scores. The pattern is not totally consistent, however, and a domain-by-domain consideration of the data is appropriate.

Only one of the domains, work, shows strong language maintenance. This domain is one which lies at the core of the K'iche' culture with men's work being considered to be synonymous with corn cultivation. It is not surprising, therefore, that the language maintenance index should be high.

There are four domains in Chichicastenango that can be classified as domains where there is moderate language maintenance: home and hearth, personal encounters, market, and mass media. The cell chi-square values for these domains show that each of these depart from the expected normal distribution in the direction of increased use of K'iche' or decreased use of Spanish. All of these are intimate and solidary domains where K'iche' would be expected to be predominant and all have language maintenance indices that are comfortably within the moderate language-maintenance range.

The remaining five domains show only weak language maintenance. These domains are recreation, religion, stores, formal education, and government offices. All have LMI scores at the upper end of the weak language maintenance range. Government offices has the lowest index, 1.06, followed rather closely by religion and formal education both with LMIs of 1.13. Recreation[33] and stores have identical LMIs at 1.21. These domains are more public, formal situations which would be likely to be more strongly associated with the H(igh) language in a diglossic situation. Even in these domains in Chichicastenango, however, K'iche' is used and maintained to some extent, though less strongly than in the informal and intimate domains described above.

An examination of the level of code-mixing in each domain might provide an indicator to the degree of leakage present in that domain. Those domains which show more code-mixing than expected in a normal distribution could well be those which are leaking. If this is the case, then, few domains in Chichicastenango could be classified as leaking domains since few depart from the expected normal distribution for code-mixing. We should keep in mind, however, that the norms in this case are based on a general pattern of relatively weak language maintenance. The most notable domain in this category is that of religion where the cell chi-square value for code-mixed utterances is very large indeed. Our observations of Protestant church services and religious radio broadcasting provided ample evidence of high levels of code-mixing. Protestant forms of religion seem to be clearly associated with Spanish, and yet, in the rural areas in particular, are predominantly practiced by K'iche's. It may well be that this code-mxing is the result of the efforts of nonproficient speakers to produce Spanish utterances in that domain.

A more general alternative approach to the analysis of the domains of use is to characterize the domains in terms of their formality. Generally in diglossic situations, H(igh) is associated with more formal domains while L(ow) is associated with informal domains of use. If diglossia is breaking down and compartmentalization is being lost, it would be expected that significant differences in language use would not be identified. Using the formality values assigned to the topic/location categories in chapter 3 (see table 3.2) an analysis of language use by formality of domain can be attempted. Table 6.9 shows the distribution of the speech transactions between the formal and informal domains by language used. Of the 3,113 K'iche'-produced speech transactions analyzed for Chichicastenango, 44.2% (1,375) were classified as formal and 55.8% (1,738) were classified as informal. Of the total, 61.4% (1,910) were produced in K'iche', 25.0% (779) were produced in Spanish and 13.6% (424) were classified as code-mixed.

The chi-square analysis shows that there is a significant difference in the language use patterns between the two levels of formality which can

---

[33]In Chichicastenango, Totonicapán, and Santa Cruz del Quiché, I consider the recreation domain to be a more formal domain. I will discuss this decision more fully in chapter 7.

be taken as a general indication that there is a diglossic relationship being maintained between K'iche' and Spanish in Chichicastenango.

However, the LMI scores calculated for the two categories of domains show that neither demonstrates strong language maintenance. Rather the LMI for formal domains is within the range of weak language maintenance and the informal domain LMI is centered in the range of moderate language maintenance and is very close to the mean of the sample of language maintenance index scores.

**6.1.4 Summary.** The data for Chichicastenango show an overall pattern of moderate K'iche' maintenance though the level of maintenance is relatively weak in some domains. The chi-square analyses of the roles of race, age, and domain all show that there are significant differences in language use among those categories, a fact which is indicative of continuing diglossia. The age data, however, provide evidence of increasing levels of bilingualism. The LMI analysis also shows that the levels of language maintenance may be weakening. Using all of the speech transactions produced by all speakers, including those excluded for various reasons from the age and domain analysis, the global language maintenance index for Chichicastenango is 1.36, within the moderate maintenance range.

Table 6.9: Language use by formality level in Chichicastenango

| Language | Domain Formality | | Total |
|---|---|---|---|
| | Formal | Informal | |
| | K'iche' | | |
| Frequency | 734 | 1176 | 1910 |
| Expected | 843.64 | 1066.4 | |
| Cell chi-square | 14.249 | 11.273 | |
| | Spanish | | |
| Frequency | 394 | 385 | 779 |
| Expected | 344.08 | 434.92 | |
| Cell chi-square | 7.2421 | 5.7295 | |
| | Code-Mixed | | |
| Frequency | 247 | 177 | 424 |
| Expected | 187.28 | 236.72 | |
| Cell chi-square | 19.044 | 15.067 | |
| Total | 1375 | 1738 | 3113 |
| LMI | 1.25 | 1.46 | |

($X^2 = 72.064$ $p < .001$, df = 2)

## 6.2 Language use in Cunén

The language use data for Cunén consist of 808 observations of 1,852 participants producing 2,408 speech transactions.[34]

**6.2.1 Race and sex.** The tabulation of the speech transactions suitable for this analysis for Cunén is shown in table 6.10 which gives the frequency counts by language variety used according to the race and sex of the speaker and race and sex of the interlocutor. The results of the categorical models analysis for a saturated model are shown in table 6.11.

The results show that the four-way interaction between RACE, SEX, IRACE, and ISEX has a significant effect on language use. This interaction involves all four of the independent variables that have been analyzed. It indicates that in Cunén the differences in language use are sharply drawn, not only along the lines of race, but also along the gender division.

The interaction of the four variables is complex but can best be understood if viewed as a plot of the frequency counts, expressed as a percentage. This percentage has been calculated by dividing the number of speech transactions in each category by the total number of speech transactions produced by speakers of the same race and sex.

---

[34] In Cunén and Sacapulas the varieties of K'iche' spoken in the community are counted together without distinction.

Table 6.10 Speech transactions in Cunén by race and sex of speaker and interlocutor

| Speakers | | Interlocutor | | | | | | | | | | | | | |
|---|---|---|---|---|---|---|---|---|---|---|---|---|---|---|---|
| | | K'iche' | | | | | | | Ladino | | | | | | |
| | | Females | | | | Males | | | Females | | | | Males | | |
| Race Sex | CM | S | K | Total K/F | CM | S | K | Total K/M | CM | S | K | Total L/F | CM | S | K | Total L/M | Total Spkrs |
| K'iche' Females | 0 | 3 | 295 | 298 | 0 | 12 | 211 | 223 | 1 | 23 | 30 | 54 | 0 | 13 | 8 | 21 | 596 |
| K'iche' Males | 1 | 15 | 212 | 228 | 101 | 92 | 656 | 849 | 1 | 20 | 19 | 40 | 27 | 132 | 10 | 169 | 1286 |
| K'iche' Subtotal | 1 | 18 | 507 | 526 | 101 | 104 | 867 | 1072 | 2 | 43 | 49 | 94 | 27 | 145 | 18 | 190 | 1882 |
| Ladino Females | 2 | 39 | 14 | 55 | 0 | 28 | 10 | 38 | 0 | 17 | 0 | 17 | 0 | 11 | 0 | 11 | 121 |
| Ladino Males | 1 | 20 | 2 | 23 | 23 | 142 | 5 | 170 | 0 | 9 | 0 | 9 | 2 | 81 | 0 | 83 | 285 |
| Ladino Subtotal | 3 | 59 | 16 | 78 | 23 | 170 | 15 | 208 | 0 | 26 | 0 | 26 | 2 | 92 | 0 | 94 | 406 |
| Grand Total | 4 | 77 | 523 | 604 | 124 | 274 | 882 | 1280 | 2 | 69 | 49 | 120 | 29 | 237 | 18 | 284 | 2288 |

Speech transactions are either code-mixed (CM), Spanish (S), or K'iche' (K).

## 6.2 Language use in Cunén

Table 6.11 Maximum likelihood analysis-of-variance
Race and sex data from Cunén

| Source | DF | Chi-Square | Prob |
|---|---|---|---|
| SEX | 2 | 65.03 | 0.0000 |
| RACE | 2 | 231.02 | 0.0000 |
| SEX*RACE | 2 | 52.05 | 0.0000 |
| ISEX | 2 | 64.23 | 0.0000 |
| SEX*ISEX | 2 | 33.09 | 0.0000 |
| RACE*ISEX | 2 | 37.96 | 0.0000 |
| SEX*RACE*ISEX | 2 | 69.62 | 0.0000 |
| IRACE | 2 | 137.78 | 0.0000 |
| SEX*IRACE | 2 | 40.30 | 0.0000 |
| RACE*IRACE | 2 | 119.09 | 0.0000 |
| SEX*RACE*IRACE | 2 | 54.31 | 0.0000 |
| ISEX*IRACE | 2 | 43.16 | 0.0000 |
| SEX*ISEX*IRACE | 2 | 73.29 | 0.0000 |
| RACE*ISEX*IRACE | 2 | 55.91 | 0.0000 |
| SEX*RACE*ISEX*IRACE | 2 | 49.14 | 0.0000 |
| Likelihood ratio | 2 | 187.97 | 0.0000 |

Table 6.12 shows the tally of the speech transactions and the percentages calculated for each category of speech transaction. Figure 6.7 shows how all of the speech transactions produced by K'iche' males speaking to other K'iche's of either sex follow the same general pattern of little Spanish use and considerably greater K'iche' use.

This pattern does not occur in any of the speech transactions involving a ladino participant, either as speaker or interlocutor. It is important to note, however, that K'iche' female speakers use more K'iche' when speaking to other K'iche' females but use slightly less K'iche' than Spanish when their interlocutor is a K'iche' male. They also use more Spanish than K'iche' when conversing with any ladino. Thus, the patterns of language use for K'iche' females are more like those of ladinos when they are speaking to K'iche' males. In addition, K'iche' males, when speaking with K'iche' females, use more K'iche' than Spanish, but the level of Spanish use is much higher in these situations than when K'iche' males are conversing among themselves. This difference is all the more notable because conversational interactions between the sexes are generally less frequent than same-sex conversations so the higher percentages cannot be easily attributed to the unbalanced nature of the sample.

Table 6.12 Tally of language use for SEX*RACE*ISEX*IRACE in Cunén

| Speaker/Interlocutor | Code-Mixed Count | % | Spanish Count | % | K'iche' Count | % |
|---|---|---|---|---|---|---|
| Female K'iche'/Female K'iche' | 0 | 0.0 | 3 | 1.0 | 295 | 99.0 |
| Female K'iche'/Female Ladino | 1 | 1.9 | 23 | 42.6 | 30 | 55.6 |
| Female K'iche'/Male K'iche' | 0 | 0.0 | 12 | 5.4 | 211 | 94.6 |
| Female K'iche'/Male Ladino | 0 | 0.0 | 13 | 61.9 | 8 | 38.1 |
| Female Ladino/Female K'iche' | 2 | 3.6 | 39 | 70.9 | 14 | 25.5 |
| Female Ladino/Female Ladino | 0 | 0.0 | 17 | 100.0 | 0 | 0.0 |
| Female Ladino/Male K'iche' | 0 | 0.0 | 28 | 73.7 | 10 | 26.3 |
| Female Ladino/Male Ladino | 0 | 0.0 | 11 | 100.0 | 0 | 0.0 |
| Male K'iche'/Female K'iche' | 1 | 0.4 | 15 | 6.6 | 212 | 93.0 |
| Male K'iche'/Female Ladino | 1 | 2.5 | 20 | 50.0 | 19 | 47.5 |
| Male K'iche'/Male K'iche' | 101 | 11.9 | 92 | 10.8 | 656 | 77.3 |
| Male K'iche'/Male Ladino | 27 | 16.0 | 132 | 78.1 | 10 | 5.9 |
| Male Ladino/Female K'iche' | 1 | 4.3 | 20 | 87.0 | 2 | 8.7 |
| Male Ladino/Female Ladino | 0 | 0.0 | 9 | 100.0 | 0 | 0.0 |
| Male Ladino/Male K'iche' | 2 | 13.5 | 142 | 83.5 | 5 | 2.9 |
| Male Ladino/Male Ladino | 2 | 2.4 | 81 | 97.6 | 0 | 0.0 |

Ladinos, as would be expected, always use more Spanish than K'iche', regardless of the sex of the speaker and the race and sex of the interlocutor. There are some important differences, however, in the distribution of Spanish use depending on speaker and interlocutor variables. As with K'iche's, there is a general tendency for males to converse more with males, and females to converse with females, thus creating higher percentages of the sample for same-sex speech transactions. There is also a clear tendency for ladino females to use more K'iche' than ladino males when their interlocutor is a K'iche' female. This can be attributed to the higher level of contact between females of the two races in the market domain where K'iche' is the predominant language. The most significant anomaly in the language use of ladinos is the pattern of divergence which is demonstrated when ladinos interact with K'iche's causing higher levels of Spanish use than would be expected. This pattern among ladino females is somewhat ameliorated by the convergence pattern in the market domain. However, among ladino males the divergence is quite clear with very high levels of Spanish use occurring when the interlocutor is a K'iche' male. The pattern is similar, but on a smaller scale because there are so few interracial different-sex speech transactions, when ladino males converse with K'iche' females. Ladino males make no effort to accommodate to the language of their K'iche' interlocutors. This is one of the primary

## 6.2 Language use in Cunén

sources of pressure on K'iche' participants to accommodate to their ladino interlocutors. The pressure is applied primarily on K'iche' males who have the greatest amount of contact with ladino males. It is not felt so greatly by K'iche' females because they have limited contact with ladino males and because of the convergence demonstrated by ladino females.

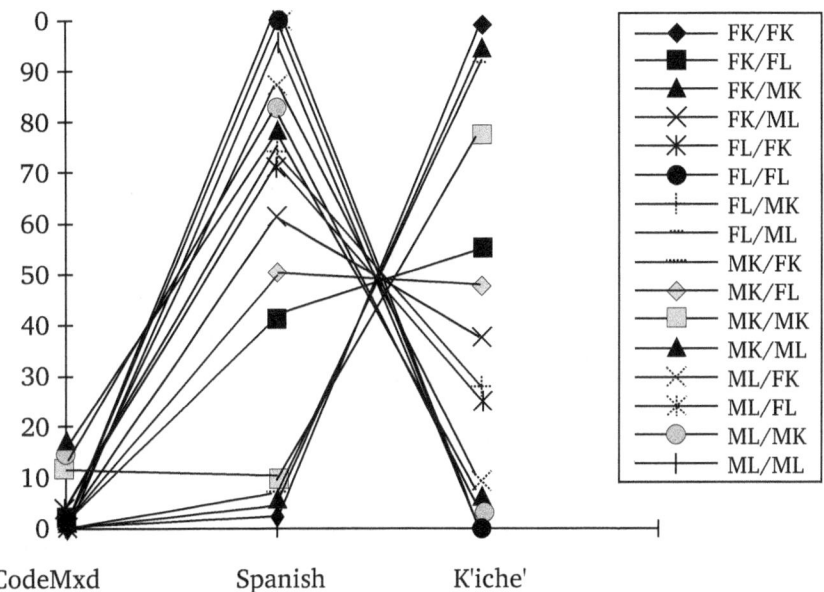

Figure 6.7 Language use by SEX*RACE*ISEX*IRACE in Cunén

These patterns of interaction in Cunén show quite clearly how the four variables have a significant effect on language use. Based on these data, the compartmentalization along racial lines in Cunén can be said to be quite robust. The anomalous behavior of female K'iche's, however, shows the beginning of convergence patterns, which is particularly ominous given the crucial role of females in the intergenerational transmission of language behavior. In addition, the ladino male lack of accommodation creates a situation where K'iche' males are under pressure to use more Spanish.

**6.2.2 Age.** There were 1,924 K'iche'-produced speech transactions analyzed for Cunén. Of these, 76.3% (1,468) were produced in K'iche', 16.1% (310) were produced in Spanish, and 7.6% (146) were classified as code-mixed. Table 6.13 shows the distribution of the speech transactions among the age groups by language used and the calculated LMI for each age group.

Table 6.13 K'iche' language use by age group in Cunén

| Age | 1–12 | 13–24 | 25–34 | 35–44 | 45–54 | 55+ | Total |
|---|---|---|---|---|---|---|---|
| K'iche' | | | | | | | |
| Frequency | 108 | 444 | 357 | 417 | 100 | 42 | 1468 |
| Expected | 85.455 | 439.48 | 349.45 | 423.46 | 129.71 | 40.439 | |
| Cell chi-square | 5.9477 | 0.0464 | 0.1631 | 0.0986 | 6.8046 | 0.0603 | |
| Spanish | | | | | | | |
| Frequency | 4 | 105 | 74 | 88 | 36 | 3 | 310 |
| Expected | 18.046 | 92.807 | 73.794 | 89.423 | 27.391 | 8.5395 | |
| Cell chi-square | 10.932 | 1.602 | 0.0006 | 0.0226 | 2.7059 | 3.5934 | |
| Code-Mixed | | | | | | | |
| Frequency | 0 | 27 | 27 | 50 | 34 | 8 | 146 |
| Expected | 8.499 | 43.709 | 34.755 | 42.115 | 12.9 | 4.0218 | |
| Cell chi-square | 8.499 | 6.3874 | 1.7303 | 1.4761 | 34.511 | 3.935 | |
| Total | 112 | 576 | 458 | 555 | 170 | 53 | 1924 |
| LMI | 1.93 | 1.59 | 1.62 | 1.59 | 1.38 | 1.74 | |

($X^2 = 88.517$ p $\leq$ .001, df = 10)

The chi-square analysis of these data indicates that there is a significant difference in language use between the age groups. This could mean that at least one age group's language use patterns differ significantly from the others. An examination of the cell chi-square values reveals that the youngest age group accounts for a great deal of the difference from the expected normal distribution. This age group uses more K'iche' than would be expected and far less Spanish and code-mixing. The greatest difference from the normal distribution, however, is found in the 45 to 54-year-old group which uses less K'iche' than expected, slightly more Spanish than expected, and considerably more code-mixing than expected. This is the group that would have experienced the effects of the language policy shifts of the 1940s most directly, and this anomalous linguistic behavior may be a reflection of that policy shift.

Figure 6.8 shows the LMI scores in a bar graph. Overall, the LMI profile of Cunén demonstrates a much more robust pattern of language maintenance than that seen in Chichicastenango, evidence which corroborates the conclusions drawn based on the analysis of race and sex in the previous section.

## 6.2 Language use in Cunén

Two of the age groups have LMI scores in the strong maintenance range (>1.65), and the youngest age group has an LMI very near the 2.00 maximum level. This is indicative of a strong pattern of intergenerational transmission of K'iche'. The oldest age group also has an LMI score in the strong maintenance range.

Although the school-aged and young adult groups (12 to 44-year-olds) show lower levels of language maintenance than either the youngest or the oldest group, these younger groups are still exhibiting moderate levels of K'iche' maintenance. The middle-aged adult group (45 to 54), the current generation of older parents, shows the weakest level of language maintenance but it is still well within the moderate maintenance range of scores. This overall profile is a very strong one in terms of K'iche' use and language maintenance.

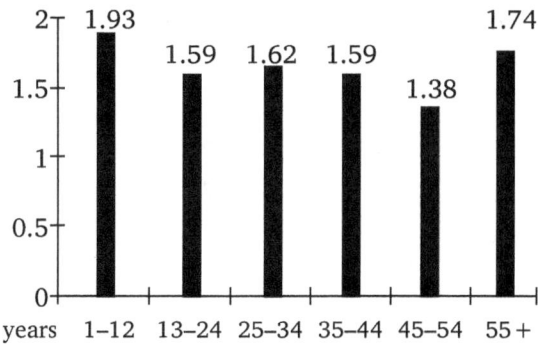

Figure 6.8 Language use by age group in Cunén

**6.2.3 Domain.** The domain analysis of the language use data for Cunén is based on a sample of 1,950 speech transactions which were produced by K'iche's. Of these, 75.7% (1,476) were produced in K'iche', 16.8% (328) were produced in Spanish, and 7.5% (146) were classified as code-mixed. Table 6.14 shows the distribution of the speech transactions among the domains by language used along with the LMI which I have calculated for each domain.

The chi-square analysis of these data indicates that there is a significant difference in language use among these domains in that at least one of the domains differs from the others in the pattern of language use which it exhibits. The domains which contribute the most to the difference from the expected normal distribution are: the home and work domains with higher than expected use of K'iche' and almost no use of Spanish; the stores domain with much lower than expected levels of code-mixing, higher K'iche' use and lower Spanish use; and the mass media and government offices domains with very low levels of K'iche' use and high levels of Spanish use.

The LMI scores also indicate a strong general pattern of language maintenance with seven of the ten domains having scores in the strong maintenance range. Figure 6.9 shows the LMI numbers for each domain in a bar graph format.

One of the domains, religion, has an LMI in the moderate maintenance range. This pattern is indicative of the generally lower levels of institutional support for K'iche' use provided by the Protestant churches and the somewhat stronger support provided by the Roman Catholic church as reported in chapter 4.

Two of the domains show weak language maintenance. These are mass media and government offices. Both of these domains are public and formal domains which would be expected to be more generally associated with Spanish. As reported above, these are also domains which differ from the expected normal distribution in the direction of increased Spanish use.

## 6.2 Language use in Cunén

Table 6.14 K'iche' language use by domain in Cunén

| Domain | Home | Street | Play | Market | Work | Religion | Stores | Media | School | Govt | Total |
|---|---|---|---|---|---|---|---|---|---|---|---|
| | | | | | K'iche' | | | | | | |
| Frequency | 176 | 168 | 85 | 179 | 252 | 34 | 328 | 104 | 39 | 111 | 1476 |
| Expected | 133.98 | 149.87 | 68.123 | 151.38 | 205.13 | 40.117 | 280.82 | 217.24 | 34.062 | 195.29 | |
| Cell chi-square | 13.182 | 2.193 | 4.1811 | 5.0376 | 10.711 | 0.9327 | 7.9272 | 59.026 | 0.716 | 36.378 | |
| | | | | | Spanish | | | | | | |
| Frequency | 1 | 30 | 5 | 19 | 13 | 11 | 42 | 113 | 3 | 91 | 328 |
| Expected | 29.772 | 33.305 | 15.138 | 33.641 | 45.584 | 8.9149 | 62.404 | 48.275 | 7.5692 | 43.397 | |
| Cell chi-square | 27.806 | 0.3279 | 6.7899 | 6.372 | 23.291 | 0.4877 | 6.6175 | 86.781 | 2.7583 | 52.217 | |
| | | | | | Code-Mixed | | | | | | |
| Frequency | 0 | 0 | 0 | 2 | 6 | 8 | 1 | 70 | 3 | 56 | 146 |
| Expected | 13.252 | 14.825 | 6.7835 | 14.974 | 20.29 | 3.9682 | 27.777 | 21.488 | 3.3692 | 19.317 | |
| Cell chi-square | 13.252 | 14.825 | 6.7385 | 11.241 | 10.065 | 4.0964 | 25.813 | 109.52 | 0.0405 | 69.662 | |
| Total | 177 | 198 | 90 | 200 | 271 | 53 | 371 | 287 | 45 | 258 | 1950 |
| LMI | 1.99 | 1.70 | 1.89 | 1.80 | 1.88 | 1.43 | 1.77 | 0.97 | 1.80 | 1.07 | |

($X^2 = 619.041$ $p < .001$ df = 18)

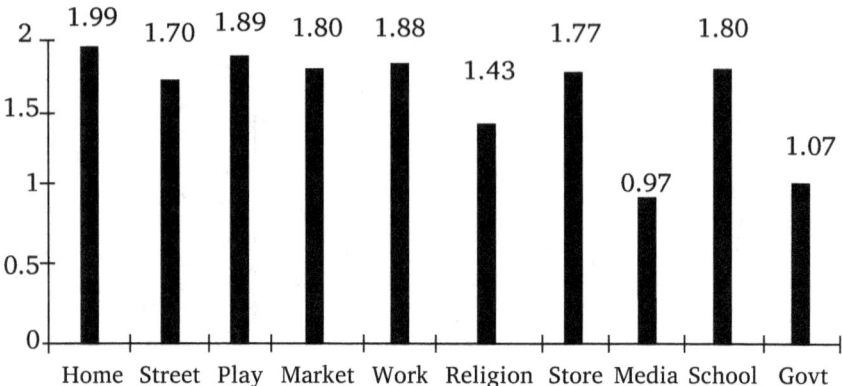

Figure 6.9 Language use by domain in Cunén

Of the 1,950 K'iche'-produced speech transactions analyzed for Cunén, 43.5% (848) were classified as occurring in formal domains, and 56.5% (1,102) were classified as occurring in informal domains. Table 6.15 shows the distribution of the speech transactions between the formal and informal domains by language used and also shows the LMI for each category. The chi-square analysis of these data shows the difference in language use between the two formality levels to be significant.

In terms of percentages, the typical diglossic association of H with formal domains and of L with informal domains is clearly demonstrated by the data from Cunén. Of the K'iche' speech transactions 33.8% (499) were classified as formal and 66.2% (977) were informal. Of the Spanish speech transactions 66.2% (217) were classified as formal and 33.8% (111) were classified as informal. Code-mixed speech transactions also were clearly associated with formal domains with 90.4% (132) classified as formal and 9.6% (14) classified as informal.

## 6.2 Language use in Cunén

Table 6.15 K'iche' language use by formality level in Cunén

| Language | Domain Formality | | Total |
|---|---|---|---|
| | Formal | Informal | |
| **K'iche'** | | | |
| Frequency | 499 | 977 | 1476 |
| Expected | 641.87 | 834.13 | |
| Cell chi-square | 31.801 | 24.471 | |
| **Spanish** | | | |
| Frequency | 217 | 111 | 328 |
| Expected | 142.64 | 185.36 | |
| Cell chi-square | 38.767 | 29.832 | |
| **Code-Mixed** | | | |
| Frequency | 132 | 14 | 146 |
| Expected | 63.491 | 82.509 | |
| Cell chi-square | 73.923 | 56.884 | |
| Total | 848 | 1102 | 1950 |
| LMI | 1.33 | 1.79 | |

($X^2 = 255.678$ $p < .001$, df = 2)

The LMI scores for each category also show the stronger association of K'iche' with the informal domains. The LMI for the informal domains is well within the strong maintenance range while the LMI for the formal domains is within the moderate maintenance range. This clear compartmentalization by formality level demonstrates the overall retention of a diglossic pattern and of a robust maintenance of K'iche' in Cunén.

**6.2.4 Summary.** The data from Cunén show one of the strongest patterns of K'iche' language maintenance found in this study. The chi-square analyses of the roles of race, sex, age, and domain all show significant differences in language use among the various categories analyzed. There is pressure on K'iche's, particularly males, to converge with Spanish speakers when they interact conversationally. Similarly, the LMI scores are in the range which indicates strong maintenance, but with some domains showing a clear tendency to be associated with Spanish. I have calculated a global LMI score of 1.59 which indicates overall moderate maintenance.

## 6.3 Language use in Joyabaj

The language use data collected for Joyabaj is not as extensive as that collected in the other communities. The data consist of 406 observations of 550 individuals producing 584 speech transactions. None of the transactions observed in Joyabaj were classifed as code-mixed by our observer who was himself a speaker of the Joyabaj variety.[35]

**6.3.1 Race and sex.** When the speech transactions with missing or ambiguous race or sex data are eliminated, there are 568 speech transactions that are amenable to statistical analysis. Table 6.16 shows the frequency counts of language used in the speech transactions according to the race and sex categories of both speakers and interlocutors. It also shows that the majority of the observed speech transactions occurred between K'iche' participants and between participants of the same sex.

The categorical models analysis results are shown in table 6.17 which shows that the interaction between the two variables RACE (race of the speaker) and IRACE (race of the interlocutor) has a significant effect on language use. Sex of speaker (SEX) and sex of interlocutor (ISEX) have no significant effect on language use nor do any of the interactions of these variables with any of the others. These results provide evidence that there is diglossia in Joyabaj along racial lines.

The tally of the frequency counts for the speech transactions, according to the possible combinations of RACE and IRACE and their percentages of the total number of speech transactions produced by each race, are shown in table 6.18.

The pattern of language use created by the interaction of RACE and IRACE can be seen in figure 6.10 which plots the percentages of the frequency counts by combinations of speaker and interlocutor according to their respective racial categories. The line graph shows that in Joyabaj the presence of a ladino as a participant in any speech transaction affects the choice of language for that transaction. While there are some differences between mixed-race speech transactions and those involving only ladinos, generally the pattern is the same with Spanish being the predominant language.

---

[35] My colleague Helen Passwater, who resided in Joyabaj for several years, reported to me that the Joyabaj variety of K'iche' is known to speakers of other varieties as one which has incorporated a great number of Spanish loan words. It may be that the observer made no distinction because the Joyabaj variety is not markedly different from code-mixed speech.

6.3 Language use in Joyabaj

Table 6.16 Speech transactions in Joyabaj by race and sex of speaker and interlocutor

| Speakers | Interlocutor | | | | | | | | | | | | | | | | |
|---|---|---|---|---|---|---|---|---|---|---|---|---|---|---|---|---|---|
| | K'iche' | | | | | | | | Ladino | | | | | | | | |
| | Females | | | | Males | | | | Females | | | | Males | | | | |
| Race/Sex | CM | S | K | Total K/F | CM | S | K | Total K/M | CM | S | K | Total L/F | CM | S | K | Total L/M | Total Spkrs |
| K'iche' Females | n.d. | 11 | 63 | 74 | n.d. | 5 | 31 | 36 | n.d. | 9 | 3 | 12 | n.d. | 24 | 7 | 31 | 153 |
| K'iche' Males | n.d. | 5 | 31 | 36 | n.d. | 15 | 79 | 94 | n.d. | 25 | 6 | 31 | n.d. | 33 | 3 | 36 | 197 |
| K'iche' Subtotal | n.d. | 16 | 94 | 110 | n.d. | 20 | 110 | 130 | n.d. | 34 | 9 | 43 | n.d. | 57 | 10 | 67 | 350 |
| Ladino Females | n.d. | 9 | 3 | 12 | n.d. | 25 | 6 | 31 | n.d. | 28 | 0 | 28 | n.d. | 20 | 2 | 22 | 93 |
| Ladino Males | n.d. | 25 | 6 | 31 | n.d. | 33 | 3 | 36 | n.d. | 20 | 2 | 22 | n.d. | 36 | 0 | 36 | 125 |
| Ladino Subtotal | n.d. | 34 | 9 | 43 | n.d. | 58 | 9 | 67 | n.d. | 48 | 2 | 50 | n.d. | 56 | 2 | 58 | 218 |
| Grand Total | n.d. | 50 | 103 | 153 | n.d. | 78 | 119 | 197 | n.d. | 82 | 11 | 93 | n.d. | 113 | 12 | 125 | 568 |

Speech transactions are either code-mixed (CM), Spanish (S), or K'iche' (K).

Table 6.17 Maximum likelihood analysis-of-variance
Race and sex data from Joyabaj

| Source | DF | Chi-Square | Prob |
|---|---|---|---|
| SEX | 1 | 3.60 | 0.0576 |
| RACE | 1 | 65.17 | 0.0000 |
| SEX*RACE | 1 | 0.00 | 0.9672 |
| ISEX | 1 | 3.12 | 0.0774 |
| SEX*ISEX | 1 | 3.43 | 0.0642 |
| RACE*ISEX | 1 | 0.01 | 0.9272 |
| SEX*RACE*ISEX | 1 | 0.18 | 0.6750 |
| IRACE | 1 | 63.08 | 0.0000 |
| SEX*IRACE | 1 | 0.01 | 0.9272 |
| RACE*IRACE | 1 | 24.99 | 0.0000 |
| SEX*RACE*IRACE | 1 | 2.02 | 0.1553 |
| ISEX*IRACE | 1 | 0.00 | 0.9672 |
| SEX*ISEX*IRACE | 1 | 0.08 | 0.7811 |
| RACE*ISEX*IRACE | 1 | 1.66 | 0.1975 |
| SEX*RACE*ISEX*IRACE | 1 | 6.63 | 0.0100 |
| Likelihood ratio | 1 | 70.62 | 0.0000 |

Speech transactions involving only ladinos have the highest use of Spanish and the lowest use of K'iche'. Ladino speakers addressing K'iche' interlocutors have the next highest level of Spanish and the highest level of K'iche' use by ladinos. K'iche' speakers with ladino interlocutors use the next highest level of Spanish. In contrast, speech transactions involving only K'iche's show an overwhelming use of K'iche' and only very low levels of Spanish use.

Table 6.18 Tally of language use for RACE*IRACE in Joyabaj

| RACE/IRACE | Spanish | | K'iche' | |
|---|---|---|---|---|
| | Count | % | Count | % |
| K'iche'/K'iche' | 36 | 15.0 | 204 | 85.0 |
| K'iche'/Ladino | 91 | 82.7 | 19 | 17.3 |
| Ladino/K'iche' | 92 | 83.6 | 18 | 16.4 |
| Ladino/Ladino | 104 | 96.3 | 4 | 3.7 |

## 6.3 Language use in Joyabaj

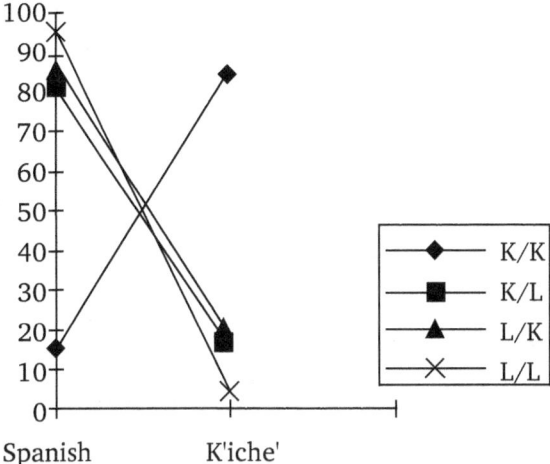

Figure 6.10 Interaction of RACE*IRACE in Joyabaj

**6.3.2 Age.** Not all of the age groups are represented in the sample from Joyabaj. There were 354 speech transactions produced by K'iche's in Joyabaj in which the ages of the speakers were identified. However, there were not enough speech transactions in the 1 to 12 year age group (n = 8), the 45 to 54 year age group (n = 7), or the 55 and older age group (n = 4) for a valid chi-square analysis or LMI calculation. The resulting sample consists of 335 speech transactions representing age groups 13 to 24 years (A02), 25 to 34 years (A03), and 35 to 44 years (A04). Though incomplete, this sample does cover the age groups which are most responsible for the intergenerational transmission of K'iche'. Table 6.19 shows the distribution of the transactions among these age groups by language used and shows the results of a chi-square analysis as well as the LMI for each age group. The LMI scores are graphed in figure 6.11.

The chi-square analysis indicates that there is no significant difference in language use among the age groups. This may be due, in part, to the limited sample that is available for analysis. It may also be due to the fact that these are the school-aged and young adult groups which have been seen to have similar language patterns in the other communities.

The LMI numbers show some differences between the three age groups in the level of language maintenance. The 13 to 24-year-old group (A02) has the lowest LMI at 1.18 and thus demonstrates weak language maintenance. The other two groups have higher LMI scores which are within the moderate language maintenance range.

Table 6.19 K'iche' language use by age group in Joyabaj

| Age | 1–12 | 13–24 | 25–34 | 35–44 | 45–54 | 55+ | Total |
|---|---|---|---|---|---|---|---|
| | | | K'iche' | | | | |
| Frequency | n.d. | 107 | 83 | 30 | n.d. | n.d. | 220 |
| Expected | n.d. | 118.87 | 74.866 | 26.269 | n.d. | n.d. | |
| Cell chi-square | n.d. | 1.1845 | 0.8838 | 0.53 | n.d. | n.d. | |
| | | | Spanish | | | | |
| Frequency | n.d. | 74 | 31 | 10 | n.d. | n.d. | 115 |
| Expected | n.d. | 62.134 | 39.134 | 13.731 | n.d. | n.d. | |
| Cell chi-square | n.d. | 2.266 | 1.6908 | 1.014 | n.d. | n.d. | |
| Total | n.d. | 181 | 114 | 40 | n.d. | n.d. | 335 |
| LMI | n.d. | 1.18 | 1.46 | 1.50 | n.d. | n.d. | |

($X^2 = 7.569$ p < .001, df = 2)

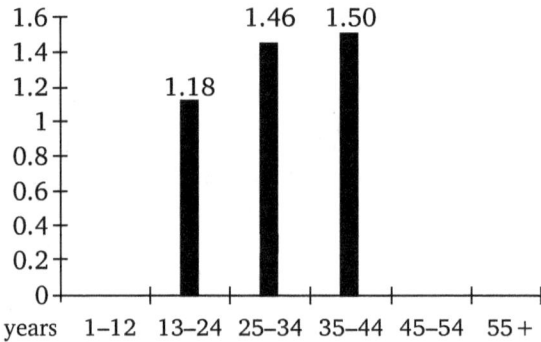

Figure 6.11 Language use by age group in Joyabaj

**6.3.3 Domain.** The language use data from Joyabaj represent only four of the ten domain groups, market, work, religion, and stores. Table 6.20 shows the distribution of the speech transactions among the domains by language used along with the results of a chi-square analysis and the computed LMI for each domain.

The chi-square analysis indicates that there is a significant difference in language use among the domains. This is evident in the range of the LMI scores for the four domains which are displayed graphically in figure 6.12.

## 6.3 Language use in Joyabaj

Table 6.20 K'iche' language use by domain in Joyabaj

| Domain | Home | Street | Play | Market | Work | Religion | Stores | Media | School | Govt | Total |
|---|---|---|---|---|---|---|---|---|---|---|---|
| | | | | | K'iche' | | | | | | |
| Frequency | n.d. | n.d. | n.d. | 164 | 36 | 21 | 8 | n.d. | n.d. | n.d. | 229 |
| Expected | n.d. | n.d. | n.d. | 162.92 | 24.863 | 26.171 | 15.049 | n.d. | n.d. | n.d. | |
| Cell chi-square | n.d. | n.d. | n.d. | 0.0072 | 4.9888 | 1.0219 | 3.3015 | n.d. | n.d. | n.d. | |
| | | | | | Spanish | | | | | | |
| Frequency | n.d. | n.d. | n.d. | 85 | 2 | 19 | 15 | n.d. | n.d. | n.d. | 121 |
| Expected | n.d. | n.d. | n.d. | 86.083 | 13.137 | 13.829 | 7.9514 | n.d. | n.d. | n.d. | |
| Cell chi-square | n.d. | n.d. | n.d. | 0.0136 | 9.4416 | 1.9339 | 6.2482 | n.d. | n.d. | n.d. | |
| Total | | | | 249 | 38 | 40 | 23 | | | | 350 |
| LMI | | | | 1.32 | 1.89 | 1.05 | 0.70 | | | | |

($X^2 = 26.957$ p < .001, df = 3)

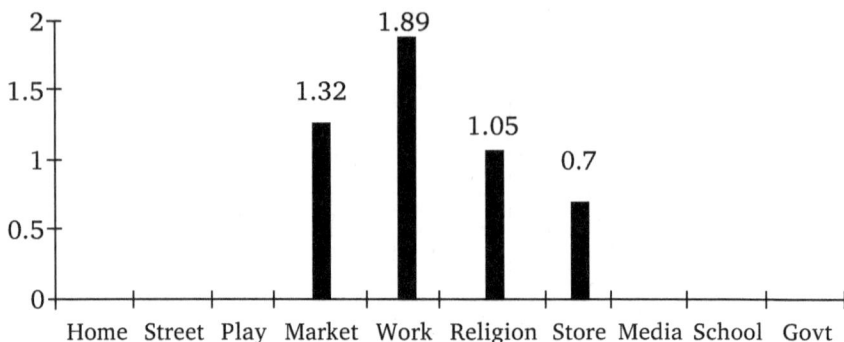

Figure 6.12: Language use by domain in Joyabaj

The domain with the highest LMI (1.89) is the work domain. This domain shows strong language maintenance and is the only domain in the sample that does so. The cell chi-square values for this domain contribute about half of the total chi-square value.

The market domain (LMI = 1.32) is within the moderate language maintenance range, and the distribution of the use of the two languages is quite close to the expected normal distribution.

The domains of religion (LMI = 1.05) and stores (LMI = 0.70) show weak language maintenance. The latter also shows a considerable divergence from the normal distribution.

The pattern of language use in the domains shown in Joyabaj is one which shows evidence of some compartmentalization between the formal and informal domains. The work and market domains are associated with K'iche', while the domains of religion and stores, to differing degrees, are associated more with Spanish.

Of the 363 speech transactions analyzed for Joyabaj, 14.6% (53) were classified as formal and 85.4% (310) were classified as informal. Of the formal speech transactions, 52.8% (28) were produced in K'iche' and 47.2% (25) were produced in Spanish. Of the informal speech transactions, 64.8% (201) were produced in K'iche' and 35.2% (109) were produced in Spanish. Table 6.21 shows the distribution of the speech transactions between the formal and informal domains by language used as well as the calculation of the LMI for these two categories.

The chi-square analysis shows the differences in language use between the formal and informal domains not to be significant. Although this may be the result of the weaknesses of the sample, it might also be an indication of an incipient loss of compartmentalization. The more detailed analysis of domains showed a general pattern of moderate language maintenance in the informal domains and quite weak language maintenance in the two more formal domains. While that analysis indicated that the differences were significant, overall the pattern of compartmentalization between the two languages is not very strong.

Table 6.21 K'iche' language use by formality level in Joyabaj

| Language | Domain Formality | | Total |
|---|---|---|---|
| | Formal | Informal | |
| **K'iche'** | | | |
| Frequency | 499 | 977 | 1476 |
| Expected | 641.87 | 834.13 | |
| Cell chi-square | 31.801 | 24.471 | |
| **Spanish** | | | |
| Frequency | 217 | 111 | 328 |
| Expected | 142.64 | 185.36 | |
| Cell chi-square | 38.767 | 29.832 | |
| **Code-Mixed** | | | |
| Frequency | 132 | 14 | 146 |
| Expected | 63.491 | 82.509 | |
| Cell chi-square | 73.923 | 56.884 | |
| Total | 848 | 1102 | 1950 |
| LMI | 1.33 | 1.79 | |

($X^2 = 2.803$ p<.001, df=1)

The LMI scores show that in the informal domains, there is moderate language maintenance although the LMI is near the bottom of the moderate range. In the formal domains there is only weak language maintenance.

**6.3.4 Summary.** Because of the incomplete data from Joyabaj, it is more difficult to see the patterns of language use and to draw firm conclusions from them. Although there is evidence that ladinos converge when interacting with K'iche' interlocutors, there is far more convergence on the part of K'iche's when their interlocutor is a ladino. The only speech transactions that are fully associated with K'iche' are those with only K'iche' participants.

The young adult age groups show moderate language maintenance but the youngest of the age groups represented demonstrates only weak K'iche' maintenance. The more formal domains show weak language maintenance, while the informal domains evidence only lackluster moderate language maintenance. The global LMI calculated for Joyabaj is

1.26 which places Joyabaj in the weak language maintenance range with the lowest global LMI of the seven communities.

## 6.4 Language use in Sacapulas

The language use data for Sacapulas consist of 631 observations of 1,257 individuals producing 1,265 speech transactions.[36] From these have been excluded those speech transactions in which the race, sex, or age of the speaker was not clearly identified.

**6.4.1 Race and sex.** The speech transactions analyzed for the effect of race and sex on language use in Sacapulas total 1,064. This analysis excludes speech transactions produced by participants who were mixed-race or mixed-gender groups. Table 6.22 shows the distribution of the speech transactions between the racial and gender groups by language.

As in the other communities the preponderance of the observations were of speech transactions between K'iche' participants. In addition, the majority of the speech transactions produced by male speakers were with male interlocutors although the speech transactions produced by female speakers are more evenly distributed between male and female interlocutors. The results of the categorical models analysis of the age and sex frequency counts are shown in table 6.23.

---

[36] The sample sizes for the omitted domain groups are: D01, n = 0, D02, n = 2, D03, n = 8, D08, n = 9, D09, n = 0, D10, n = 10. All of these speech transactions were produced in Spanish.

## 6.4 Language use in Sacapulas

Table 6.22 Speech transactions in Sacapulas by race and sex of speaker and interlocutor

| Speakers | | Interlocutor | | | | | | | | | | | | | | | | |
|---|---|---|---|---|---|---|---|---|---|---|---|---|---|---|---|---|---|---|
| | | K'iche' | | | | | | | | Ladino | | | | | | | | |
| | | Females | | | | Males | | | | Females | | | | Males | | | | |
| Race/Sex | CM | S | K | Total K/F | CM | S | K | Total K/M | CM | S | K | Total L/F | CM | S | K | Total L/M | Total Spkrs |
| K'iche' Females | 27 | 10 | 150 | 187 | 17 | 15 | 143 | 175 | 2 | 4 | 3 | 9 | 2 | 3 | 1 | 6 | 377 |
| K'iche' Males | 17 | 9 | 143 | 169 | 68 | 24 | 291 | 383 | 4 | 5 | 10 | 19 | 10 | 11 | 11 | 32 | 603 |
| K'iche' Subtotal | 44 | 19 | 293 | 356 | 85 | 39 | 434 | 558 | 6 | 9 | 13 | 28 | 12 | 14 | 12 | 38 | 980 |
| Ladino Females | 4 | 8 | 0 | 12 | 6 | 10 | 4 | 20 | 8 | 4 | 0 | 12 | 0 | 1 | 0 | 1 | 45 |
| Ladino Males | 1 | 5 | 0 | 6 | 8 | 18 | 4 | 30 | 0 | 1 | 0 | 1 | 0 | 2 | 0 | 2 | 39 |
| Ladino Subtotal | 5 | 13 | 0 | 18 | 14 | 28 | 8 | 50 | 8 | 5 | 0 | 13 | 0 | 3 | 0 | 3 | 84 |
| Grand Total | 49 | 32 | 293 | 374 | 99 | 67 | 442 | 608 | 14 | 14 | 13 | 41 | 12 | 17 | 12 | 41 | 1064 |

Speech transactions are either code-mixed (CM), Spanish (S), or K'iche' (K).

Table 6.23 Maximum likelihood analysis-of-variance
Race and sex data from Sacapulas

| Source | DF | Chi-Square | Prob |
|---|---|---|---|
| SEX | 2 | 0.85 | 0.6552 |
| RACE | 2 | 54.00 | 0.0000 |
| SEX*RACE | 2 | 0.89 | 0.6417 |
| ISEX | 2 | 0.57 | 0.7512 |
| SEX*ISEX | 2 | 1.20 | 0.5497 |
| RACE*ISEX | 2 | 2.33 | 0.3116 |
| SEX*RACE*ISEX | 2 | 0.91 | 0.6342 |
| IRACE | 2 | 1.49 | 0.4749 |
| SEX*IRACE | 2 | 0.45 | 0.7971 |
| RACE*IRACE | 2 | 9.32 | 0.0095 |
| SEX*RACE*IRACE | 2 | 0.06 | 0.9722 |
| ISEX*IRACE | 2 | 0.37 | 0.8304 |
| SEX*ISEX*IRACE | 2 | 0.56 | 0.7552 |
| RACE*ISEX*IRACE | 2 | 0.68 | 0.7119 |
| SEX*RACE*ISEX*IRACE | 2 | 0.30 | 0.8607 |
| Likelihood ratio | 2 | 10.32 | 0.0058 |

The only variable that has a significant effect on language use in Sacapulas is race of the speaker. All other variables and interactions between variables fail to achieve significance. This follows the general pattern which we have seen in the other communities where the primary demarcation in language use has been along racial lines. In Sacapulas, however, it is only the race of the speaker that is significant. As in the other communities, this provides general evidence for an intact diglossia without bilingualism where ladinos primarily use Spanish, and K'iche's primarily use K'iche'. Missing in Sacapulas is any indication that the sex of the participants has an influence on language use.

Although only RACE is significant, the pattern of language use in Sacapulas is quite similar to that which occurs in the other communities with K'iche's showing distinct differences in language use from ladinos. The differences in language use caused by the sex of the participants which were seen in the other communities are not present to any significant degree in Sacapulas. The tally of the frequency counts by RACE and the percentages which these represent of the total number of speech transactions are shown in table 6.24.

## 6.4 Language use in Sacapulas

Table 6.24 Tally of language use for race in Sacapulas

| Speaker/Interlocutor | Code-Mixed | | Spanish | | K'iche' | |
|---|---|---|---|---|---|---|
| | Count | % | Count | % | Count | % |
| K'iche' | 147 | 15.0 | 81 | 83 | 752 | 76.7 |
| Ladino | 27 | 32.1 | 49 | 58.3 | 8 | 9.5 |

Figure 6.13 plots the frequency counts by language used according to the race of the speaker and shows quite clearly the sharp divergence in language use between K'iche' and ladino speakers. What is notable in Sacapulas is the difference between ladinos and K'iche's not only in K'iche' use but also in the use of code-mixing.

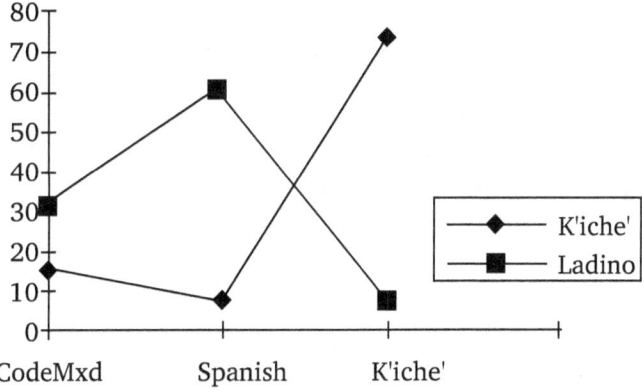

Figure 6.13 Interaction of RACE in Sacapulas

The other noteworthy characteristic of language use in Sacapulas is that the pattern is influenced by the race of the speaker and not by the race of the interlocutor, nor by the sex of either speaker or interlocutor. Both of these factors represent a somewhat strong level of compartmentalization in that there is less evidence of convergence to the code of their interlocutors by K'iche' speakers, and good evidence that ladinos in Sacapulas converge, through code-mixing, with their K'iche' interlocutors. This convergence, on the basis of the race of the interlocutor, however, was not found to be statistically significant.

**6.4.2 Age.** There were 992 K'iche'-produced speech transactions analyzed for Sacapulas. Of these, 74.8% (742) were produced in K'iche', 8.7% (86) were produced in Spanish, and 16.5% (164) were classified as code-mixed. Table 6.25 shows the distribution of the speech transactions among the age groups by language used and also shows the LMI that I have calculated for each age group.

Table 6.25 K'iche' language use by age group in Sacapulas

| Age | 1–12 | 13–24 | 25–34 | 35–44 | 45–54 | 55+ | Total |
|---|---|---|---|---|---|---|---|
| K'iche' | | | | | | | |
| Frequency | 212 | 163 | 193 | 144 | 23 | 7 | 742 |
| Expected | 198.22 | 178.02 | 195.97 | 130.9 | 28.423 | 10.472 | |
| Cell chi-square | 0.9586 | 1.2673 | 0.0451 | 1.3116 | 1.0348 | 1.151 | |
| Spanish | | | | | | | |
| Frequency | 17 | 35 | 19 | 5 | 4 | 6 | 86 |
| Expected | 22.974 | 20.633 | 22.714 | 15.171 | 3.2944 | 1.2137 | |
| Cell chi-square | 1.5533 | 10.004 | 0.6072 | 6.8192 | 0.1511 | 18.875 | |
| Code-Mixed | | | | | | | |
| Frequency | 36 | 40 | 50 | 26 | 11 | 1 | 164 |
| Expected | 43.81 | 39.347 | 43.315 | 28.931 | 6.2823 | 2.3145 | |
| Cell chi-square | 1.3924 | 0.0108 | 1.0319 | 0.297 | 3.5428 | 0.7466 | |
| Total | 265 | 238 | 262 | 175 | 38 | 14 | 992 |
| LMI | 1.74 | 1.54 | 1.66 | 1.79 | 1.50 | 1.07 | |

($X^2 = 50.800$ p<.001, df=10)

The chi-square analysis of these data shows that there is a significant difference in language use between the age groups. An inspection of these data also shows that while the percentages of use of K'iche' fluctuates from age group to age group, there is a generally low percentage of Spanish use in all but the oldest age group (where the sample size is quite small and therefore possibly untrustworthy).

The LMI scores for Sacapulas, shown in figure 6.14, show a fairly robust pattern of language maintenance with three of the age groups, 1 to 12-year-olds, 25 to 34-year-olds, and 35 to 44-year-olds. These three groups show the highest levels of language maintenance within the strong maintenance range. This bodes well for future language maintenance since these groups represent the current generation of parents and the youngest group of children in the community. Although the 13 to 24-year-old group and the 45 to 54-year-old group show somewhat lower LMI scores, both groups are demonstrating moderate language maintenance.

## 6.4 Language use in Sacapulas

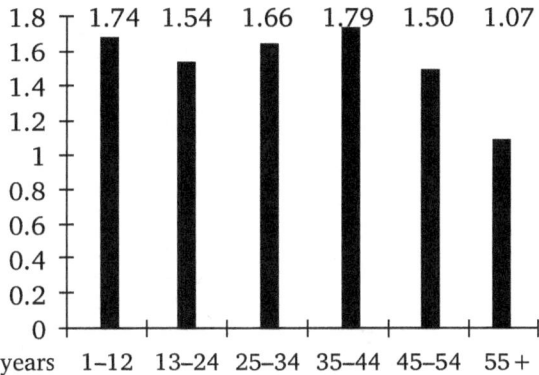

Figure 6.14 Language use by age group in Sacapulas

Interestingly, the group showing the weakest levels of language maintenance is the oldest age group, with an LMI in the weak maintenance range. As mentioned above, these results may be due to the small (n = 14), and therefore possibly unreliable, sample in the oldest age group. An alternative interpretation, however, is that these results may indicate the effect of emigration to Guatemala City for employment and the subsequent return of these individuals to Sacapulas for their retirement. Thus, while the intergenerational transmission of K'iche' is carried on by the current generation of parents (35 to 44-year-olds), the older generation shows a pattern of increased Spanish use because of their exposure to Spanish outside of Sacapulas. My impression is that while this presents a picture of a classic pattern of current language maintenance with age grading, a continuation and generalization of the pattern of emigration is likely to result in a gradual erosion of language maintenance in the generations to come.

**6.4.3 Domain.** There were 1,114 K'iche'-produced speech transactions used in this analysis by domains for Sacapulas. Of these, 74.2% (827) were produced in K'iche', 9.3% (103) were produced in Spanish, and 16.5% (184) were classified as code-mixed. Table 6.26 shows the distribution of the speech transactions among the domains by language used along with the results of the chi-square analysis and the LMI for each domain.

Table 6.26 K'iche' language use by domain in Sacapulas

| Domain | Home | Street | Play | Market | Work | Religion | Stores | Media | School | Govt | Total |
|---|---|---|---|---|---|---|---|---|---|---|---|
| | | | | | K'iche' | | | | | | |
| Frequency | 70 | 141 | 4 | 140 | 49 | 37 | 99 | 38 | 210 | 39 | 827 |
| Expected | 59.39 | 121.75 | 5.939 | 132.88 | 62.359 | 63.101 | 95.023 | 47.512 | 199.7 | 39.346 | |
| Cell chi-square | 1.8956 | 3.0441 | 0.633 | 0.381 | 2.8619 | 10.797 | 0.1664 | 1.9042 | 0.5315 | 0.003 | |
| | | | | | Spanish | | | | | | |
| Frequency | 5 | 7 | 0 | 12 | 3 | 19 | 22 | 12 | 18 | 5 | 103 |
| Expected | 7.3968 | 15.163 | 0.7397 | 16.55 | 7.7666 | 7.8591 | 11.835 | 5.9174 | 24.872 | 4.9004 | |
| Cell chi-square | 0.7766 | 4.3948 | 0.7397 | 1.251 | 2.9254 | 15.793 | 8.7311 | 6.2524 | 1.8985 | 0.002 | |
| | | | | | Code-Mixed | | | | | | |
| Frequency | 5 | 16 | 4 | 27 | 32 | 29 | 7 | 14 | 41 | 9 | 184 |
| Expected | 13.214 | 27.088 | 1.3214 | 29.566 | 13.874 | 14.039 | 21.142 | 10.571 | 44.431 | 8.754 | |
| Cell chi-square | 5.1056 | 4.5387 | 5.4301 | 0.2226 | 23.68 | 15.942 | 9.4595 | 1.1124 | 0.2649 | 0.0069 | |
| Total | 80 | 164 | 8 | 179 | 84 | 85 | 128 | 64 | 269 | 53 | 1114 |
| LMI | 1.81 | 1.82 | 1.50 | 1.72 | 1.55 | 1.21 | 1.60 | 1.41 | 1.71 | 1.64 | |

($X^2 = 130.745$ p < .001, df = 18)

## 6.4 Language use in Sacapulas

The chi-square analysis of these data indicates that there is a significant difference in language use among the domains. The domains which show the highest cell chi-square values are the work domain where there is considerably more code-mixing than expected, and the religion domain, where there is more code-mixing and Spanish and less K'iche' use than expected. In all of the more formal domains except formal education, Spanish is used more than would be expected in a normal distribution. In the formal education domain, K'iche' is used just slightly more than would be expected. In all of the more informal domains Spanish is used less than expected. In these same domains, K'iche' is used more than expected with the exception of recreation where K'iche' is used slightly less than expected and code-mixing is used more than expected.

Overall, the LMI scores, displayed graphically in figure 6.15, show a robust pattern of language maintenance with even some of the more formal domains having LMIs that show strong language maintenance.

There are four domains that have LMI scores that indicate strong language maintenance. These are home, personal encounters, market, and formal education. With the exception of the latter, these are the informal domains most expected to show strong language maintenance in a strongly diglossic situation. Formal education in Sacapulas is part of the bilingual education program and thus reflects the emphasis of that program on the use of K'iche'.

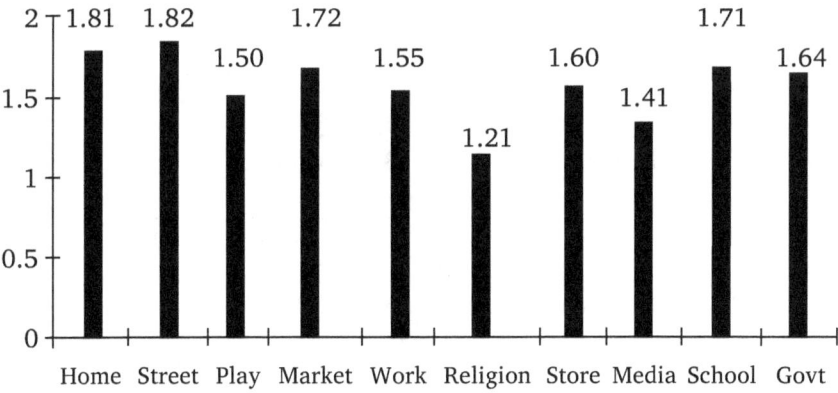

Figure 6.15 Language use by domain in Sacapulas

Five of the domains have LMI scores within the moderate language maintenance range. These are recreation, work, stores, mass media, and government offices. These domains show the level of accommodation by the ladinos in the community to the use of K'iche' in many traditionally

Spanish domains. They further show the level of participation of K'iche's in the local economy (stores) and government (government offices) as well as in commercially-based work, as opposed to purely agricultural kinds of labor which tend to be associated with K'iche'.

As in most of the other communities, religion has an LMI score that indicates weak language maintenance. Religion is a domain that is generally associated with Spanish.

Of the 1,114 speech transactions analyzed for Sacapulas, 30.2% (336) were classified as having been produced in formal domains and 69.8% (778) in informal domains. Table 6.27 shows the distribution of the speech transactions between the formal and informal domains by language used and the LMI calculated for each category.

The chi-square analysis indicates that the differences in language use between the two levels of formality are not significant. The LMI scores for each category show that, while formal domains are within the moderate maintenance range and informal domains are demonstrating strong language maintenance, the two scores are indeed quite close to each other. Formal domains have only a slightly lower level of K'iche' language maintenance than the informal domains.

Table 6.27 K'iche' language use by formality level in Sacapulas

|  | Domain Formality | | |
|---|---|---|---|
|  | Formal | Informal | Total |
|  | K'iche' | | |
| Frequency | 229 | 598 | 827 |
| Expected | 249.44 | 577.56 | |
| Cell chi-square | 1.6743 | 0.7231 | |
|  | Spanish | | |
| Frequency | 44 | 59 | 103 |
| Expected | 31.066 | 71.934 | |
| Cell chi-square | 5.3845 | 2.3254 | |
|  | Code-Mixed | | |
| Frequency | 63 | 121 | 184 |
| Expected | 55.497 | 128.5 | |
| Cell chi-square | 1.0143 | 0.438 | |
| Total | 336 | 778 | 1114 |
| LMI | 1.55 | 1.69 | |

($X^2 = 11.560$ $p < .001$, $df = 2$)

**6.4.4 Summary.** The data from Sacapulas show a strong pattern of language maintenance in most age groups and in most domains. The chi-square analyses of the race, sex, age, and domain indicate that race of the speaker is the only significant line of cleavage in language use but that there are also significant differences in language use among the age groups and in the various domains. There is no significant difference between formal and informal domains which may indicate an incipient loss of compartmentalization. The LMI scores confirm the general pattern of strong language maintenance with the weakest language maintenance occurring in the oldest age groups and in the domain of religion. The global LMI calculated for Sacapulas is 1.65, the highest of all of the communities in this study.

### 6.5 Language use in San Andrés Sajcabajá

The language use data for San Andrés Sajcabajá consist of 418 observations of 1,033 individuals producing 1,368 speech transactions.

**6.5.1 Race and sex.** The speech transactions produced by participants whose race and sex were unambiguously identified by the observers total 1,259. The distribution of these speech transactions is shown in table 6.28. The data follow the pattern seen in the other communities with most of the speech transactions, particularly among K'iche' participants, taking place between same-sex participants.

Table 6.28 Speech transactions in San Andrés Sajcabajá by race and sex of speaker and interlocutor

| Speakers | | Interlocutor | | | | | | | | | | | | | | |
|---|---|---|---|---|---|---|---|---|---|---|---|---|---|---|---|---|
| | | K'iche' | | | | | | | | Ladino | | | | | | |
| | | Females | | | | Males | | | | Females | | | | Males | | |
| Race/Sex | CM | S | K | Total K/F | CM | S | K | Total K/M | CM | S | K | Total L/F | CM | S | K | Total L/M | Total Spkrs |
| K'iche' Females | 14 | 1 | 105 | 120 | 0 | 4 | 46 | 50 | 1 | 12 | 25 | 38 | 0 | 4 | 13 | 17 | 225 |
| K'iche' Males | 0 | 6 | 55 | 61 | 23 | 36 | 323 | 382 | 1 | 31 | 23 | 55 | 5 | 56 | 44 | 95 | 593 |
| K'iche' Subtotal | 14 | 7 | 160 | 181 | 23 | 40 | 369 | 432 | 2 | 43 | 48 | 88 | 5 | 60 | 57 | 112 | 818 |
| Ladino Females | 2 | 12 | 20 | 34 | 2 | 35 | 12 | 49 | 0 | 61 | 2 | 63 | 2 | 36 | 2 | 40 | 186 |
| Ladino Males | 1 | 3 | 12 | 16 | 5 | 72 | 32 | 109 | 2 | 34 | 3 | 39 | 2 | 76 | 3 | 81 | 245 |
| Ladino Subtotal | 3 | 15 | 32 | 50 | 7 | 107 | 44 | 158 | 2 | 95 | 5 | 102 | 4 | 112 | 5 | 121 | 431 |
| Grand Total | 17 | 22 | 192 | 231 | 30 | 147 | 413 | 590 | 4 | 138 | 53 | 190 | 9 | 172 | 62 | 233 | 1249 |

Speech transactions are either code-mixed (CM), Spanish (S), or K'iche' (K).

## 6.5 Language use in San Andrés Sajcabajá

The data were subjected to a categorical models analysis and the results are shown in table 6.29. It shows that the four-way interaction between SEX, RACE, ISEX, and IRACE has a significant effect on language use in San Andrés.

Table 6.29 Maximum likelihood analysis-of-variance
Race and sex data from San Andrés Sajcabajá

| Source | DF | Chi-Square | Prob |
| --- | --- | --- | --- |
| SEX | 2 | 49.98 | 0.0000 |
| RACE | 2 | 210.78 | 0.0000 |
| SEX*RACE | 2 | 83.02 | 0.0000 |
| ISEX | 2 | 51.25 | 0.0000 |
| SEX*ISEX | 2 | 16.04 | 0.0003 |
| RACE*ISEX | 2 | 16.41 | 0.0003 |
| SEX*RACE*ISEX | 2 | 39.95 | 0.0000 |
| IRACE | 2 | 191.11 | 0.0000 |
| SEX*IRACE | 2 | 33.44 | 0.0000 |
| RACE*IRACE | 2 | 50.83 | 0.0000 |
| SEX*RACE*IRACE | 2 | 32.69 | 0.0000 |
| ISEX*IRACE | 2 | 65.72 | 0.0000 |
| SEX*ISEX*IRACE | 2 | 33.41 | 0.0000 |
| RACE*ISEX*IRACE | 2 | 22.96 | 0.0000 |
| SEX*RACE*ISEX*IRACE | 2 | 40.90 | 0.0000 |
| Likelihood ratio | 2 | 144.74 | 0.0000 |

The pattern in San Andrés is similar to that found in Cunén. Table 6.30 shows the tally of the combinations of the speech transactions for the combinations of the values for each of the four variables. The percentages are calculated using the total number of speech transactions produced by speakers of the same race and sex. Figure 6.16 plots the frequency counts of the speech transactions by language used according to the RACE and IRACE variables.

Table 6.30 Tally of language use for SEX*RACE*ISEX*IRACE in San Andrés Sajcabajá

| Speaker/Interlocutor | Code-Mixed Count | % | Spanish Count | % | K'iche' Count | % |
|---|---|---|---|---|---|---|
| Female K'iche'/Female K'iche' | 14 | 11.7 | 1 | 0.8 | 105 | 87.5 |
| Female K'iche'/Female Ladino | 1 | 2.6 | 12 | 31.6 | 25 | 65.8 |
| Female K'iche'/Male K'iche' | 0 | 0.0 | 4 | 8.0 | 46 | 92.0 |
| Female K'iche'/Male Ladino | 0 | 0.0 | 4 | 23.5 | 13 | 76.5 |
| Female Ladino/Female K'iche' | 2 | 5.9 | 12 | 35.3 | 20 | 58.8 |
| Female Ladino/Female Ladino | 0 | 0.0 | 61 | 96.8 | 2 | 3.2 |
| Female Ladino/Male K'iche' | 2 | 4.1 | 35 | 71.4 | 12 | 24.5 |
| Female Ladino/Male Ladino | 2 | 5.0 | 36 | 90.0 | 2 | 5.0 |
| Male K'iche'/Female K'iche' | 0 | 0.0 | 6 | 9.8 | 55 | 90.2 |
| Male K'iche'/Female Ladino | 1 | 1.8 | 31 | 56.4 | 23 | 41.8 |
| Male K'iche'/Male K'iche' | 23 | 6.0 | 36 | 9.4 | 323 | 84.6 |
| Male K'iche'/Male Ladino | 5 | 4.8 | 56 | 53.3 | 44 | 41.9 |
| Male Ladino/Female K'iche' | 1 | 6.3 | 3 | 18.8 | 12 | 75.0 |
| Male Ladino/Female Ladino | 2 | 5.1 | 34 | 87.2 | 3 | 7.7 |
| Male Ladino/Male K'iche' | 5 | 4.6 | 72 | 66.1 | 32 | 29.4 |
| Male Ladino/Male Ladino | 2 | 2.5 | 76 | 93.8 | 3 | 3.7 |

The most notable characteristic of these language use patterns is the effect of the presence of a ladino participant in a speech transaction which greatly increases the likelihood of the use of Spanish. Speech transactions with only K'iche' participants show a much greater use of K'iche'. However, the pattern in San Andrés shows some evidence that ladinos will use K'iche' when speaking to K'iche's, as well as a slightly stronger tendency for K'iche's to address ladinos in K'iche'. These data coincide with the ethnographic observations of language use in San Andrés described in chapter 4.

The pattern of language use based on the sex of the participants involved is also similar to the patterns observed in Chichicastenango and Cunén. There is a slightly greater level of Spanish use among men than among women though the difference in San Andrés is not as sharply defined as in Cunén. The evidence for this is seen in the tendency of male speakers to address females in K'iche' more often than female speakers address males in K'iche'.

There is ample evidence in San Andrés of convergence on the part of the ladino participants with their K'iche' interlocutors. Both males and females will accommodate to the code of their K'iche' interlocutors. K'iche's, on the other hand, show very little inclination to converge with their ladino interlocutors. This provides evidence of the lack of bilingualism among K'iche's.

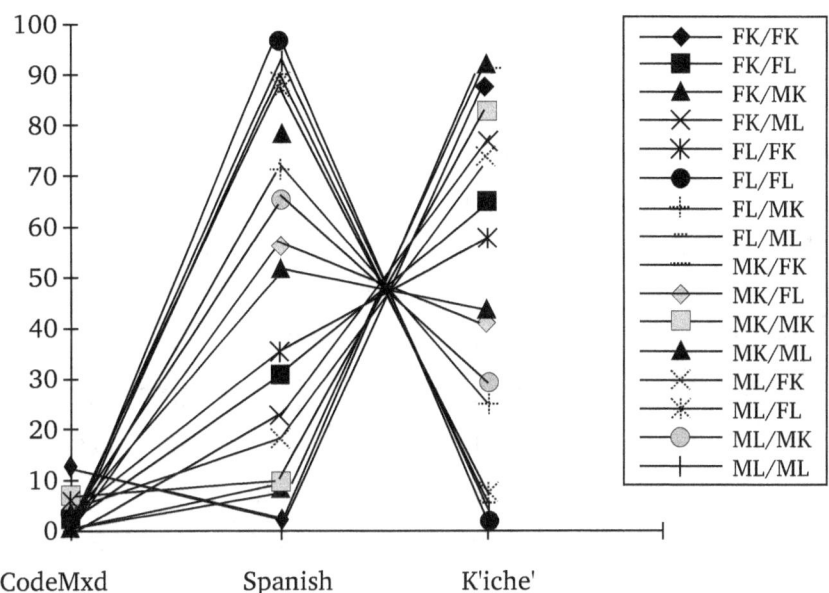

Figure 6.16 Interaction of RACE*SEX*IRACE*ISEX in San Andrés Sajcabajá

**6.5.2 Age.** There were 856 K'iche'-produced speech transactions analyzed for San Andrés Sajcabajá. Of these, 76.2% (652) were produced in K'iche', 18.3% (157) were produced in Spanish, and 5.5% (47) were classified as code-mixed. Table 6.31 shows the distribution of the speech transactions among the age groups by language used along with the results of the chi-square analysis and the LMI for each age group.

Table 6.31 K'iche' language use by age group in San Andrés Sajcabajá

| Age | 1–12 | 13–24 | 25–34 | 35–44 | 45–54 | 55+ | Total |
|---|---|---|---|---|---|---|---|
| | | | K'iche' | | | | |
| Frequency | 83 | 192 | 179 | 107 | 71 | 40 | 652 |
| Expected | 57.126 | 207.94 | 186.61 | 100.54 | 67.028 | 32.752 | |
| Cell chi-square | 0.604 | 1.2218 | 0.3105 | 0.4148 | 0.2354 | 1.6038 | |
| | | | Spanish | | | | |
| Frequency | 7 | 57 | 60 | 20 | 11 | 2 | 157 |
| Expected | 13.756 | 50.071 | 44.936 | 24.21 | 16.14 | 7.8867 | |
| Cell chi-square | 3.318 | 0.9588 | 5.0501 | 0.7322 | 1.637 | 4.3939 | |
| | | | Code-Mixed | | | | |
| Frequency | 5 | 24 | 6 | 5 | 6 | 1 | 47 |
| Expected | 4.118 | 14.989 | 13.452 | 7.2477 | 4.8318 | 2.361 | |
| Cell chi-square | 0.1889 | 5.4164 | 4.1283 | 0.6971 | 0.2825 | 0.7845 | |
| Total | 75 | 273 | 245 | 132 | 88 | 43 | 856 |
| LMI | 1.75 | 1.49 | 1.48 | 1.66 | 1.68 | 1.88 | |

($X^2 = 31.978$ p < .001, df = 10)

The chi-square analysis shows that there is a significant difference in the language use between the age groups. As would be expected in a situation where there is strong language maintenance, the youngest and oldest age groups show lower than expected levels of Spanish use. However, the 12 to 24-year-old group (A02) shows higher than expected levels of code-mixing accompanied by lower than expected levels of K'iche' use, and the 25 to 34-year-olds show both more code-mixing and more Spanish use than would be expected in a normal distribution.

Figure 6.17 shows the LMI scores for each age group in bar graph form.

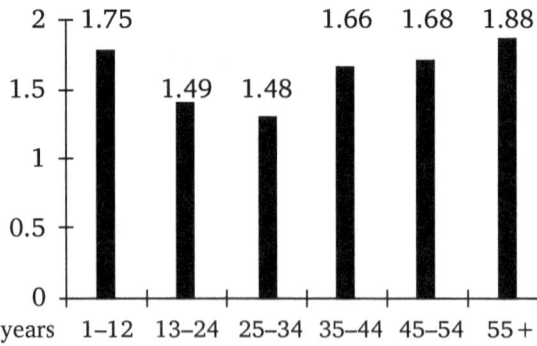

Figure 6.17 Language use by age group in San Andrés Sajcabajá

Overall, the pattern of language maintenance among the age groups in San Andrés Sajcabajá is quite strong. All but two of the age groups have LMI scores in the strong maintenance range. Only the age groups comprising individuals between the ages of 13 and 34 show moderate language maintenance. The older age groups, 35 years old and older, show quite strong maintenance levels as does the very youngest age group (1–12 years).

**6.5.3 Domain.** Although there were a total of 866 K'iche'-produced speech transactions for San Andrés Sajcabajá, the number of code-mixed observations were insufficient for the chi-square analysis, when divided among the ten domain groups, and so were excluded.[37]

This low level of observed code-mixing may be the result of the sampling methods used in data gathering, but more likely is an accurate representation of language use in San Andrés. Code-mixing does not occur to any great degree. This leaves a total of 817 speech transactions which were analyzed for San Andrés Sajcabajá. Of these, 80.7% (659) were produced in K'iche' and 19.3% (158) were produced in Spanish. Table 6.32 shows the distribution of the speech transactions among the domains by language used, along with the results of the chi-square analysis and the computed LMI scores for each domain.

The chi-square analysis indicates that there is a significant difference in language use among the domains. The greatest amount of difference from the expected normal distribution is found in the school domain where there is a high level of Spanish use and lower than expected use of K'iche'. The domain of religion also differs considerably from the normal distribution in the direction of Spanish use. On the other hand, the market domain is strongly associated with K'iche' use. One ominous sign is the higher than expected use of Spanish in the home.

Figure 6.18 is a bar graph presentation of the LMI scores for each domain.

---

[37]Nor have these data been included in the calculation of the LMI scores for each domain since the difference in the resulting index is negligible (±.02). In no case does the difference change the classification of the domain in terms of the language maintenance levels associated with the LMI scores.

Table 6.32 K'iche' language use by domain in San Andrés Sajcabajá

| Domain | Home | Street | Play | Market | Work | Religion | Stores | Media | School | Govt | Total |
|---|---|---|---|---|---|---|---|---|---|---|---|
| | | | | | K'iche' | | | | | | |
| Frequency | 60 | 116 | 9 | 206 | 146 | 18 | 41 | 17 | 17 | 29 | 659 |
| Expected | 66.142 | 108.09 | 8.0661 | 186.33 | 133.09 | 25.812 | 45.17 | 15.326 | 34.684 | 36.297 | |
| Cell chi-square | 0.5703 | 0.5795 | 0.1081 | 2.0772 | 1.2522 | 2.364 | 0.385 | 0.1829 | 9.0165 | 1.4671 | |
| | | | | | Spanish | | | | | | |
| Frequency | 22 | 18 | 1 | 25 | 19 | 14 | 15 | 2 | 26 | 16 | 158 |
| Expected | 15.858 | 25.914 | 1.9339 | 44.673 | 31.909 | 6.1885 | 10.83 | 3.6744 | 8.3158 | 8.7026 | |
| Cell chi-square | 2.3789 | 2.4171 | 0.451 | 8.6637 | 5.227 | 9.8602 | 1.6057 | 0.763 | 37.607 | 6.1192 | |
| Total | 82 | 134 | 10 | 231 | 165 | 32 | 56 | 19 | 43 | 45 | 817 |
| LMI | 1.46 | 1.73 | 1.80 | 1.78 | 1.77 | 1.12 | 1.46 | 1.79 | 0.79 | 1.29 | |

($X^2 = 93.091$ $p < .001$, $df = 9$)

## 6.5 Language use in San Andrés Sajcabajá

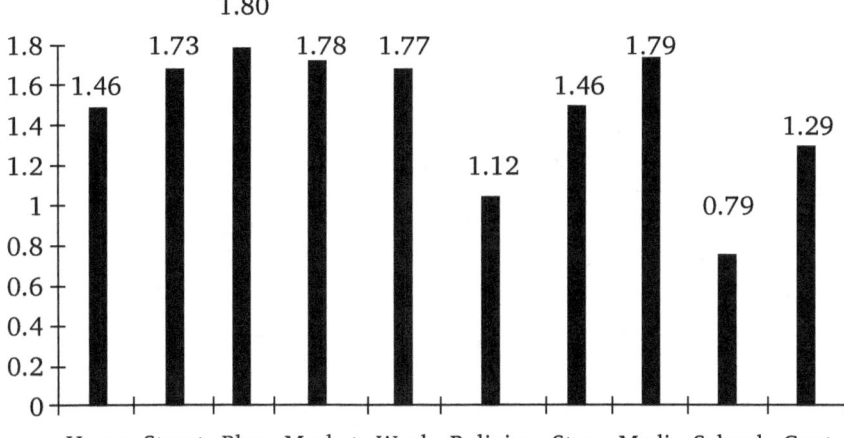

Figure 6.18 Language use by domain in San Andrés Sajcabajá

The profile of San Andrés provided by the domain analysis is somewhat different than might be expected based on the analysis of language use by age groups. Of the ten domains, only five have LMI scores that indicate strong language maintenance. Three show moderate language maintenance, and in two domains there is only weak language maintenance.

The five domains that demonstrate strong language maintenance are personal encounters, recreation, market, work, and mass media. Of these, the observations of the recreation domain consist of a very small sample of only ten speech transactions. These are all examples of the more informal kinds of recreational activities among friends, probably children, rather than observations of formal, organized team sports as in some of the other larger communities.

Notably absent from the group of strong maintenance domains is the home domain, which shows moderate language maintenance. It should be noted that in spite of the overall impression of strong language maintenance in San Andrés, the home and hearth domain, a crucial domain for intergenerational language transmission, has one of the lowest LMI scores for that domain of any of the communities included in this study.

The other domains with LMI scores indicative of moderate language maintenance are stores and government offices. As in the other communities these are ladino-dominated domains where the use of K'iche' is an accommodation to the communicative needs of the K'iche's in the community.

The domains of religion and formal education have LMI scores in the weak language maintenance range. This is a reflection of the general trend for the religious domain to be Spanish-dominant, and of the small role that has been given to the bilingual education program in the few schools that exist in San Andrés.

The speech transactions were also analyzed by formality level with 20.9% (181) being classified as formal and 79.1% (685) classified as informal. Table 6.33 shows the distribution of the speech transactions between the formal and informal domains along with the chi-square analysis results and an LMI score computed for each category.

Table 6.33 K'iche' language use by formality level in San Andrés Sajcabajá

|  | Domain Formality | | |
|---|---|---|---|
|  | Formal | Informal | Total |
| K'iche' | | | |
| Frequency | 92 | 567 | 659 |
| Expected | 137.74 | 521.26 | |
| Cell chi-square | 15.187 | 4.0128 | |
| Spanish | | | |
| Frequency | 67 | 91 | 158 |
| Expected | 33.023 | 124.98 | |
| Cell chi-square | 34.958 | 9.2371 | |
| Code-Mixed | | | |
| Frequency | 22 | 27 | 49 |
| Expected | 10.241 | 38.759 | |
| Cell chi-square | 13.501 | 3.5674 | |
| Total | 181 | 685 | 866 |
| LMI | 1.14 | 1.70 | |

($X^2 = 80.463$, $p < .001$ df = 2)

The chi-square analysis indicates that the difference between language use in formal and informal domains is significant and the difference is seen in the LMI scores for the two categories. In the domains that have been classified as formal, the LMI score indicates only weak language maintenance while in the informal domains the LMI score shows strong language maintenance.

**6.5.4 Summary.** The profile of San Andrés Sajcabajá that emerges from these data is one that is nearly as robust in terms of K'iche' maintenance as that described for Cunén. There is clear compartmentalization of language use along racial and gender lines. All of the age groups are maintaining K'iche' and most of the domains are doing so as well. The few areas of weakness are in the lack of accommodation to K'iche' use in the formal education domain and the weak language maintenance observed in the domains of religion and government offices. Perhaps, most significantly, the home domain is characterized by only weak language maintenance. The global LMI computed for San Andrés Sajcabajá is 1.58.

## 6.6 Language use in Santa Cruz del Quiché

The language use data for Santa Cruz del Quiché consist of a total of 876 observations of 2,267 individuals producing 4,375 speech transactions.

**6.6.1 Race and sex.** For the purposes of the race and sex analysis, speech transactions with participants whose race or sex were not clearly identified have been excluded. This results in 4,045 speech transactions that were amenable to the categorical models analysis. The distribution of the frequency counts for the speakers and interlocutors according to race and sex categories and language used is shown in table 6.34.

The results of the categorical models analysis are shown in table 6.35. These results indicate that the interaction of all four participant variables, RACE, SEX, IRACE, and ISEX, is significant.

Table 6.36 reorganizes the speech transaction tallies according to the combinations of the speaker and interlocutor variables and shows the percentages of the total number of speech transactions produced by speakers of the same race and sex.

These percentages are plotted in figure 6.19 which shows the clear differences in language use between K'iche's and ladinos. As has been the pattern in the other communities, speech transactions occurring between K'iche' speakers and interlocutors show high levels of K'iche' use and lower levels of Spanish use. In Santa Cruz, both races use very low levels of code-mixing—the highest levels are produced by males when speaking to K'iche' male interlocutors.

The effect of the presence of a ladino in a speech transaction, either as speaker or interlocutor, produces language use patterns that are essentially identical to those which exist in ladino-only speech transactions. Almost no K'iche' is used in such cases. The only speech situations where K'iche' is used in Santa Cruz del Quiché is when both of the participants are K'iche's.

Table 6.34 Speech transactions in Santa Cruz del Quiché by race and sex of speaker and interlocutor

| Speakers | Interlocutor ||||||||||||||
| Race/Sex | K'iche' |||||||| Ladino |||||||
| | Females |||| Males |||| Females |||| Males ||||
| | CM | S | K | Total K/F | CM | S | K | Total K/M | CM | S | K | Total L/F | CM | S | K | Total L/M | Total Spkrs |
|---|---|---|---|---|---|---|---|---|---|---|---|---|---|---|---|---|---|
| K'iche' Females | 9 | 246 | 594 | 849 | 4 | 73 | 291 | 368 | 0 | 126 | 6 | 132 | 0 | 46 | 20 | 66 | 1415 |
| K'iche' Males | 9 | 71 | 288 | 368 | 93 | 201 | 1088 | 1382 | 2 | 33 | 12 | 47 | 20 | 100 | 31 | 151 | 1948 |
| K'iche' Subtotal | 18 | 317 | 882 | 1217 | 97 | 274 | 1379 | 1750 | 2 | 159 | 18 | 179 | 20 | 146 | 51 | 217 | 3363 |
| Ladino Females | 1 | 129 | 4 | 134 | 0 | 45 | 3 | 48 | 0 | 126 | 2 | 128 | 0 | 9 | 2 | 11 | 321 |
| Ladino Males | 1 | 54 | 16 | 71 | 18 | 136 | 14 | 168 | 0 | 11 | 2 | 13 | 2 | 97 | 10 | 109 | 361 |
| Ladino Subtotal | 2 | 183 | 20 | 205 | 18 | 181 | 17 | 216 | 0 | 137 | 4 | 141 | 2 | 106 | 12 | 120 | 682 |
| Grand Total | 20 | 500 | 902 | 1422 | 115 | 455 | 1396 | 1966 | 2 | 296 | 22 | 320 | 22 | 252 | 63 | 337 | 4045 |

Speech transactions are either code-mixed (CM), Spanish (S), or K'iche' (K).

## 6.6 Language use in Santa Cruz del Quiché

Table 6.35 Maximum likelihood analysis-of-variance
Race and sex data from Santa Cruz del Quiché

| Source | DF | Chi-Square | Prob |
|---|---|---|---|
| SEX | 2 | 44.26 | 0.0000 |
| RACE | 2 | 239.63 | 0.0000 |
| SEX*RACE | 2 | 105.14 | 0.0000 |
| ISEX | 2 | 115.81 | 0.0000 |
| SEX*ISEX | 2 | 484.41 | 0.0000 |
| RACE*ISEX | 2 | 76.78 | 0.0000 |
| SEX*RACE*ISEX | 2 | 269.58 | 0.0000 |
| IRACE | 2 | 270.37 | 0.0000 |
| SEX*IRACE | 2 | 85.84 | 0.0000 |
| RACE*IRACE | 2 | 307.88 | 0.0000 |
| SEX*RACE*IRACE | 2 | 86.15 | 0.0000 |
| ISEX*IRACE | 2 | 83.16 | 0.0000 |
| SEX*ISEX*IRACE | 2 | 286.60 | 0.0000 |
| RACE*ISEX*IRACE | 2 | 89.01 | 0.0000 |
| SEX*RACE*ISEX*IRACE | 2 | 224.82 | 0.0000 |
| Likelihood ratio | 2 | 604.90 | 0.0000 |

Table 6.36 Tally of language use for SEX*RACE*ISEX*IRACE
in Santa Cruz del Quiché

| Speaker/Interlocutor | Code-Mixed | | Spanish | | K'iche' | |
|---|---|---|---|---|---|---|
| | Count | % | Count | % | Count | % |
| Female K'iche'/Female K'iche' | 9 | 1.1 | 246 | 29.0 | 594 | 70.0 |
| Female K'iche'/Female Ladino | 0 | 0.0 | 126 | 95.5 | 6 | 4.5 |
| Female K'iche'/Male K'iche' | 4 | 1.1 | 73 | 19.8 | 291 | 79.1 |
| Female K'iche'/Male Ladino | 0 | 0.0 | 46 | 69.7 | 20 | 30.3 |
| Female Ladino/Female K'iche' | 1 | 0.7 | 129 | 96.3 | 4 | 3.0 |
| Female Ladino/Female Ladino | 0 | 0.0 | 126 | 98.4 | 2 | 1.6 |
| Female Ladino/Male K'iche' | 0 | 0.0 | 45 | 93.8 | 3 | 6.3 |
| Female Ladino/Male Ladino | 0 | 0.0 | 9 | 81.8 | 2 | 18.2 |
| Male K'iche'/Female K'iche' | 9 | 2.4 | 71 | 19.3 | 288 | 78.3 |
| Male K'iche'/Female Ladino | 2 | 4.3 | 33 | 70.2 | 12 | 25.5 |
| Male K'iche'/Male K'iche' | 93 | 6.7 | 201 | 14.5 | 1088 | 78.7 |
| Male K'iche'/Male Ladino | 20 | 13.2 | 100 | 66.2 | 31 | 20.5 |
| Male Ladino/Female K'iche' | 1 | 1.4 | 54 | 76.1 | 16 | 22.5 |
| Male Ladino/Female Ladino | 0 | 0.0 | 11 | 84.6 | 2 | 15.4 |
| Male Ladino/Male K'iche' | 18 | 10.7 | 136 | 81.0 | 14 | 8.3 |
| Male Ladino/Male Ladino | 2 | 1.8 | 97 | 89.0 | 10 | 9.2 |

There are also differences of language use between males and females among the K'iche' participants. As in the other communities, there is a strong tendency for speech transactions between same-sex participants to demonstrate higher levels of K'iche' use than between participants of different sexes. In addition, K'iche' females tend to have a greater percentage of their speech transactions in Spanish than do the K'iche' males. This does not bode well for the intergenerational transmission of K'iche'.

Among the ladinos, there are only weak indications of accommodation to K'iche' interlocutors. Most of this is demonstrated by ladino male speakers through slightly greater use of K'iche' or of code-mixing. There is almost no evidence of ladino females using K'iche'.

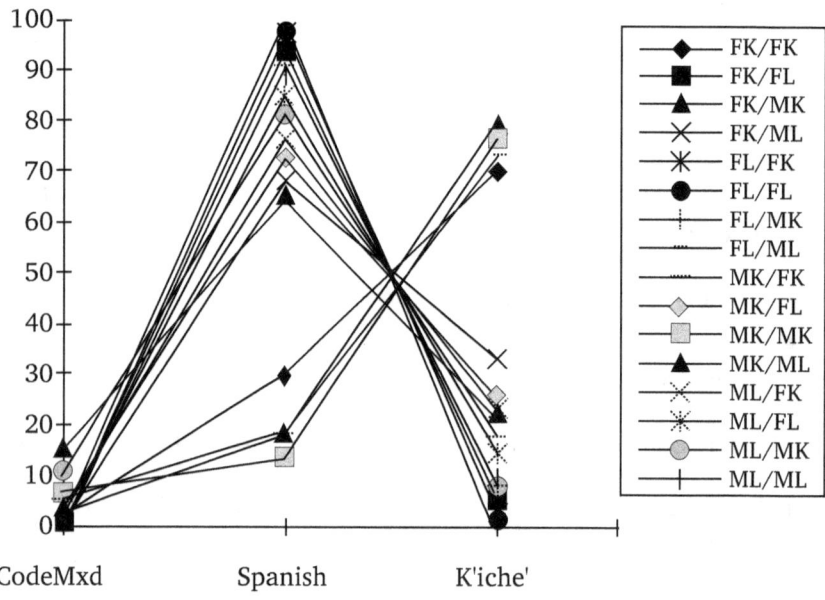

Figure 6.19 Interaction of SEX*RACE*ISEX*IRACE in Santa Cruz del Quiché

**6.6.2 Age.** There were 3,336 K'iche'-produced speech transactions subjected to analysis for Santa Cruz del Quiché. Of these, 68.5% (2,286) were produced in K'iche', 27.3% (910) were produced in Spanish, and 4.2% (140) were classified as code-mixed.

Table 6.37 shows the distribution of the speech transactions among the age groups by language used, as well as the results of the chi-square analysis and the computed LMI scores for each age group.

## 6.6 Language use in Santa Cruz del Quiché

The chi-square analysis shows that there is a significant difference in language use between the age groups. The age groups with the greatest divergence from the expected normal distribution is the youngest age group. They have much higher levels of Spanish use and commensurately lower levels of K'iche' use than expected. The second youngest age group, the 13 to 24-year-olds, also shows lower than expected use of K'iche' and higher than expected use of Spanish. Only those 25 years old and older show any significant level of K'iche' maintenance, and it is only the 35 to 44-year-old age group that shows markedly low levels of Spanish use.

Table 6.37 K'iche' language use by age group in Santa Cruz del Quiché

| Age | 1–12 | 13–24 | 25–34 | 35–44 | 45–54 | 55+ | Total |
|---|---|---|---|---|---|---|---|
| K'iche' | | | | | | | |
| Frequency | 282 | 512 | 543 | 661 | 207 | 81 | 2286 |
| Expected | 405.67 | 616.04 | 483.1 | 528.33 | 187.01 | 65.784 | |
| Cell chi-square | 37.701 | 17.571 | 7.4264 | 33.316 | 2.1225 | 3.5194 | |
| Spanish | | | | | | | |
| Frequency | 295 | 364 | 132 | 65 | 41 | 13 | 910 |
| Expected | 161.49 | 245.23 | 192.31 | 210.31 | 74.469 | 26.187 | |
| Cell chi-square | 110.39 | 57.522 | 18.914 | 100.4 | 15.042 | 6.6406 | |
| Code-Mixed | | | | | | | |
| Frequency | 15 | 23 | 30 | 45 | 25 | 2 | 140 |
| Expected | 24.844 | 37.728 | 29.586 | 32.356 | 11.457 | 4.0288 | |
| Cell chi-square | 3.9006 | 5.7493 | 0.0058 | 4.9409 | 16.009 | 1.0216 | |
| Total | 592 | 899 | 705 | 771 | 273 | 96 | 3336 |
| LMI | 0.98 | 1.16 | 1.58 | 1.77 | 1.61 | 1.71 | |

($X^2 =$ 442.192 $p < .001$, df $= 10$)

This profile is also demonstrated by the LMI scores, displayed graphically in figure 6.20, which provide a clear picture of weak language maintenance in the two youngest age groups. The remaining four age groups show moderate to strong language maintenance with a general increase in the LMI scores from the youngest to the oldest age groups. The 25 to 34-year-old age group and the 45 to 54-year-old group are those whose LMI scores are within the moderate language maintenance range. The 45 to 54-year-old group and those 55 and older have LMI scores which are within the strong language maintenance range. The pattern is one that would be expected if there is intergenerational language shift beginning to take place as the younger age groups begin to use K'iche' less and less.

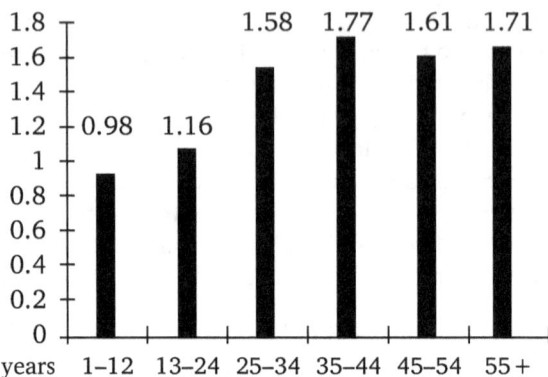

Figure 6.20 Language use by age group in Santa Cruz del Quiché

**6.6.3 Domain.** There were 3,453 K'iche'-produced speech transactions subjected to the analysis by domains for Santa Cruz del Quiché. Of these, 68.7% (2,373) were produced in K'iche', 27.2% (939) were produced in Spanish, and 4.1% (141) were classified as code-mixed. Table 6.38 shows the distribution of the speech transactions among the domains by language used, along with the results of the chi-square analysis and the LMI computed for each domain.

The chi-square analysis indicates that there is a significant difference in language use among the domains. The domain that contributes most to the difference from the expected normal distribution is formal education where there is an overwhelming use of Spanish and only low levels of K'iche' use. Spanish use is also much higher in the recreation domain than would be expected. This follows the general pattern for the larger towns where many of the recreation observations involved formal organized team sports, thus introducing an unexpected level of formality to a usually informal domain. In spite of these strongly divergent domains, however, there is a general pattern of greater Spanish use in the more formal domains and of lower Spanish use (and greater K'iche' use) in the more informal domains.

An examination of the LMI scores for each domain, which are graphically represented in figure 6.21, shows a less-than-strong language maintenance profile for Santa Cruz del Quiché. Of the ten domains, only two show strong language maintenance. These are market and mass media. The latter, usually a Spanish-dominant domain, is K'iche'-dominant probably because of the local Roman Catholic church-sponsored radio station which broadcasts in K'iche' and is one of the few sources of local news available.

## 6.6 Language use in Santa Cruz del Quiché

Table 6.38 K'iche' language use by domain in Santa Cruz del Quiché

| Domain | Home | Street | Play | Market | Work | Religion | Stores | Media | School | Govt | Total |
|---|---|---|---|---|---|---|---|---|---|---|---|
| | | | | | K'iche' | | | | | | |
| Frequency | 181 | 643 | 53 | 507 | 513 | 43 | 80 | 232 | 50 | 71 | 2373 |
| Expected | 173.18 | 536.73 | 117.52 | 415.09 | 496.09 | 69.41 | 85.904 | 181.43 | 233.66 | 63.912 | |
| Cell chi-square | 0.353 | 21.043 | 35.419 | 20.353 | 0.5703 | 10.049 | 0.4057 | 14.096 | 144.36 | 0.786 | |
| | | | | | Spanish | | | | | | |
| Frequency | 66 | 135 | 118 | 86 | 120 | 56 | 40 | 30 | 256 | 22 | 939 |
| Expected | 68.528 | 212.38 | 46.501 | 164.25 | 196.34 | 27.466 | 33.992 | 71.791 | 92.459 | 25.29 | |
| Cell chi-square | 0.0933 | 28.195 | 109.93 | 37.279 | 29.681 | 29.645 | 1.0618 | 24.328 | 325.73 | 0.428 | |
| | | | | | Code-Mixed | | | | | | |
| Frequency | 5 | 3 | 0 | 11 | 89 | 2 | 5 | 2 | 24 | 0 | 141 |
| Expected | 10.29 | 31.891 | 6.9826 | 24.664 | 29.482 | 4.1242 | 5.1043 | 10.78 | 13.884 | 3.7976 | |
| Cell chi-square | 2.7197 | 26.174 | 6.9826 | 7.5698 | 120.15 | 1.0941 | 0.0021 | 7.1512 | 7.3714 | 3.7976 | |
| Total | 252 | 781 | 171 | 604 | 722 | 101 | 125 | 264 | 340 | 93 | 3453 |
| LMI | 1.46 | 1.65 | 0.62 | 1.70 | 1.54 | 0.87 | 1.32 | 1.76 | 0.36 | 1.53 | |

($X^2 = 1016.822$ $p < 001$ df = 18)

Five domains have LMI scores which indicate moderate language maintenance. These are home, personal encounters, work, stores, and government offices. Three domains, recreation, religion, and formal education, have LMI scores indicating weak language maintenance.

This profile shows not only that some domains are thoroughly dominated by Spanish but that some of the moderate maintenance and weak maintenance domains are those which are normally associated with the L language in a diglossic situation.

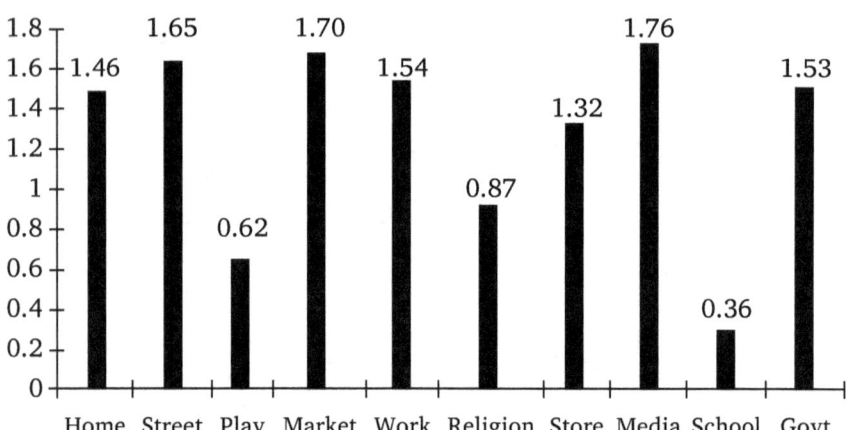

Figure 6.21 Language use by domain in Santa Cruz del Quiché

The domain data was also subjected to a chi-square analysis in terms of the level of formality of the domains. Of the 3,453 speech transactions analyzed, 12.7% (437) were classified as formal and 87.3% (3,016) were classified as informal. Table 6.39 shows the distribution of the speech transactions between the formal and informal domains by language used and shows the results of the chi-square analysis as well as the computed LMI for each category.

Table 6.39 K'iche' language use by formality level in Santa Cruz del Quiché

|  | Domain Formality | | |
|---|---|---|---|
|  | Formal | Informal | Total |
| **K'iche'** | | | |
| Frequency | 279 | 2094 | 2373 |
| Expected | 300.32 | 2072.7 | |
| Cell chi-square | 1.5134 | 0.2193 | |
| **Spanish** | | | |
| Frequency | 149 | 790 | 939 |
| Expected | 118.84 | 820.16 | |
| Cell chi-square | 7.6561 | 1.1093 | |
| **Code-Mixed** | | | |
| Frequency | 9 | 132 | 141 |
| Expected | 17.844 | 123.16 | |
| Cell chi-square | 4.3837 | 0.6352 | |
| Total | 437 | 3016 | 3453 |
| LMI | 1.30 | 1.43 | |

($X^2 = 15.517$ p<.001, df=2)

The chi-square analysis indicates that the difference in language use between levels of formality is significant. The LMI scores for the two categories of speech transactions show that neither category demonstrates strong language maintenance. Both formal and informal domains are characterized by moderate maintenance of K'iche'. This lack of a sharp distinction between the two sets of domains indicates that the compartmentalization between K'iche' and Spanish domains is leaking, and that leakage is more clearly evident in the informal domains.

**6.6.4 Summary.** The profile of Santa Cruz del Quiché that has been developed from these analyses of race, sex, age, and domain shows language maintenance in this community to be weaker than that of several of the other communities in this study. Though there is still evidence of differences in language use based on race and sex of the speakers and interlocutors, the analysis of the speech transactions by age groups shows that the youngest age groups are not maintaining the use of K'iche'. Rather, they are showing evidence of potential language shift. Unlike the other communities where K'iche' is being maintained in many domains, Santa Cruz shows evidence that Spanish is becoming dominant in several domains. The linguistic distinction between formal and informal domains is being lost as Spanish is increasingly used in the informal domains. The global LMI that I have calculated for Santa Cruz del Quiché is 1.41.

## 6.7 Language use in Totonicapán

The language use data for Totonicapán consist of 883 observations of 1,941 individuals producing 3,275 speech transactions.

**6.7.1 Race and sex.** For this analysis there were 3,219 speech transactions which had unambiguous identifications of participants and interlocutors by race and sex. Table 6.40 shows the distribution of the speech transactions according to the race and sex of speaker and interlocutor and language used.

The majority of the observations are of K'iche' speakers interacting with other K'iche's and most of the K'iche'-produced speech transactions occur between members of the same sex. The results of the categorical models analysis of these data are shown in table 6.41. It shows that Totonicapán has a complex pattern of language use quite similar to that of Chichicastenango where the interaction between RACE and IRACE is significant, as is the interaction between SEX and IRACE and between SEX and ISEX.

The tallies of the speech transactions by race of the speaker and race of the interlocutor are reorganized in table 6.42, and the percentage of the total number of speech transactions produced by speakers of the same race is also calculated.

6.7 Language use in Totonicapán 207

Table 6.40 Speech transactions in Totonicapán by race and sex of speaker and interlocutor

| Speakers | Interlocutor | | | | | | | | | | | | | | | |
|---|---|---|---|---|---|---|---|---|---|---|---|---|---|---|---|---|
| | K'iche' | | | | | | | | Ladino | | | | | | | |
| | Females | | | | Males | | | | Females | | | | Males | | | |
| Race/Sex | CM | S | K | Total K/F | CM | S | K | Total K/M | CM | S | K | Total L/F | CM | S | K | Total L/M | Total Spkrs |
| K'iche' Females | 29 | 132 | 658 | 819 | 21 | 111 | 295 | 427 | 0 | 37 | 19 | 56 | 2 | 23 | 8 | 33 | 1335 |
| K'iche' Males | 34 | 83 | 299 | 416 | 115 | 292 | 524 | 931 | 0 | 33 | 3 | 36 | 8 | 91 | 3 | 102 | 1485 |
| K'iche' Subtotal | 63 | 215 | 957 | 1235 | 136 | 403 | 819 | 1358 | 0 | 70 | 22 | 92 | 10 | 114 | 11 | 135 | 2820 |
| Ladino Females | 0 | 60 | 4 | 64 | 0 | 41 | 0 | 41 | 0 | 38 | 0 | 38 | 0 | 24 | 0 | 24 | 167 |
| Ladino Males | 0 | 29 | 5 | 34 | 0 | 105 | 1 | 106 | 0 | 25 | 0 | 25 | 0 | 67 | 0 | 67 | 232 |
| Ladino Subtotal | 0 | 89 | 9 | 98 | 0 | 146 | 1 | 147 | 0 | 63 | 0 | 63 | 0 | 91 | 0 | 91 | 399 |
| Grand Total | 63 | 304 | 966 | 1333 | 136 | 549 | 820 | 285 | 0 | 133 | 22 | 155 | 10 | 205 | 11 | 226 | 3219 |

Speech transactions are either code-mixed (CM), Spanish (S), or K'iche' (K).

Table 6.41 Maximum likelihood analysis-of-variance Race and sex data from Totonicapán

| Source | DF | Chi-Square | Prob |
|---|---|---|---|
| SEX | 2 | 14.22 | 0.0008 |
| RACE | 2 | 100.19 | 0.0000 |
| SEX*RACE | 2 | 8.38 | 0.0152 |
| ISEX | 2 | 7.12 | 0.0284 |
| SEX*ISEX | 2 | 97.22 | 0.0000 |
| RACE*ISEX | 2 | 3.63 | 0.1627 |
| SEX*RACE*ISEX | 2 | 4.17 | 0.1244 |
| IRACE | 2 | 70.38 | 0.0000 |
| SEX*IRACE | 2 | 16.46 | 0.0003 |
| RACE*IRACE | 2 | 30.78 | 0.0000 |
| SEX*RACE*IRACE | 2 | 2.84 | 0.2419 |
| ISEX*IRACE | 2 | 4.60 | 0.1001 |
| SEX*ISEX*IRACE | 2 | 13.11 | 0.0014 |
| RACE*ISEX*IRACE | 2 | 0.53 | 0.7683 |
| SEX*RACE*ISEX*IRACE | 2 | 1.49 | 0.4750 |
| Likelihood ratio | 2 | 870.79 | 0.0000 |

Table 6.42 Tally of language use for RACE*IRACE in Totonicapán

| Speaker/Interlocutor | Code-Mixed | | Spanish | | K'iche' | |
|---|---|---|---|---|---|---|
| | Count | % | Count | % | Count | % |
| K'iche'/K'iche' | 199 | 7.7 | 618 | 23.8 | 1776 | 68.5 |
| K'iche'/Ladino | 10 | 4.4 | 184 | 81.1 | 33 | 14.5 |
| Ladino/K'iche' | 0 | 0.0 | 235 | 95.9 | 10 | 4.1 |
| Ladino/Ladino | 0 | 0.0 | 154 | 100.0 | 0 | 0.0 |

Figure 6.22 shows the plot of the percentages of the speech transactions by language used according to RACE and IRACE. The pattern which it displays shows the now-familiar convergence effect of the presence of a ladino in a speech transaction. A K'iche''s language use patterns are nearly indistinguishable from those of a ladino if the interlocutor is a ladino. These results correspond to those of the other communities.

## 6.7 Language use in Totonicapán

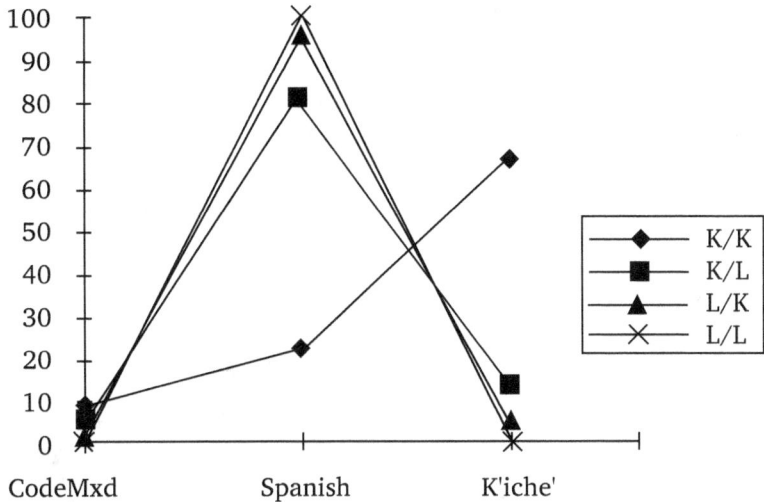

Figure 6.22 Interaction of RACE*IRACE Totonicapán

Clearly the race of the participants is the most significant factor influencing language use, but there is also the important effect of the sex of the participants.

Table 6.43 shows the tallies of the speech transactions by the combinations of sex of speaker and interlocutor, and the percentage of the total number of speech transactions produced by participants of the same sex.

Figure 6.23 plots the frequency counts of the speech transactions by language used according to SEX and ISEX.

Surprisingly, the resulting pattern is one where males speaking to males show a propensity to use Spanish while females speaking to females show a lower level of Spanish use. This provides evidence that males in Totonicapán are in the lead of the trend to acquire Spanish and that females generally have lower proficiency in Spanish. While this is not as ominous a situation as exists in some of the other communities where intergenerational language transmission is at risk, it still represents a dangerous trend in terms of K'iche' maintenance.

Table 6.43 Tally of language use for SEX*ISEX in Totonicapán

| Speaker/Interlocutor | Code-Mixed | | Spanish | | K'iche' | |
|---|---|---|---|---|---|---|
| | Count | % | Count | % | Count | % |
| Female/Female | 29 | 3.0 | 267 | 27.3 | 681 | 69.7 |
| Female/Male | 23 | 4.4 | 199 | 37.9 | 303 | 57.7 |
| Male/Female | 34 | 6.7 | 170 | 33.3 | 307 | 60.1 |
| Male/Male | 123 | 10.2 | 555 | 46.0 | 528 | 43.8 |

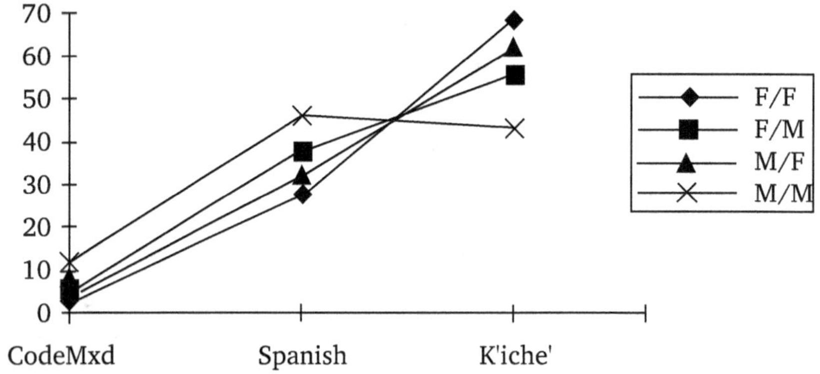

Figure 6.23 Interaction of SEX*ISEX in Totonicapán

The third significant interaction in Totonicapán is that between SEX and IRACE. Table 6.44 shows the tallies of the speech transactions produced by speakers of each sex with interlocutors of each race. The percentages are calculated using the total number of speakers of each sex.

Table 6.44 Tally of language use for SEX*IRACE in Totonicapán

| Speaker/Interlocutor | Code-Mixed | | Spanish | | K'iche' | |
|---|---|---|---|---|---|---|
| | Count | % | Count | % | Count | % |
| Female/K'iche' | 50 | 3.7 | 344 | 25.5 | 957 | 70.8 |
| Female/Ladino | 2 | 1.3 | 122 | 80.8 | 27 | 17.9 |
| Male/K'iche' | 149 | 10.0 | 509 | 34.2 | 829 | 55.7 |
| Male/Ladino | 8 | 3.5 | 216 | 93.9 | 6 | 2.6 |

Figure 6.24 plots the percentages by language used according to the values of these two variables. The graph shows even more clearly the basic difference in language use between the two races but particularly demonstrates the difference between male and female speakers. The male propensity to use more Spanish is evident and follows the general pattern

expected of speech transactions involving ladinos even when the interlocutor is a K'iche'. Female speakers use proportionately less Spanish than males and proportionately more K'iche' than males. This is further evidence of the male tendency to use Spanish more frequently and presumably with greater proficiency.

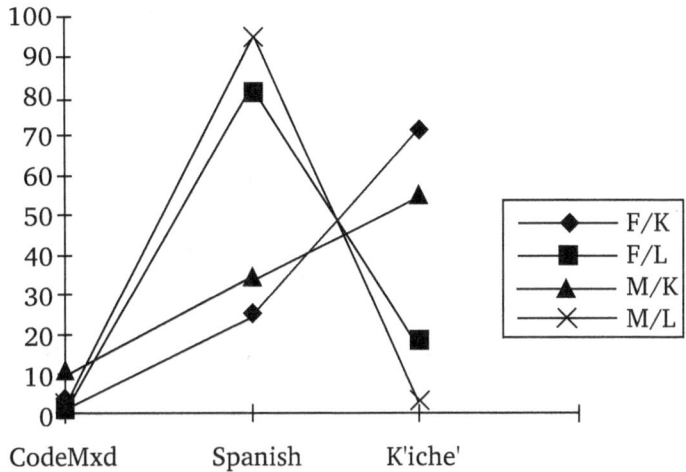

Figure 6.24 Interaction of SEX*IRACE in Totonicapán

**6.7.2 Age.** There were 2,834 K'iche'-produced speech transactions subjected to analysis for Totonicapán. Of these, 64.1% (1,816) were produced in K'iche', 28.4% (806) were produced in Spanish, and 7.5% (212) were classified as code-mixed.

Table 6.45 shows the distribution of the speech transactions among the age groups by language used as well as the results of a chi-square analysis and the LMI computed for each age group.

The chi-square analysis shows that there is a significant difference in language use between the age groups. The age group which contributes the greatest amount to the total chi-square value is the 13 to 24 age group. This group shows higher levels of Spanish use and lower levels of K'iche' use than expected in a normal distribution. The data from the youngest age group show only a slight tendency to use more K'iche' than expected. It is only in the 35 to 44-year-old age group that any marked level of K'iche' dominance is clearly evident in Totonicapán.

Table 6.45 K'iche' language use by age group in Totonicapán

| Age | 1–12 | 13–24 | 25–34 | 35–44 | 45–54 | 55+ | Total |
|---|---|---|---|---|---|---|---|
| K'iche' | | | | | | | |
| Frequency | 309 | 224 | 344 | 441 | 333 | 165 | 1816 |
| Expected | 289.64 | 340.65 | 351.79 | 415.87 | 287.07 | 131.36 | |
| Cell chi-square | 1.2944 | 39.724 | 0.1727 | 1.5182 | 7.3472 | 8.6137 | |
| Spanish | | | | | | | |
| Frequency | 129 | 262 | 159 | 149 | 75 | 32 | 806 |
| Expected | 128.55 | 151.02 | 156.14 | 184.58 | 127.41 | 58.303 | |
| Cell chi-square | 0.0016 | 81.559 | 0.0525 | 6.8578 | 21.561 | 11.866 | |
| Code-Mixed | | | | | | | |
| Frequency | 14 | 45 | 46 | 59 | 40 | 8 | 212 |
| Expected | 33.812 | 39.722 | 41.068 | 48.549 | 33.513 | 15.335 | |
| Cell chi-square | 11.609 | 0.7013 | 0.5922 | 2.2497 | 1.2556 | 3.5086 | |
| Total | 452 | 531 | 549 | 649 | 448 | 205 | 2834 |
| LMI | 1.40 | 0.93 | 1.34 | 1.45 | 1.58 | 1.65 | |

($X^2 = 200.484$ p<.001, df=10)

The LMI scores, graphically displayed in figure 6.25, show that none of the age groups can be characterized as showing strong language maintenance. Five of the age groups have LMI scores which demonstrate moderate language maintenance. These are the youngest age group, the 25 to 34 age groups, the 35 to 44-year-old age group, the 45 to 54-year-old age group and the oldest age group. The teenaged group has an LMI score of 0.93 which is indicative of weak maintenance.

The profile which the LMI scores give is one indicative of a potential for intergenerational language shift. Although parents do seem to be passing on K'iche' to the youngest age group, education and other influences outside of the home seem to be eroding the use of K'iche'. With the only marginal exception of the youngest age group, the LMI scores parallel the age of the speakers with higher language maintenance being evidenced by older participants.

6.7 Language use in Totonicapán 213

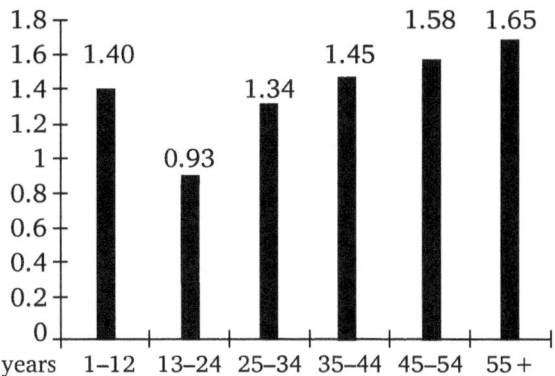

Figure 6.25 Language use by age group in Totonicapán

**6.7.3 Domain.** There were 2,843 K'iche'-produced speech transactions subjected to the domain analysis for Totonicapán. Of these, 64.1% (1,823) were produced in K'iche', 28.4% (808) were produced in Spanish, and 7.5% (212) were classified as code-mixed.

Table 6.46 shows the distribution of the speech transactions among the domains by language used, the results of the chi-square analysis, and the LMI computed for each domain.

The chi-square analysis indicates that there is a significant difference in language use among the domains. The domain with the greatest divergence from the expected normal distribution is religion. It shows very high levels of code-mixing and moderately high levels of Spanish use accompanied by lower than expected levels of K'iche' use. The recreation domain also shows higher than expected levels of Spanish and code-mixing as is the pattern in the other larger communities. The market domain is clearly associated with K'iche' use with higher than expected levels of K'iche' and lower than expected levels of Spanish. The Home domain is also associated with K'iche' use.

The LMI scores, shown graphically in figure 6.26, indicate that there are only two of the ten domains which can be classified as showing strong language maintenance. There are three domains which demonstrate moderate language maintenance, and five domains which demonstrate weak levels of language maintenance.

Table 6.46 K'iche' language use by domain in Totonicapán

| Domain | Home | Street | Play | Market | Work | Religion | Stores | Media | School | Govt | Total |
|---|---|---|---|---|---|---|---|---|---|---|---|
| K'iche' | | | | | | | | | | | |
| Frequency | 280 | 217 | 11 | 510 | 115 | 71 | 109 | 30 | 230 | 250 | 1823 |
| Expected | 197.5 | 184.03 | 39.115 | 381.53 | 121.83 | 146.2 | 150.05 | 42.321 | 284.06 | 276.37 | |
| Cell chi-square | 34.465 | 5.9062 | 20.208 | 43.26 | 0.3832 | 38.679 | 11.229 | 3.5869 | 10.289 | 2.5157 | |
| Spanish | | | | | | | | | | | |
| Frequency | 6 | 60 | 32 | 66 | 53 | 92 | 119 | 36 | 195 | 149 | 808 |
| Expected | 87.536 | 81.567 | 17.337 | 169.1 | 53.999 | 64.799 | 66.504 | 18.758 | 125.9 | 122.49 | |
| Cell chi-square | 75.947 | 5.7027 | 12.402 | 62.862 | 0.0185 | 11.418 | 41.438 | 15.849 | 37.92 | 5.7359 | |
| Code-Mixed | | | | | | | | | | | |
| Frequency | 22 | 10 | 18 | 19 | 22 | 65 | 6 | 0 | 18 | 32 | 212 |
| Expected | 22.967 | 21.401 | 4.5487 | 44.369 | 14.168 | 17.002 | 17.449 | 4.9216 | 33.034 | 32.139 | |
| Cell chi-square | 0.0407 | 6.0739 | 39.778 | 14.505 | 4.3293 | 135.51 | 7.5123 | 4.9216 | 6.8422 | 0.0006 | |
| Total | 308 | 287 | 61 | 595 | 190 | 228 | 234 | 66 | 443 | 431 | 2843 |
| LMI | 1.89 | 1.55 | 0.66 | 1.75 | 1.33 | 0.91 | 0.96 | 0.91 | 1.08 | 1.23 | |

($X^2 = 659.326$ p < .001, df = 18)

## 6.7 Language use in Totonicapán

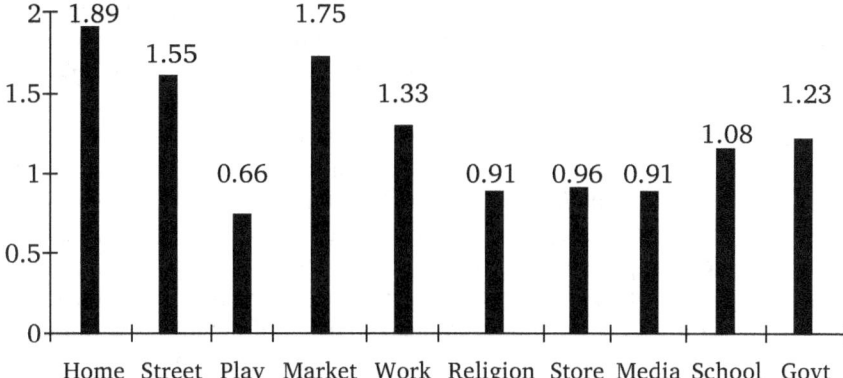

Figure 6.26 Language use by domain in Totonicapán

The domains whose LMI scores are within the strong maintenance range are home and market. These are the more informal and solidary domains where K'iche' use is expected to be predominant.

The domains whose LMI scores are within the moderate language maintenance range are personal encounters, work, and government offices. The first two are generally more informal and solidary domains, while the third is a ladino-dominated domain. The use of K'iche' in this domain represents the accommodation of ladinos to the communicative needs of K'iche's.

There are five domains in Totonicapán which demonstrate weak language maintenance. The only other community in the study with so many domains in this category is Chichicastenango. These weak maintenance domains are recreation, religion, stores, mass media, and formal education. In all of the communities, these are the domains that have consistently shown lower levels of K'iche' maintenance. None of the other communities, however, had LMI scores in the weak language maintenance range of all five of these domains simultaneously.

Of the speech transactions analyzed by formality level, 33.4% (950) were classified as formal and 66.6% (1,893) were classified as informal. Table 6.47 shows the distribution of the speech transactions between the formal and informal domains by language used, the chi-square analysis results, and the LMI.

The chi-square analysis, corroborated by the LMI scores, shows that there is a significant difference in language use between the two levels of formality. The informal domains have an LMI score which is within the range of moderate language maintenance, and the formal domains have an LMI score which indicates weak language maintenance.

**6.7.4 Summary.** The combined profile for Totonicapán derived from these data shows generally weak language maintenance occurring in the community. There is relatively strong compartmentalization in language use, based on race and sex of the participants, though there is evidence that men use more Spanish than K'iche'. Based on the LMI scores for both the youngest age group and the home and hearth domain, many parents seem to be transmitting K'iche' to their children. Yet, in spite of these signs of language maintenance, the overall pattern in the community is that the younger age groups are not maintaining K'iche' as strongly as the older generations. The more intimate and solidary domains show moderate, and even strong, language maintenance but a few of the informal domains are also showing weak language maintenance. Totonicapán and Chichicastenango have more domains characterized by weak language maintenance than any of the other communities in the study. The global LMI calculated for Totonicapán is 1.36.

Table 6.47 K'iche' language use by formality level in Totonicapán

|  | Domain Formality | | |
| --- | --- | --- | --- |
|  | Formal | Informal | Total |
| K'iche' | | | |
| Frequency | 465 | 1358 | 1823 |
| Cell chi-square | 609.16 | 1213.8 | |
| Spanish | | | |
| Frequency | 414 | 394 | 808 |
| Expected | 270 | 538 | |
| Cell chi-square | 76.805 | 38.544 | |
| Code-Mixed | | | |
| Frequency | 71 | 141 | 212 |
| Expected | 70.841 | 141.16 | |
| Cell chi-square | 0.0004 | 0.0002 | |
| Total | 950 | 1893 | 2843 |
| LMI | 1.05 | 1.51 | |

($X^2 = 166.589$ p < .001, df = 2)

# 7
# Integration of the Two Data Sets

In chapters 4 and 5, I described the communities using the framework of ethnolinguistic identity theory. In chapter 6, I described the observed language use patterns in the communities. The first set of data is qualitative, the second is quantitative. In order to arrive at a fuller understanding of the dynamics of identity and language use, the two data sets need to be integrated for each community. The resulting overall profile can be used to compare the communities to each other and to relate their levels of language and identity maintenance to the social changes which have taken place in Guatemalan society. This process, though not statistically rigorous, can then be used to test the second hypothesis of this study: that there is a significant relationship between loss (or maintenance) of diglossia in the communities and their degree of acceptance (or rejection) of modern identity factors.

The procedure I use in categorizing the communities in terms of their acceptance of modern identity factors is to synthesize and summarize the various aspects of their ethnolinguistic vitality profiles, as developed in chapters 4 and 5, and to compare those to their overall language maintenance profiles developed in chapter 6. This global perspective should provide a means of discerning the relationship between identity shift and language shift as well as bringing into clearer focus those areas where further research is needed.

## 7.1–7.4 Ethnolinguistic identity measures

As described in chapter 2, the ethnolinguistic identity theory attempts to identify the factors which motivate individuals in a society to "maintain or sacrifice their ethnolinguistic identity in the short term of social interaction as well as in the longer term of the group retaining or relinquishing their language as a communicative code" (Giles 1987:70). By describing seven K'iche' communities in terms of the ethnolinguistic identity factors identified by the theory, I have attempted to arrive at a measure of the strength of each community's ethnolinguistic identity and in turn to provide a means of linking measurement to observed language use. The following sections bring together the ethnolinguistic vitality descriptions and language maintenance measures for the seven communities under the rubrics provided by the ethnolinguistic identity theory.

### 7.1 Demographic factors

The demographic factors include information concerning population factors (density, growth, age), racial composition, urban versus rural, and marriage and migration patterns. Table 7.1 provides a summary of the demographic data for each of the seven communities.

The categories which are compared are based on the Guatemalan government census figures, primarily from the 1981 census. The table provides data on population density in terms of number of persons per square kilometer, the percentage of the total population identified as Mayans, the percentage of the total population which resides in the rural areas (i.e., outside of the town centers), the percent increase from 1955 to 1981, and the percentage of the total population which is under 19 years of age.

In addition, the table provides qualitative information based on the ethnographic observations of the investigators in each community. These data are expressed as measures of the amount of exogamous marriage and the amount of migration and travel on a scale which includes the terms LITTLE, MODERATE, and FREQUENT. Each community is also characterized as to its status as a vacant town.

**7.1.1 Population density.** An examination of table 7.1 reveals that the three most cosmopolitan communities in the study, Chichicastenango, Santa Cruz del Quiché, and Totonicapán, are those with the highest population density.

## 7.1 Demographic factors

Table 7.1 Summary of demographic factors

| Demographic factor/Town | Pop./Km² | % Mayan | % Rural | % Inc. '55–'81 | % <19 yrs | Exog. Marr. | Migration & Travel | Vacant Town |
|---|---|---|---|---|---|---|---|---|
| Chichicastenango | 141.5 | 97.5 | 94.3 | 104.3 | 58.6 | Little | Frequent | Yes |
| Cunén | 79.6 | 86.0 | 87.6 | 126.9 | 58.9 | Moderate | Little | No |
| Joyabaj | 117.5 | 75.1 | 93.1 | 149.1 | 59.0 | No Data | Little | Yes |
| Sacapulas | 97.4 | 94.4 | 91.8 | 91.2 | 59.0 | No Data | Frequent | Yes |
| San Andrés Sajcabajá | 50.5 | 84.2 | 92.6 | 17.7 | 55.9 | No Data | Little | Yes |
| Santa Cruz del Quiché | 275.8 | 79.5 | 74.6 | 15.4* | 55.1 | Moderate | Frequent | No |
| Totonicapán | 190.3 | 95.1 | 88.0 | 90.6 | 54.5 | No Data | Frequent | No |

*Data available only for period from 1964–1981.

Both Totonicapán and Santa Cruz del Quiché were separated from the other communities because I recognized them as being more city-like because of their status as departmental capitals. Chichicastenango, although treated as a town in chapter 4, has much more exposure to outside influences than the other towns because of the attraction of its tourist market and the tourism infrastructure.

The community with the most dispersed population is San Andrés Sajcabajá which was described as a very rural and isolated community. The other communities fall into an intermediate range of population density.

**7.1.2 Racial composition.** The communities vary somewhat in their racial composition. Several communities have high percentages of the total population identified as being Mayan. Those with the highest percentages are Chichicastenango (97.5%), Totonicapán (95.1%), and Sacapulas (94.4%). The community with the lowest percentage of Mayans is Joyabaj (75.1%), followed by Santa Cruz del Quiché (79.5%). Cunén and San Andrés Sajcabajá fall in a middle range with 86.0% and 84.2% Mayan populations, respectively.

**7.1.3 Urban versus rural.** The percentage of the population that is rural seems to parallel the identification of the community as a vacant town. All of the communities so identified (Chichicastenango, Joyabaj, Sacapulas, and San Andrés Sajcabajá) have rural population percentages above 90%. The three communities not identified as vacant towns have rural population percentages of 74.6% in Santa Cruz del Quiché, 87.6% in Cunén and 88.0% in Totonicapán.

**7.1.4 Population growth.** All of the communities have shown growth in the last twenty-five years but at vastly different rates. The community with the greatest increase in population in the period between 1955 and 1981 is Joyabaj which has shown a 149.1% increase over the period. Two other communities show large increases in population: Chichicastenango with a 104.3% increase and Cunén with a 126.9% increase. The community with the smallest increase in population is Santa Cruz del Quiché with a 15.4% increase over the period from 1964 to 1981. San Andrés Sajcabajá has shown a similar small increase since the 1955 census with a 17.7% increase. The other communities, Sacapulas with 91.2%, and Totonicapán with 90.6%, show more moderate but still considerable growth. It is difficult to assess the impact of growth on the communities. While overall population growth may be viewed by the members of the community as an indicator of group success, thus boosting overall ethnolinguistic vitality, such growth complicates social network interactions and, to some degree, causes a disintegration of the face-to-face nature of the society. Social norms, including linguistic norms, are less easily enforced when the social networks become more numerous and less closely interlocked with each other.

**7.1.5 Age of the population.** The one statistic that is nearly equivalent for all of the communities is the percentage of the total population that is young, i.e., under the age of 19. The communities range from a low of 55.1% in Santa Cruz del Quiché to a high of 59.0% in Joyabaj and Sacapulas. This high number is of particular importance when correlated with the language use patterns of the age groups described in chapter 6. The language use patterns of the two youngest age groups, those between 1 and 24-years-old, provide evidence for the language use of a majority of the population in every community.

**7.1.6 Marriage and migration patterns.** The two qualitative factors, exogamous marriage and migration and travel, provide a more impressionistic characterization of the communities. No data were provided by the observers for four of the communities regarding the existence of patterns of exogamous marriage. Of the three communities where there is data provided, Chichicastenango is reported to have little exogamous marriage, while Cunén and Santa Cruz del Quiché are reported to have moderate levels. One crucial distinction, however, is that the exogamous marriage in Cunén and in Chichicastenango is with other Mayans, either speakers of other varieties of K'iche' (as in Cunén) or of other Mayan languages (as in Chichicastenango). In Santa Cruz del Quiché, there is a greater incidence of intermarriage (though still not enough for it to be considered commonplace) between Mayans and ladinos.

Migration and travel not related to temporary agricultural work on the Pacific coast varies from little in Cunén, Joyabaj, and San Andrés Sajcabajá, to frequent in Chichicastenango, Sacapulas, Santa Cruz del Quiché, and Totonicapán. These patterns reflect economic realities in these communities. Those with little migration and travel are those with little economic activity which extends beyond their own community. Those with more frequent travel patterns are those communities whose merchants travel to sell their produce. Even those communities which have been described as having frequent migration and travel are characterized by different levels of pervasiveness of this activity throughout the community. In some communities, such as Chichicastenango and

Totonicapán, a larger percentage of the population engages in itinerant merchandising. In Sacapulas, a great many of those who travel to other markets to sell are women.

## 7.2 Institutional support factors

Institutional support refers to the kind of recognition and use given to a linguistic variety by societal institutions and can be either formal or informal. The former refers to recognition and use which is part of the structures of the societal institutions themselves. The latter refers to organized efforts to support the use and recognition of a particular variety produced by members of the society apart from, or even in opposition to, the structural postures and policies of the societal institutions. As pointed out in chapter 2, institutions correspond in many ways to domains of language use, and some institutions/domains can be expected to be more crucial in their influence on ethnolinguistic vitality. Two such crucial institutions mentioned specifically in the literature are education and religion.

Table 7.2 is a compendium of the ethnographic data on institutional support for the seven communities. The presence or absence of institutional support in the societal institutions is indicated as a plus or minus. The table distinguishes between the presence or absence of both formal (F) and informal (I) support for each institution and is based on my interpretation of the ethnographic data.

Table 7.2 also compiles the data for five globally-conceived societal institutions: government, church, education, business, and culture. These are the general rubrics under which institutional support was described in chapters 4 and 5. Within each general category however, there is considerable complexity. Where appropriate and useful, I have attempted to break down the categorizations to recognize the diversity within the larger institutional categorization. I have also considered the language use data for the domains of use where the domains coincide with the institutional categorizations.

At times, the sub-institutions/domains can be seen to be at odds with each other in terms of their level of use and recognition of K'iche'.

**7.2.1 Government.** In the institution of government there is little or no formal recognition or use given to K'iche' in any of the communities. Still, low-level government functionaries are confronted daily with the communicative difficulties presented by citizens who are not proficient in Spanish. In the smaller communities, informal support of K'iche' is provided through the use of interpreters who are not formally recognized nor

## 7.2 Institutional support factors

employed by the government as such. Notably, the two communities which I have classified as cities, Santa Cruz del Quiché and Totonicapán, were not observed to provide even this level of government support for K'iche', though inevitably K'iche' is still used in some government offices. In these communities, Spanish is the expected language of government.

The actual language use patterns described for these communities in chapter 6 show that, in spite of this lack of formal and informal governmental support, K'iche' is still used in the government domain. The LMI scores for government for Santa Cruz del Quiché and Totonicapán are within the moderate language maintenance range.

**7.2.2 Religion.** Apart from the traditional Mayan religion which is pervasive in all of the communities and is a bulwark of K'iche' use,[38] religious institutions in the communities show a mixed pattern of support for the use and maintenance of K'iche'. The general pattern is that whatever institutional support exists in the religious institutions, does so informally. Furthermore, institutional support in some of the communities is found only in the Roman Catholic church, and only weakly or not at all in the Protestant churches. The communities with the strongest formal support of K'iche' by the Roman Catholic church are Chichicastenango, Joyabaj, and San Andrés Sajcabajá. This pattern, however, is not a result of church policy at higher levels, but is coincidental with the ideological leanings of the local priest in each community and is, therefore, subject to change when the priest is transferred. Thus, church support in any community can come and go with the assignment and reassignment of the K'iche'-speaking priests.

Protestant churches almost universally provide only minimal support for the use of K'iche'. Nevertheless, much K'iche' is used for nonpublic or nonformal functions in the churches. As in the Roman Catholic church, there is no formal policy of K'iche' support among the Protestant churches, and each congregation provides only as much support as it deems appropriate. While Protestant pastors can have some influence in affecting the local attitudes and practices, typically their influence is not as great as the Roman Catholic priest's is in his parish.

---

[38]The use of K'iche' for ritual purposes in the traditional religion is confined to the shamans who, though numerous, do not constitute a significant portion of the population.

Table 7.2 Summary of institutional support factors

| Institution | Government | | Religion | | | Education | | Business | | | Culture | | |
|---|---|---|---|---|---|---|---|---|---|---|---|---|---|
| Town | F | I | | F | I | F | I | | F | I | | F | I |
| Chichicastenango | - | + | R.C. | + | + | + | - | Market | + | + | Cofradia | + | + |
| | | | Prot. | - | + | | | Stores | - | - | Other | - | - |
| Cunén | - | + | R.C. | - | + | - | + | Market | + | + | Cofradia | + | + |
| | | | Prot. | - | + | | | Stores | - | + | Other | + | + |
| Joyabaj | - | + | R.C. | + | + | - | - | Market | + | + | Cofradia | + | + |
| | | | Prot. | - | + | | | Stores | - | + | Other | - | - |
| Sacapulas | - | + | R.C. | - | + | + | - | Market | + | + | Cofradia | + | + |
| | | | Prot. | - | + | | | Stores | - | + | Other | - | - |
| San Andrés Sajcabajá | - | + | R.C. | + | + | - | - | Market | + | + | Cofradia | + | + |
| | | | Prot. | - | - | | | Stores | - | + | Other | - | - |
| Santa Cruz del Quiché | - | - | R.C. | - | - | - | + | Market | - | + | Cofradia | + | - |
| | | | Prot. | - | + | | | Stores | - | + | Other | - | - |
| Totonicapán | - | - | R.C. | - | + | - | - | Market | - | + | Cofradia | + | + |
| | | | Prot. | - | + | | | Stores | - | - | Other | - | - |

Significantly, the Protestant churches have experienced rapid growth in the last twenty years and serve as one of the few easily-accessible resources that K'iche' monolinguals have for the acquisition of Spanish. The LMI scores for the religious domain reflect this lack of support and are universally among the lowest of all of the domains.

**7.2.3 Education.** Education is another source of relinguification. Generally, the communities see education as a resource for progress and development. Education is seen as a means of gaining power. In spite of bilingual methodology and the rhetoric of multiculturalism, the general function of education is to provide support for the use of Spanish and disincentive for the use of K'iche'. The use of K'iche' in bilingual education is a stepping stone to Spanish proficiency. Only in a few communities is there evidence of formal, official support for the maintenance of K'iche'. In all of the other communities, school officials view K'iche' as an obstacle to education and bilingual education as either misguided at worst or as a strategy to relinguify and equip students for success in the Spanish educational setting at best. In Cunén and Santa Cruz del Quiché, the bilingual education program is functioning in spite of the school leaders' misgivings, primarily because of the enthusiasm and persistence of the young bilingual teachers.

**7.2.4 Business.** Business institutions show a sharp cleavage between those parts of the economy that are Mayan-controlled and those that are ladino-controlled. The market in most of the communities is a Mayan institution where K'iche' is used and supported. Only in the two cities, Santa Cruz del Quiché and Totonicapán, where the markets are more cosmopolitan, is there a lack of formal institutional support though in both cases informal support is quite strong.

Stores in most of the communities are owned by ladino merchants and tend to provide little formal support for K'iche' maintenance. This is seen in the LMI scores for this domain which are among the lowest in each of the communities. Nevertheless, in most of the communities, there is a nominal level of informal support for the use of K'iche' as evidenced by the accommodation to K'iche' speakers by some merchants and their employees.[39]

**7.2.5 Cultural institutions.** The most difficult area of institutional support to summarize is that of the general culture which encompasses a great deal of "social space" and a large number and variety of institutions. These institutions range from the civil-religious brotherhoods to local and regional development agencies and committees of various types, to the

---

[39]In some cases, it seemed that at least one of the employees in a store would be a Mayan so that there was always one clerk available to deal with monolingual Mayan customers.

institutionalized migrant labor system. The *cofradía*, the religious brotherhood, is almost universally a stronghold of support for the cultural values and practices which are most closely associated with the use of K'iche'. Only in Santa Cruz del Quiché was there any evidence that this institution might be weakening in its support of K'iche', although in several of the communities no firm conclusions could be drawn because no data were available.

The migrant labor system, though a well-entrenched part of the Mayan's annual economic cycle, is still a ladino institution. It represents the pervading and persistent economic and social oppression to which Mayans have accommodated themselves. Though the labor contractors may speak K'iche' (and in fact often are themselves Mayans), and though the participants in the system are Mayans, the effect of the dislocation, exposure to other Mayan languages, and communicative pressures of the work situation, all conspire against the use of K'iche' and promote the adoption of Spanish as a lingua franca.

Other social and cultural agencies also exist in the communities. As might be expected in summarizing so diverse a collection of institutions, different institutions are promoting different outcomes in terms of language use and maintenance in these K'iche' communities. Overall, however, the trend seems to be away from the support of the K'iche' language. Cunén, with its indigenous agricultural cooperatives, is one exception, and surprisingly, Santa Cruz del Quiché, at least in its rural *cantones,* is another, though in both cases the goals of these local development institutions are not in support of traditional K'iche' culture. Local development committees unreservedly use K'iche' if only because it is the only linguistic code at their disposal.

## 7.3 Status factors

Status factors are those which deal with the relative prestige of the linguistic varieties and are derived from the prestige of the speakers of the varieties more than from any inherent features of the varieties themselves. The four kinds of status recognized by Giles, Bourhis, and Taylor (1977) are economic status, ascribed (social) status, sociohistorical status, and language status. The community descriptions in chapters 4 and 5 attempt to account for these aspects of status.

Based on those data, I have evaluated the status of the speakers of K'iche' in each community in each of the four status categories and characterized their status as either high or low. I have attempted to characterize each community from the prevailing perspective of all of the population, both Mayan and ladino, while recognizing that these two groups may have very different perspectives on the status of K'iche' speakers. I have attempted to weigh the relative power differential of the two groups, the strength of the perceptions of status, and other intuitive measures. In short, these summary evaluations are my impressions of the communities based on the data and on experience in the communities themselves. Table 7.3 shows my summation of the various status factors for each community. As can be seen, the combined status characteristics of the communities range from a totally low status profile as in Joyabaj, San Andrés Sajcabajá, and Santa Cruz del Quiché to a fairly high status profile in Totonicapán. Chichicastenango, Cunén, and Sacapulas have mixed profiles with Sacapulas the lowest of the three, and Chichicastenango and Cunén having ambivalent profiles.

Table 7.3 Summary of status factors

| Town | Economic Status | Social Status | Sociohistorical Status | Language Status |
|---|---|---|---|---|
| Chichicastenango | High | Low | High | Low |
| Cunén | High | Low | Low | High |
| Joyabaj | Low | Low | Low | Low |
| Sacapulas | Low | Low | Low | High |
| San Andrés Sajcabajá | Low | Low | Low | Low |
| Santa Cruz del Quiché | Low | Low | Low | Low |
| Totonicapán | High | High | High | Low |

**7.3.1 Economic status.** Economic status is high in the three communities where Mayans participate in the major cash-producing activities of the communities. Chichicastenango and Totonicapán depend on tourism-based products and the cultivation of fruits and vegetables as cash crops. These communities are moving away from subsistence farming as the primary economic activity, though agricultural production for domestic consumption is still important as a cultural activity.

Cunén is in the beginning stages of an economic transition to cash crop production with the formation of agricultural cooperatives and the introduction of garlic and brussels sprouts as supplements to the earlier introduction of wheat. In the communities which are still based on subsistence farming and local, rather than regional, trade, the economic status of Mayans is low.

**7.3.2 Social status.** Quite generally, the social status of Mayans is low. Even in those communities where Mayans are participating in the economy and have other positive indicators of status, they are perceived as being socially inferior and, to some extent, so perceive themselves. Only in Totonicapán have I evaluated social status as high. This is because of the overwhelming predominance of Mayans in the community and their participation in almost every area of social life. While the ladinos of Totonicapán, no doubt, still perceive Mayans as being their social inferiors, the ladinos have so little social and economic leverage in the community that their perceptions are largely unheeded by the Mayan majority. Chichicastenango shows some of these same characteristics but much of the economic power in Chichicastenango is in the hands of ladinos who operate the larger hotels and restaurants and so are much more visible as a more prestigious social group. There may also be a similar pattern at work in Sacapulas where ladinos are largely invisible numerically, but still hold important political and economic positions.

**7.3.3 Sociohistorical status.** Only in Chichicastenango and Totonicapán do I view sociohistorical status as being high. Both of these communities are identified as sites where great events from the past took place and have maintained their contemporary connections with the great traditions from the past. Chichicastenango is well-known as the site where the *Popol Wuj,* the K'iche' recounting of creation and the exploits of the gods and the ancestors, was discovered. Totonicapán has strong connections with Tecun Uman, the Mayan warrior chieftain who died battling the Spanish conquerors. Some Mayan residents of other communities erroneously identified Totonicapán as the place where K'iche' came from. In spite of the fact that Santa Cruz del Quiché has a strong historical and geographical link to the ancient Quichean capital city, Utatlán, that link is not prominent in the minds of most of the Mayan residents of the community and is not maintained with any strong level of pride or enthusiasm except by a few.

**7.3.4 Language status.** Language status in the communities, the last status category, can be categorized as generally low with only Cunén and Sacapulas providing exceptions. Most residents of the communities, including many Mayans, perceive the K'iche' language to be inferior to Spanish at least in instrumental terms. Spanish is perceived as the language of power, progress, and most certainly, of upward mobility. Sentimental attachment to K'iche' is still strong as the language of tradition and cultural continuity and so use of K'iche' is greater in the informal domains. In most of the communities the status of K'iche' is being promoted by the bilingual teachers. A few others are attempting to "undo diglossia" by promoting the expansion of K'iche' into the more formal domains, particularly in the areas of education and government. In spite of these efforts, however, the general trend is towards the acquisition and use of Spanish.

## 7.4 Subjective vitality factors

Subjective vitality is a measure of a group's self-perception independent of the objective measures of their ethnolinguistic vitality. Groups which perceive themselves to be successful will behave accordingly while groups which perceive themselves to be weakening are likely to engage in more overt efforts to preserve their language and culture. If they are unwilling to do so, they may capitulate to the pressures of the encroaching culture and conform to the social and linguistic norms of the outgroup. Subjective vitality has much to do with boundary maintenance and convergence and divergence behaviors.

In evaluating and summarizing the subjective vitality perceptions of the communities in this study, I use the taxonomy provided by Paulston (1987) which classifies ethnic groups in terms of their awareness of and stance towards language and identity. In Paulston's framework, a group which is largely unaware of its own identity, that takes its identity and vitality for granted, is called an ethnicity. When a group is more self-conscious and therefore less passive about the preservation of its identity, it assumes the stance of an ethnic movement. Such a group is marked by a higher level of militancy about language and culture preservation and usually is characterized by the emergence of a leader who articulates the more militant stance towards language maintenance. An ethnic movement is not so militant as the third stage along the continuum which Paulston calls ethnic nationalism which can be distinguished from an ethnic movement by the more widely held militance. Ethnic nationalism, while sharing the militancy of an ethnic movement, relies less on individual leaders to give it focus and direction. Ethnic nationalism also tends to have a regional rather than a local, community-based focus and so is less directly applicable to the community-by-community analysis which I am carrying out here. A fourth stage which does not apply to any of the individual K'iche' communities at this point is that of geographic nationalism which is characterized by efforts to achieve political sovereignty over the group's traditional territory.

The communities in this study are at the less militant end of the continuum for the most part and I have classified the towns as showing either the characteristic responses of an ethnicity or of an ethnic movement. Though the parallels are not perfect, communities with the posture of an ethnicity are those which are demonstrating the centuries-old patterns of passive resistance. Residents in these communities maintain their cultural ways without making any overt language or culture maintenance efforts.

The imposed culture and language is simply tolderated. While there is some sense of threat present in these communities, the response is a Mayan one. The other communities see themselves as unsuccessful and endangered and have engaged in more overt and militant boundary maintenance behaviors. I have classified these communities as ethnic movements and I consider them to have demonstrated an identity shift in that they have opted to fight ladino culture on ladino terms.

I have classified five of the seven towns as ethnicities. This indicates a general passivity regarding language maintenance which is a result, I believe, of the overall lack of conscious awareness of the status of K'iche' in the communities. Most of the residents of these communities are simply not aware that there is any threat to their language and do not perceive their own linguistic behavior to be a threat to the ongoing maintenance of K'iche'. Table 7.4 shows the categorizations which I have applied to each community.

Table 7.4 Summary of subjective vitality factors

| Town | Subjective vitality |
|---|---|
| Chichicastenango | Ethnicity |
| Cunén | Ethnicity |
| Joyabaj | Ethnicity |
| Sacapulas | Ethnicity |
| San Andrés Sajcabajá | Ethnicity |
| Santa Cruz del Quiché | Ethnic Movement |
| Totonicapán | Ethnic Movement |

This general perception that K'iche' is being successfully maintained, however, is not universal. In all of the communities there are a few who are actively promoting not only maintenance but an expanded set of roles and functions for K'iche'. These activists were still in the minority when these data were collected. Unless their efforts are buttressed by institutions such as the Roman Catholic church (as in Chichicastenango and San Andrés Sajcabajá) or, more effectively, the educational system (as in Cunén, Sacapulas and, less effectively, Santa Cruz del Quiché) their efforts are likely to achieve only limited results.

The two communities classified as assuming the more active stance of an ethnic movement, Santa Cruz del Quiché and Totonicapán, are the two where the strength of the educational infrastructure produces a more favorable climate for activism as well as a system for distribution of the message. The fact that most of the K'iche'-speaking bilingual teachers are from these two communities is not unimportant. The economic and institutional supports which have brought about a certain degree of success

## 7.4 Subjective vitality factors

for Mayans in the ladino economic and social systems in Totonicapán and Chichicastenango and, to a lesser degree in Sacapulas and Cunén, have also resulted in K'iche' maintenance reinforcing behaviors as a result of the self-perception of success. The first two of these are also the communities where the threat to K'iche' maintenance is more starkly visible as can be seen by an examination of language use.

That there is little awareness of threats to language maintenance in the other communities does not necessarily mean that the threat does not exist. It does mean that the residents of those communities have not become aware of the potential sources of language shift which exist in their communities or have not believed those who do see the existence of such threats. To this point these K'iche' speakers have not mobilized themselves around any leader and so remain in the passive stance of an ethnicity. As the threat becomes more apparent, depending on the identity which the residents of each community wish to assume, they may respond as an ethnic movement or ethnic nationalism. K'iche' language and culture maintenance behaviors increasingly may be based on an adopted ladino world view; or, they may respond by abandoning K'iche' and embracing the linguistic and cultural behaviors which will further develop a progressive, modern, and ladinoized identity.

## 7.5 Language maintenance indices

In chapter 6, I examined the results of the observations of language use in the seven communities from the perspectives of race, sex, age, and domain of use. The overall impression provided by that analysis is that broad diglossia is intact in most of the communities although each of the communities has a different profile of language use and maintenance from age group to age group and domain to domain.

**7.5.1 Race and sex.** In all of the communities, race, whether of speaker or interlocutor or both is the primary factor influencing language use. The "ladino effect" was observed, where the presence of a ladino in a speech situation increased the tendency for Spanish to be used. In some of the communities, this effect was so strong that language use patterns of Mayans were indistinguishable from those of ladinos if a ladino was present as one of the participants.

Sex of speaker and interlocutor have a secondary influence on language use with different tendencies observed in the communities. In all of the communities where the interaction between the race of the speaker and the race of the interlocutor is significant, there is a tendency for speech transactions between same-sex speakers to have higher levels of K'iche' use. At the same time, in some communities, there is a marked difference between the language use of Mayan males and Mayan females. In Cunén, San Andrés Sajcabajá, and Totonicapán, for example, Mayan males tend to use more Spanish than Mayan females. On the other hand, in Santa Cruz del Quiché, females are taking the lead in Spanish acquisition and use, a pattern which has serious implications for intergenerational transmission of K'iche'. In other communities (e.g., Joyabaj, Sacapulas) there was no significant difference in language use between the sexes.

**7.5.2 Age.** Since language shift generally occurs through the lack of transmission of a language from one generation to the next, it would be expected that if K'iche' is not being maintained, there would be indications of lower levels of language maintenance in the younger age groups. Table 7.5 shows the LMI scores calculated for the communities by age group and exhibits the differences in language use and maintenance between the age groups in each community.

The community with the lowest levels of language maintenance in the younger age groups is Santa Cruz del Quiché, where the two youngest age groups have LMI scores that are quite low. Cunén, on the other hand, has a nearly perfect LMI score for the youngest age group. While Totonicapán shows moderate language maintenance in the youngest age group, the next age group has an LMI that is lower than any other in the study. The other communities, with the exception of Joyabaj where there are no data, show relatively high levels of language maintenance in the younger age groups. All of the communities, however, show a decrease in K'iche' maintenance among the school-aged and young adult residents.

Table 7.5 Summary of language use by age groups

| Town | 1–12 | 13–24 | 25–34 | 35–44 | 45–54 | 55+ |
|---|---|---|---|---|---|---|
| Chichicastenango | 1.54 | 1.37 | 1.35 | 1.31 | 1.57 | 1.30 |
| Cunén | 1.93 | 1.59 | 1.62 | 1.59 | 1.38 | 1.74 |
| Joyabaj | | 1.18 | 1.46 | 1.50 | | |
| Sacapulas | 1.74 | 1.54 | 1.66 | 1.79 | 1.50 | 1.07 |
| San Andrés Sajcabajá | 1.75 | 1.49 | 1.48 | 1.66 | 1.68 | 1.88 |
| Santa Cruz del Quiché | 0.98 | 1.16 | 1.58 | 1.77 | 1.61 | 1.71 |
| Totonicapán | 1.40 | 0.93 | 1.34 | 1.45 | 1.58 | 1.65 |

Though there are some anomalies, generally the communities show higher levels of language maintenance among the older age groups.

## 7.5 Language maintenance indices

Chichicastenango and Sacapulas have unexpected dramatically lower levels of language maintenance in the oldest age group. This may be the result, at least in the case of Sacapulas, of emigration from the community by residents for employment (and Spanish acquisition) followed by their return for their older years.

The data show that although the language maintenance profiles based on age differ in their details, there is a general tendency for relatively higher levels of K'iche' maintenance to be seen in the very youngest and in the older age groups. Lower maintenance levels are generally seen in the more economically active middle range groups. This indicates that in most of the communities K'iche' is being transmitted to the youngest age group in the home domain. When the children begin school, however, and then move on to young adulthood, they are exposed to both the opportunities and the pressures to learn and use Spanish. Though I have not examined the distribution of language use in each age group by domain, it is likely that the clearest indications of domain leakage are to be found in these young adult age groups. This is one important aspect of the data that merits further investigation.

**7.5.3 Domain.** A similar comparative analysis can be performed using the data from the analysis by domains. Table 7.6 provides the LMI data for each community by domain of use. In a situation characterized by broad diglossia, it is expected that the more intimate, more solidary domains are those most likely to show higher levels of maintenance. If broad diglossia obtains in the K'iche' communities, we should expect to find higher levels of K'iche' maintenance in the more intimate domains and lower levels in the less intimate domains.

Table 7.6 Summary of language maintenance indices by domain

| Town | Home | Street | Play | Market | Work | Religion | Stores | Media | School | Govt |
|---|---|---|---|---|---|---|---|---|---|---|
| Chichicastenango | 1.53 | 1.54 | 1.21 | 1.55 | 1.76 | 1.13 | 1.21 | 1.51 | 1.13 | 1.06 |
| Cunén | 1.99 | 1.70 | 1.89 | 1.80 | 1.88 | 1.43 | 1.77 | 0.97 | 1.80 | 1.07 |
| Joyabaj | — | — | — | 1.32 | 1.89 | 1.05 | 0.70 | — | — | — |
| Sacapulas | 1.81 | 1.82 | 1.50 | 1.72 | 1.55 | 1.21 | 1.60 | 1.41 | 1.71 | 1.64 |
| San Andrés Sajcabajá | 1.46 | 1.73 | 1.80 | 1.78 | 1.77 | 1.12 | 1.46 | 1.79 | 0.79 | 1.29 |
| Santa Cruz del Quiché | 1.46 | 1.65 | 0.62 | 1.70 | 1.54 | 0.87 | 1.32 | 1.76 | 0.36 | 1.53 |
| Totonicapán | 1.89 | 1.55 | 0.66 | 1.75 | 1.33 | 0.91 | 0.96 | 0.91 | 1.08 | 1.23 |

<————— INTIMATE —————————— LESS INTIMATE —————>

## 7.5 Language maintenance indices

As with the effect of age on language use, the home domain, like the youngest age groups, is crucial for the successful intergenerational transmission of K'iche'. It is in the home and through the family that K'iche' is most likely to be transmitted to new speakers. Bilingual education, religious practice, and the other institutional and cultural supports in the communities are, at best, providing opportunities for use and supporting the retention of an already-acquired K'iche'. There are few, if any, resources for the acquisition of K'iche' outside of the home.

In this regard, the six communities for which there are data show relatively high levels of language maintenance in the home domain. Cunén shows the highest level at a nearly perfect 1.99. Santa Cruz del Quiché shows the lowest LMI in the home domain at 1.46. Surprisingly, San Andrés Sajcabajá has an LMI for this domain that is just as low. Chichicastenango is slightly higher at 1.53. Sacapulas and Totonicapán have more vigorous LMI scores at 1.81 and 1.89, respectively.

The scaling from high to low LMI scores across the domains from most intimate to less intimate is not clear in most of the communities. While the LMI scores in the more formal domains are generally lower than those in the more intimate domains, the scalability of the data is not very strong. In part, this can be accounted for by an examination of the kinds of speech transactions which were included in each of the domain groupings and by placing these speech transactions in their social context. One anomalous domain in all of the communities is recreation. In Cunén, Sacapulas, and San Andrés Sajcabajá, the LMI scores for this domain are quite high. In Chichicastenango, the LMI is in the weak maintenance range and in Santa Cruz del Quiché and Totonicapán they are quite low. Recreation includes observations of both adults and children at play and includes children in both informal recreational activities and organized team sports. While all of the towns have teams of various kinds, it is likely that the larger towns (Santa Cruz del Quiché, Totonicapán, and Chichicastenango) have more active and well-organized amateur soccer and basketball teams. In the smaller communities the teams are less well-organized and thus, less likely to be observed either at practice or in competition. In the smaller communities (Cunén, Sacapulas, and San Andrés Sajcabajá), the observations are more likely to be dominated by children at play. Consequently, they are more likely to show higher levels of K'iche' use than in the more formal and public organized team play. This mixing of disparate social situations accounts for the anomalous results in this domain grouping.

The religious domain is another where the expected scaling of the data is interrupted by generally lower-than-expected LMI scores. In this domain there is a marked tendency for the Roman Catholic church to be more open to the use of K'iche' and even to promote its use, than the Protestant churches which are marked by a general preference for the use of Spanish. Where this divergence between the two groups exists, the tendency would be for the two sets of observations to cancel each other out. The measure of language maintenance in this domain can be linked directly to the strength of the Protestant movement and to the lack of institutional support of K'iche' use from the Roman Catholic church leadership. Thus, in Santa Cruz del Quiché and Totonicapán, where there is a strong Protestant presence and little institutional support of K'iche' from the Roman Catholic hierarchy,[40] the LMI scores for this domain are quite low. In Chichicastenango, Joyabaj, and Sacapulas, where there was institutional support of K'iche' from the church, there is also a strong Protestant segment of the society resulting in slightly higher but still weak levels of language maintenance. Only in Cunén, where there is some institutional support for the language from the church and a weaker Protestant presence, is there any indication of moderate language maintenance in the religious domain.

This difference in language use between the religious groups can also be taken as evidence that there is a difference in the evaluation of religion between the two groups. For those Roman Catholics who retain and promote the use of K'iche' in religious services, religion is an intimate, solidary domain. For the Protestants who show a preference to use Spanish in their church services, religion is a domain that has come to be associated with modernity and progressiveness. This represents an identity shift on the part of those who have become Protestants as they have adopted the values and associated linguistic behavior of the out-group.

A third domain that is significant as an indicator of the prospects for future language maintenance is that of formal education. Though much of the education of K'iche' children is achieved through informal means in the home and work domains, increasingly social and governmental pressures are causing K'iche' parents to send their children to schools. This is another domain where the data are mixed since formal schooling is in the midst of an ideological struggle. This means that some students are exposed to the assimilationist message left over from the period of *indigenismo,* while some are hearing a strong message of linguistic revival and ethnic nationalism. In addition, the bilingual program has only been implemented in grades 1 through 4, while the data have been collected from both elementary and secondary schools. Data from the lower

---

[40]This refers specifically to the use of K'iche' in church. As mentioned in chapter 5, the Roman Catholic church operates a radio station which broadcasts a considerable amount of religious and cultural programming using the K'iche' language.

*7.5 Language maintenance indices*                                                             237

elementary grades would be expected to show evidence of K'iche' use, while it would be surprising to find any K'iche' used in the higher grades.

A third source of confounding data for this domain is the differences between urban and rural schools and between speech transactions observed inside and outside of the classroom in the school setting. Classroom utterances are more likely to be in Spanish while those between students, or even between students and teachers, outside of the classroom might be expected to show some greater tendency to use K'iche'.

Given these caveats regarding the education domain data, the LMI scores for this domain can be read as an indicator of the assimilationist effect of formal education. This effect is only now beginning to be counteracted by the activities of the bilingual education program which is, for the most part, in the hands of promotors of ethnic nationalism. Those communities which have low LMI scores for formal education are those where the bilingual program has not been effective or has not yet been implemented. These communities are Santa Cruz del Quiché, where bilingual education is only available in a few rural communities, San Andrés Sajcabajá, where schools are few and far between and the bilingual program has not been fully implemented nor supported by school officials. In such situations, Spanish is the language of formal education.

In Chichicastenango and Totonicapán, the LMI scores are higher but still represent only a weak level of language maintenance in this domain. This shows the stronger presence of the bilingual program in these communities. The highest LMI scores are for Cunén and Sacapulas which were reported to have active bilingual teachers working not only in the school setting but in general community and economic development as well.

When these anomalous domains are accounted for in the data, a clearer, but still not definitive, distinction emerges between the informal domains and the more formal domains in most of the communities. This lack of definition and the lack of overall scalability, in spite of the problems with the categorizations of some of the speech transactions, is evidence of a weakening of the strong compartmentalization which would be expected in stable broad diglossia.

**7.5.4 Global language maintenance indices.** For each of the communities, I calculated a global language maintenance index using the same methodology as that used for the calculation of the LMIs for age and domain. It included all of the speech transactions observed for the community in which the language used was unambiguously identified as either K'iche', Spanish, or code-mixed. Table 7.7 shows the global LMI scores for each of the communities.

Table 7.7 Global language maintenance indices

| Town | LMI |
|---|---|
| Chichicastenango | 1.36 |
| Cunén | 1.59 |
| Joyabaj | 1.26 |
| Sacapulas | 1.65 |
| San Andrés Sajcabajá | 1.58 |
| Santa Cruz del Quiché | 1.41 |
| Totonicapán | 1.36 |

This analysis reveals that Joyabaj, with an LMI of 1.26, albeit based on somewhat restricted data, has the lowest level of language maintenance of the seven communities and is the only one whose global LMI falls within the weak language maintenance range.

Interestingly, Chichicastenango and Totonicapán have identical LMI scores at 1.36. This is the next lowest score among the communities. These two communities share other similarities as well, most notably their maintenance of Mayan identity and sociohistorical status, accompanied by a shift to cash crops and textile production as the principle economic activities. Both are cosmopolitan centers with large central markets which serve as regional centers of exchange, though this is more clearly so for Totonicapán than for Chichicastenango where outside contacts are predominantly with foreign tourists. The LMI scores for these two communities fall between the first and second quartiles of all of the LMI scores computed for the age and domain analyses.

On the other hand, it is Totonicapán and Santa Cruz del Quiché which, because of their size and status as governmental centers, are classified as cities rather than towns. Furthermore, both of these communities have the subjective vitality stance of an ethnic movement. The LMI score for Santa Cruz (1.41) is slightly higher than that for Totonicapán but is still lower than the LMI scores for most of the other communities. Santa Cruz is thus at the lower end of the moderate language maintenance category. Based on these similarities in the communities and the scores, it seems practical to consider these three communities at about the same general level of language maintenance.

The remaining three communities have higher LMI scores and, using the same criteria as used above, can be grouped together. Cunén and San Andrés Sajcabajá have nearly identical LMI scores at 1.59 and 1.58, respectively. Sacapulas has the highest LMI score at 1.65.

## 7.5 Language maintenance indices

These higher-maintenance communities are the three which are most remote, less economically diversified (though in Cunén diversification has just begun), and have some level of institutional support for the use and maintenance of K'iche'. Education is generally less available in these communities, though the bilingual teachers in Sacapulas and Cunén are quite active. The Protestant churches in these communities, which have a tendency to be associated with Spanish use, are also less numerous and generally smaller and less influential.

### 7.6 Summary

In summary, the communities included in this study demonstrate a complex and confusing combination of ethnolinguistic vitality, identity, and language use factors. Nevertheless, these combine to provide a unique profile for each community and to demonstrate how social, economic, political, and psychological factors work together to affect language use.

The data also provide a means of determining if the first and second hypotheses of this study are true. There are several possible interpretations of the data depending on the outcomes of the tests of the two hypotheses. The first hypothesis, that broad diglossia is being lost in the communities, was tested by examining the language use data, looking for areas of compartmentalization based on either race, sex, age, or domain. The results of that analysis shows that within each community the use of K'iche' and Spanish generally follows the pattern which would be expected if broad diglossia is extant. Compartmentalization seems to be intact along racial lines and in some cases along gender lines as well. Age also was shown to be a significant factor in affecting language use, with younger people (except for the very young) generally showing a weaker tendency to maintain the use of K'iche' than older people. This fact is significant in that, in all of the communities, more than half of the population is in the younger category. Domains of use show a very general tendency to follow the expected pattern for a diglossic situation with K'iche' use being higher in the intimate domains and lower in the formal and public domains. Few domains, however, were found to be exclusively associated with one language or the other, and no strong degree of scalability from more intimate to less intimate domains was found. In spite of this overall pattern of the domains relative to each other, the general level of K'iche' usage is different when the communities are compared to each other. The general pattern seems to be not so much one of K'iche' retreating a domain at a time, but rather a general erosion of K'iche' use in all domains simultaneously. The global differences in K'iche' maintenance can be seen if the global

LMI scores for each community are compared by means of a bar graph. Figure 7.1 shows this relationship between the communities.

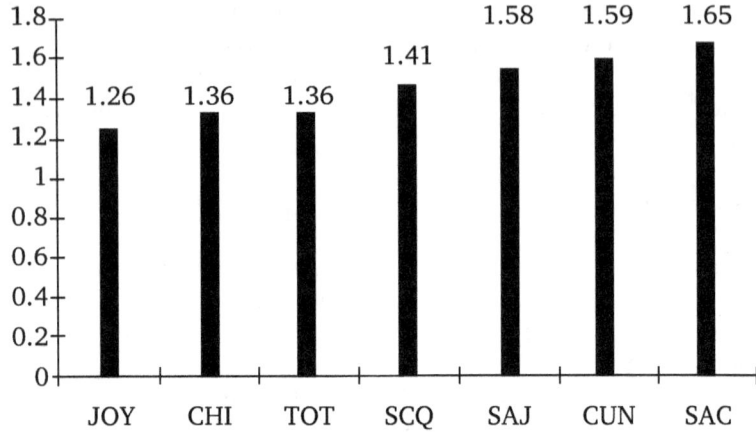

Figure 7.1 Global language maintenance indices

When I embarked upon this study I assumed that if the communities were maintaining a stable diglossic relationship between Spanish and K'iche', the second hypothesis, that there has been an accompanying shift in identity, would be moot. However, if the diglossic pattern is being maintained but at lower and lower levels of strength, while compartmentalization is being maintained, then an examination of the second hypothesis to see if there is a connection between the identity orientation of the communities and language use is not only useful, but illuminating, in terms of a broader understanding of the relationship between diglossia and language maintenance and shift.

In part, that analysis has been done in the sections above where I have summarized the various aspects of ethnolinguistic identity for each community. I pointed out there how the lower global LMI scores can be connected partially with demographic factors, but more significantly with institutional support, status, and subjective vitality factors in each case. The connections between the ethnolinguistic identity factors and language maintenance, however, are complex and are not uniform from community to community. While a community may enjoy institutional support for K'iche' maintenance, it may suffer from a lack of economic activity which lowers subjective perceptions of group success. Each community is a unique mix of factors that are maintenance-supporting and

## 7.6 Summary

maintenance-inhibiting which together establish a community-specific climate for K'iche' maintenance. The data provide ample evidence of the complex nature of the social psychological processes which contribute to ethnolinguistic identity, as well as indicating the need for the development of more precise measures of ethnolinguistic vitality.

The differences in the global language maintenance indices serve as a general index of the level of language maintenance in each community relative to the other communities. While the age and domain language maintenance indices provide baseline data which can be used for future studies of the progress of language maintenance and shift in each of the communities individually, the comparative analysis between the communities shows a progression of language shift which can be tied to the ethnolinguistic vitality measures.

In spite of the complexity of the factors and their interrelationships, the communities can be ranked in terms of their ethnolinguistic vitality and language maintenance. Figure 7.2 shows a line graph of the age-group language maintenance indices for the seven communities.[41] In spite of the denseness of the graph, the general trends followed by all of the communities, as well as the overall differences in language maintenance levels, can be seen.

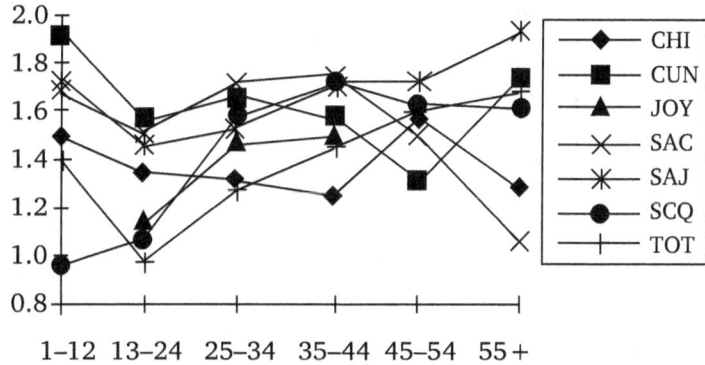

Figure 7.2 Comparative language use by age groups

Some generalizations can be made. All of the communities, except Santa Cruz del Quiché, are characterized by higher K'iche' use in the youngest age group, than in the next older age group. The three

---

[41] A similar line graph could be produced for the domain data, but the number of data points and the number of towns produces a tangled web of lines which is exceedingly difficult to interpret. While the age data graph is also quite dense, it is a more readable representation of the stratification of the communities.

school-aged and young adult age groups (13–44 years) show a parallel tendency to have lower levels of K'iche' maintenance in the younger group. This tendency may be attributable to the effect of schooling and may be a means of measuring the time-depth of the introduction of schooling as a significant influence on language use in each community. There are also some anomalies in the language maintenance levels of the oldest age groups, which have been discussed above.

Based on the curves produced in the figure, the communities can be subjectively ranked relative to each other in terms of their language maintenance. The communities ranked in ascending order of language maintenance, with the data from Joyabaj interpolated, are Totonicapán, Chichicastenango, Joyabaj, Santa Cruz del Quiché, Sacapulas, Cunén, and San Andrés Sajcabajá. This ranking does not coincide exactly with the ranking produced by the global LMI scores as shown in figure 7.1, but does agree in grouping Cunén, Sacapulas, and San Andrés Sajcabajá together because of higher levels of language maintenance and in grouping Chichicastenango, Joyabaj, Santa Cruz del Quiché, and Totonicapán as the towns with lower levels of language maintenance. This dichotomous division of the communities can be linked quite well with demographic, institutional support, status, and subjective vitality characteristics of the communities.

On the basis of the foregoing, I conclude that the second hypothesis of this study can be taken to be true. There is a relationship between ethnolinguistic identity factors and the level of language maintenance in each community.

## 7.7 Conclusions

One goal of the research undertaken here was to provide a comprehensive overview of K'iche' language use, and this study takes some steps in that direction. There is much yet to be learned, however, about the dynamics of language use and language maintenance in the K'iche'-speaking area of Guatemala.

By combining qualitative and quantitative data, a more comprehensive picture of the K'iche' situation has been developed and the links between ethnolinguistic identity factors and actual language use have been made clearer. More study is needed in the K'iche' communities of the identity factors, particularly the factors for which only scanty data were collected in this study. These areas include the patterns of migration, endogamous and exogamous marriage, cultural institutions such as the *cofradías* and their role in language and culture maintenance, the apparent division

## 7.7 Conclusions

between Roman Catholics and Protestants in language use, and the relative status of the communities and of the groups within the communities. I have done very little analysis of boundary maintenance in the communities except to note the shift in some towards the posture of an ethnic movement or ethnic nationalism. In addition, I have done no analysis of the effect of the role relations of the participants on language choice in this study and there is very little understood, at this point, about how those role relations affect language use.

As mentioned above, the language use data for each community can serve as baseline data for future studies which will more adequately be able to document the progress of language shift in each community. The picture presented here is a static one, a snapshot in time, of the language use patterns in each community. While the comparisons between the communities seem to indicate a drift towards language shift, this drift can only be corroborated as future studies are undertaken and as they reveal changes over time.

Another needed area of investigation is an examination of the degree and nature of code-mixing which is taking place as the communities move along the continuum of language shift. While code-mixed utterances were included in this study, there is much yet to be discovered about how code-mixing can be identified, analyzed, and related to language maintenance in each community and, more crucially, between communities.

The story of language contact between K'iche' and Spanish is not completed. The forces which have brought about the current changes are not necessarily permanent ones. The future is hard to predict but several scenarios are possible. One scenario assumes that the first hypothesis of this study is true, that diglossia has become destabilized, but that the second hypothesis is false, there has been no shift in identity. Accordingly, language maintenance efforts will result once the people are made aware of their situation because their underlying identity is still strongly associated with the K'iche' language. In some of the communities there are already activists promoting language maintenance. In others, the threat has not yet been perceived. When and if the threat reaches a critical mass and rises to the level of popular awareness, we might well expect a popular movement to reestablish K'iche' and to strengthen K'iche' maintenance.

If, however, both the first and second hypotheses of this study are true, another, more pessimistic scenario is a possibility. If the stability of diglossia has been lost and there has also been an accompanying shift in identity, then it might be expected that large numbers of K'iche' speakers will choose to acquire Spanish and associate themselves and their Mayan identity with the Spanish language.

The conclusions that I have drawn from this study are that language shift is underway in some of the K'iche' communities and that this shift is related to identity shift as Mayans have changed their subjective vitality assessments in response to a changing demographic, political, economic, social, and cultural environment. Just as the seven communities are at different levels of language maintenance, with the most rural and isolated communities showing the highest levels of language maintenance, so the communities are at different stages in their identity shift. It is not isolation, however, that is the crucial factor but rather the combined effects of demographics, institutional support, status, and subjective vitality which seem to play the more important roles. Notably, the most isolated community, San Andrés Sajcabajá, classified as having strong levels of language maintenance, has lower language maintenance levels in many respects than do the other two, more accessible, communities which I have classified as demonstrating strong language maintenance. At the same time, two of the larger, more urban, and cosmopolitan communities, Chichicastenango and Totonicapán, are showing moderate evidence of language maintenance, in spite of their size, accessibility, and urbanization. The economic situation of the communities has a lot to do with subjective vitality. Santa Cruz del Quiché, in spite of its importance as a governmental center, has little or no economic vitality, and so is characterized by higher levels of emigration, lower status, little institutional support, and a general sociocultural malaise which is accompanied by language shift. Cunén, on the other hand, with the perceived economic threat of rival groups has rallied and reorganized its economic life, revived institutional support for K'iche', and shows strong levels of language maintenance. Nevertheless, there is considerable evidence of identity shift as the Mayans of Cunén adopt ladino economic and social values. They are doing so, however, in and through the K'iche' language.

What seems to actually be taking place, however, is what was not foreseen when this study was initially conceived. The communities in this study all seem to be characterized by a relatively intact broad diglossia while at the same time experiencing weakening levels of language maintenance. This calls into question some of our assumptions about the relationship between diglossia and language maintenance. Can a language be lost in a situation where there is increasing bilingualism and diglossia?

This study also raises concerns regarding the relationship of language and identity, as several of the communities are clearly demonstrating an identity shift, with the adoption of ladino cultural values, but are at the same time demonstrating that shift through their now-militant efforts to

## 7.7 Conclusions

maintain the K'iche' language. I have not adequately analyzed the dynamics of this phenomenon and it remains an object for further research.

Although reculturization can take place without relinguification, it is not the usual nor the easiest course. Those communities which are adopting modern identities while at the same time maintaining K'iche' can only be viewed as happy exceptions which, at least for the moment, are defying the odds.

# Appendix

# Community Resource Profile Questions

### Demographics and boundary maintenance-related questions

001 Make a map of your primary *municipio,* i.e., the town where you live. Note especially the locations of churches, schools, government buildings, etc.

002 Make a list of the Mayan languages and dialects used in the area. Spend a few market days observing the languages used in transactions or observe what varieties are represented (though perhaps not used) in church services. What is your general impression of mutual comprehension if different varieties are used? If you don't feel like you know enough yet to be able to identify different varieties, keep a list of *trajes* (local, distinctive clothing) which you have seen in the market. Did you notice many ladinos using the vernacular?

005 If you are aware of more than one variety in your area describe the linguistic features which distinguish them as best you can.

013 Keep a journal of your observations on language use, attitudes, linguistic features, anomalies, etc. Also note any needs (linguistic, literature, or otherwise) expressed by the people themselves. Note any comments concerning reading, writing, use of the vernacular, etc.

014 Where do the people find their ethnic identity: in their town? in their *traje*? in their language? something else? Give your impression.

017 Try to observe where the visiting salesmen and vendors in the market come from? What do they sell? Who buys it? Do the people from the area go elsewhere to buy or sell? Where? When? How often?

018 With the knowledge you now have of the area, estimate the extent of bilingualism?

    a. adult males (25 years and above)
    b. adult females (25 years and above)
    c. young males (15–25 years)
    d. young females (15–25 years)
    e. children (under 15 years)

032 Estimate the percentage of the mother tongue (MT) speakers who are literate in the MT.

    a. adult males
    b. adult females
    c. young males
    d. young females
    e. children

083 Who are the innovators? How do they introduce new ideas?

103 What is the attitude of the government to this language group? How is the language policy worked out in any school or government-sponsored adult program?

107 How do people react to innovations?

108 Who accepts change first? (which groups, or types of individuals, etc.)

109 What dangers do people see in accepting change?

110 What is the level of cross-cultural tension? Can outsiders be brought into (come into) the community without undue problems or stress?

111 Who are the local personnel to whom you must relate and with whom you should establish contact? (local government, churches, military, school, organizations, etc.) What degree of cooperation might you expect from them?

112 What are the local problems which could affect development of a literacy, translation, distribution/promotion, or community development program?

114 How is information communicated in the area? For example, how does the school let parents know what children need to bring, how does the *alcaldía* communicate to townspeople, how do churches get general information out?

115 From your knowledge of the community, its resources, needs, interests, marketing procedures and outlets, how might literature be promoted and distributed?

**Status-related questions**

003 Give your tentative opinion on where the vernacular is used: the *alcaldía,* churches in town, churches in *aldeas,* the market, others?

004 What is your impression of the use of K'iche' in church? Is it used for preaching, singing, praying, announcements, Scripture reading? Elaborate. Is there a difference between Roman Catholics and Protestants in how (much) the vernacular is used?

006 Have you detected any difference in status between speakers of the K'iche' and Spanish?

007 Is there a PRONEBI teacher/school in the area? Arrange to meet the teacher(s).

008 Interview a school teacher or official in your area and get the following information:

    a. number of schools in the area
    b. classify the schools by:

        *centro de castellanización,*
        primary (1–3),
        primary (4–6),
        others,
        indicate which are involved with PRONEBI

    c. how many of these schools have a teacher who speaks K'iche'?
    d. how many children start the school year, how many finish? classify these by grade level
    e. why don't they finish?

  f. what have parents reported to the teacher/official as their attitude toward using K'iche' in school?

009 Begin to compile a list of vernacular publications that you are sure are in print in the variety from your area.

010 Has anyone expressed to you a desire to have a specific type of literature in the variety? Who was it, what was it, why?

011 List distribution outlets (if any) in your area that sell K'iche' literature. What titles? What variety(ies)? Interview them concerning sales. What titles sell? Why?

012 Is anyone producing literature in the variety? Make a list. Have you noticed people who would be good authors with training?

013 Keep a journal of your observations on language use, attitudes, linguistic features, anomalies, etc. Also note any needs (linguistic, literature, or otherwise) expressed by the people themselves. Note any comments concerning reading, writing, use of the vernacular, etc.

016 What is the principal means of income in the community? Do the majority have the same kind of work? Do you have an idea of what the average income would be? Do the people migrate to the coast yearly? Who goes (men, women, the whole family)? How long do they stay? When do they go? Why then?

019 How stable is the language situation?

020 What is the attitude of the various age groups towards the MT?

021 In what situations is the MT used?

  a. town government
  b. town churches
  c. *aldea* churches
  d. marketing
  e. other

022 What is the attitude of the political leadership towards the use of the MT?

023 What is the attitude of the church leadership towards the use of the MT?

  a. Roman Catholic
  b. Protestant

*Status related questions*

024 What is the attitude of the public school leadership towards the use of the MT? (i.e., *promotores, maestros, supervisores*)

026 Which language do children learn first at home?

    a. Mayan language
    b. Spanish

027 Which language does father use with children under 15?

028 Which language does mother use with children under 15?

031 With the knowledge you now have of your area, estimate the percentage of MT speakers who are literate in Spanish?

    a. adult males (25 years and above)
    b. adult females (25 years and above)
    c. young males (15–25 years)
    d. young females (15–25 years)
    e. children (under 15 years)

032 Estimate the percentage of the MT speakers who are literate in the MT.

    a. adult males
    b. adult females
    c. young males
    d. young females
    e. children

033 What is the attitude of the MT speakers towards reading in their MT?

034 What is the people's idea of a literate person? An educated person?

035 What language/s can be/are being used in nonformal education?

036 What types of nonformal educational programs exist in the area? Under whose direction?

037 What groups are involved in literacy work in the area?

    a. in the MT
    b. in Spanish

038 What materials are being used by other literacy programs in the area?

039 What population group/s are being reached? Approximate number being reached? Degree of success?

040 What is the motivating factor in each of these programs?

041 Of the literacy work done up to this point, comment on the success and failures and reasons, methods used, materials.

042 Of the groups involved in Spanish literacy, comment on their attitude towards MT literateness.

043 List the agencies of individuals in your area who are in any way concerned with educating the local populations (e.g., national government, local government, agriculture, church mission, health, etc.)

046 What buildings, equipment might be available?

047 What means do you see for remuneration for teachers?

049 Are there any areas of their lives where the people see themselves as disadvantaged if they are not able to read and write?

050 To whom does a nonliterate turn when he needs something read or written?

060 Name any committees or individuals that have shown a real interest in learning to read. (through survey or other contacts)

061 What reasons has anyone given for wanting to learn to read? Is this a general attitude or specific to individuals?

071 How does the community view profit-making?

072 Is honesty a value?

073 Who is a responsible person?

075 What is the attitude of the traditional leaders to:
   a. education in general?
   b. education for adults?
   c. education for children?

076 What is the attitude of other categories of leaders (e.g., pastors) to:
   a. education in general?
   b. education for adults?
   c. education for children?

077 What would the leaders like to see accomplished as a result of an educational program?

078 How do they think education should be acquired?

079 In what areas are there different leaders? (traditional, or cultural specialists, government, church, etc.)

080 Do these leaders (see 079) have influence beyond their own particular area? If so, in what way?

081 Is there any person/group that has overall power?

082 How are the decisions made (by individuals, group consensus, etc.)?

083 Who are the innovators? How do they introduce new ideas?

084 Are there different factions within the community that give allegiance to different leaders (class, political)?

087 What topics are consciously taught?

096 Will people give labor as a form of payment?

097 Will people give goods as a form of payment?

098 Do people expect to be paid for mental or physical labor?

099 What do people buy and sell?

100 What marketing system is in use?

101 How are saleable goods distributed and vendors compensated?

102 How much can people be expected to spend on books or education?

104 What is the chain of command by which decisions made at a national level are implemented at the local level? How effective is this?

113 Should someone wish to produce literature, are there any local means of production the people could operate (typewriters, mimeo, silkscreen)? Comment on standard of printing acceptable to the people.

114 How is information communicated in the area? For example, how does the school let parents know what children need to bring, how does the *alcaldía* communicate to townspeople, how do churches get general information out?

115 From your knowledge of the community, its resources, needs, interests, marketing procedures and outlets, how might literature be promoted and distributed?

## Subjective vitality-related questions

014 Where do the people find their ethnic identity: in their town? in their *traje*? in their language? something else? Give your impression.

015 Begin to observe the belief system(s). What religious groups can you identify (traditional, syncretism, Roman Catholics (of various kinds), Protestants (of various kinds)? Are there missionaries present? Are the leaders of the churches ladino or Mayan? Are the congregations predominantly Mayan or ladino?

017 Try to observe where the visiting salesmen and vendors in the market come from? What do they sell? Who buys it? Do the people from your area go elsewhere to buy or sell? Where? When? How often?

018 With the knowledge you now have of your area, estimate the extent of bilingualism.

  a. adult males (25 years and above)
  b. adult females (25 years and above)
  c. young males (15–25 years)
  d. young females (15–25 years)
  e. children (under 15 years)

020 What is the attitude of the various age groups towards the MT?

025 What language do young adults speak among themselves?

  a. young adults in towns
  b. young adults in *aldeas*

026 Which language do children learn first at home?

  a. Mayan language
  b. Spanish

030 Which language does husband use with wife?

031 With the knowledge you now have of your area, estimate the percentage of MT speakers who are literate in Spanish.

  a. adult males (25 years and above)
  b. adult females (25 years and above)
  c. young males (15–25 years)
  d. young females (15–25 years)
  e. children (under 15 years)

044 What trained personnel could be available?

045 What local funds are available?

048 Are there ways in which the team can foresee arousing a felt need for literacy?

051 What are the main topics of discussion—at home, in meetings, at various seasons?

052 What kinds of things excite people and produce action?

053 For what kinds of things will people save money?

054 What are the subjects of humorous stories?

055 What are the subjects of traditional stories?

056 Are they interested in any of the history of their people?

057 Are there any strong interests which could provide motivation for an instructional program?

    a. in total community
    b. one sector (i.e., church, cooperative)
    c. a few individuals

058 Is there any spiritual motivation for reading religious writings?

059 What desire is there to send or receive letters?

062 What are the attributes of a 'good man'?

063 What are the attributes of a 'bad man'?

064 What is considered 'hard work'?

065 How do they view a person who works hard?

066 Who is a person who has power and prestige?

067 Is knowledge, in itself, valued?

068 Is independence encouraged?

069 How do the people view someone who shows initiative?

070 Is perseverance a value?

074 How are the emotions shown? When? By whom?

085 Are people family, individual, or total community oriented?

086 Who could effectively stir motivation (chiefs, pastors, etc.)?

088 Who teaches whom, when, what age, where?

089 Who teaches what?

090 What is the period of instruction?

091 How is teaching done? Methods?

092 What rewards accrue to the educator (status, material, etc.)?

093 How is motivation for learning developed?

094 Who works on different projects? Are there group projects? Who works on these? Who organizes these?

095 Do different ages/sexes work together?

105 What are the felt needs/problems expressed by the people themselves? (Comment on how these are expressed, by whom, to whom.)

106 Are there any felt needs for which the people are seeking outside help?

112 What are the local problems which could affect development of a literacy, translation, distribution/promotion, or community development program?

# References

Bunzel, Ruth. 1952. Chichicastenango. Seattle: American Ethnological Society, University of Washington Press.
Cancian, Frank. 1967. Political and religious organizations. In Manning Nash (ed.), Social anthropology, 283–298. Handbook of Middle American Indians 6. Austin: University of Texas Press.
Carmack, Robert. 1981. The Quiché Mayas of Utatlán. Norman: University of Oklahoma.
Chiodi, Francesco, ed. 1990. La educación indígena en américa latina 1. Quito, Ecuador: P. EBI(MEC-GTZ) and ABYA-YALA. Santiago, Chile: UNESCO/OREALC.
Cojtí Macario, Narciso. 1987. Bosquejo del análisis dialectal area quiché. Unpublished ms.
Combs, Martin. 1977. Cultural considerations in language change and communication. In Richard Loving and Gary Simons (eds.), Language variation and survey techniques, 217–230. Workpapers in Papua New Guinea Languages 21. Ukarumpa, Papua New Guinea: Summer Institute of Linguistics.
Congreso de la República de Guatemala. 1986. Decreto Numero 43–86: Ley de Alfabetización.
Congreso de la República de Guatemala. 1987. Acuerdo Gubernativo 1046–87: Acuerdo Gubernativo de los Alfabetos Mayas 3.
Crossley, Charissa. 1989. El uso del idioma K'iche' en los hogares de Chuixchimal, Totonicapán, Guatemala. WINAK: Boletín Intercultural 5(1):3–33.

deBorgheyi, Stephan F. 1956/71. Settlement patterns in the Guatemalan highlands: Past and present. In Gordon R. Willey (ed.), Prehistoric settlement patterns in the new world, 101–106. Viking Fund Publications in Anthropology 23. New York: Johnson Reprint Corp.

de Vries, John. 1984. Factors affecting the survival of linguistic minorities: A preliminary comparative analysis of data for Western Europe. Journal of Multilingual and Multicultural Development 5:207–216.

Dorian, Nancy C. 1981. Language death: The life cycle of a Scottish Gaelic dialect. Philadelphia: University of Pennsylvania Press.

Dubois, John W. 1981. The Sacapultec language. Ph.D dissertation. University of California, Berkeley.

Fasold, Ralph. 1984. The sociolinguistics of society. Language in Society 5. Oxford: Blackwell.

Ferguson, Charles A. 1959. Diglossia. Word 15:325–340.

Fishman, Joshua A. 1965a. Varieties of ethnicity and varieties of language consciousness. In James E. Alatis (ed.), Georgetown University Monograph Series in Languages and Linguistics 18:69–79. Washington D.C.: Georgetown University Press.

Fishman, Joshua A. 1965b. Who speaks what to whom and when? Linguistique 2:67–88.

Fishman, Joshua A. 1967. Bilingualism with and without diglossia; diglossia with and without bilingualism. Journal of Social Issues 13(2):29–38.

Fishman, Joshua A. 1968/1972. Societal bilingualism: Stable and transitional. In Joshua A. Fishman (ed.), Language in Sociocultural Change, 135–152. Stanford: Stanford University Press.

Fishman, Joshua A. 1986a. Bilingualism and biculturism as individual and as societal phenomena. In Joshua A. Fishman, Michael H. Gertner, Esther G. Lowy, and William G. Milan (eds.), The rise and fall of the ethnic revival: Perspectives on language and ethnicity, 39–56. The Hague: Mouton.

Fishman, Joshua A. 1986b. Language maintenance and ethnicity. In Joshua A. Fishman, Michael H. Gertner, Esther G. Lowy, and William G. Milan (eds.), The rise and fall of the ethnic revival: perspectives on language and ethnicity, 57–76. The Hague: Mouton.

Fishman, Joshua A. 1991. Reversing language shift. Philadelphia: Multilingual Matters, Ltd.

Fought, John. 1985. Patterns of sociolinguistic inequality in Mesoamerica. In Nessa Wolfson and Joan Manes (eds.), Language of Inequality, 21–39. Amsterdam: Mouton.

Gal, Susan. 1978. Peasant men can't get wives: Language change and sex roles in a bilingual community. Language in Society 7(1):1–16.

Garvin, Paul, and Madeleine Mathiot. 1956. The urbanization of the Guarani language. In Anthony F. C. Wallace (ed.), Men and cultures: Selected papers from the Fifth International Congress of Anthropological and Ethnological Sciences, 365–374. Philadelphia: University of Pennsylvania Press.

Giles, Howard, Richard Yvon Bourhis, and D. M. Taylor. 1977. Towards a theory of language in ethnic group relations. In Howard Giles (ed.), Language, ethnicity and intergroup relations. European Monographs in Social Psychology 13. London: Academic Press.

Giles, Howard, and J. Byrne. 1982. The intergroup model of second language acquisition. Journal of Multilingual and Multicultural Development 3:17–40.

Giles, Howard, Nikolas Coupland, Angie Williams, and Laura Leets. 1991. Integrating theory in the study of minority languages. In Robert Cooper and Bernard Spolsky (eds.), The influence of language on culture and thought: Essays in honor of Joshua A. Fishman's sixty-fifth birthday, 112–136. New York: Mouton de Gruyter.

Giles, Howard, and Patricia Johnson. 1987. Ethnolinguistic identity theory: A social psychological approach to language maintenance. International Journal of the Sociology of Language 68:69–100.

Goubaud Carrera, Antonio. 1945. Indigenismo guatemalteco. In Antonio Goubaud Carrera (ed.), Indigenismo en Guatemala. Guatemala: Centro Editorial "José de Pineda Ibarra". Ministerio de Educación Pública.

Goubaud Carrera, Antonio. 1945/64. Del conocimiento del indio guatemalteco. In Antonio Goubaud Carrera (ed.), Indigenismo en Guatemala. Guatemala: Centro Editorial "José Pineda de Ibarra". Ministerio de Educación Pública.

Goubaud Carrera, Antonio. 1964. Indigenismo en Guatemala. Guatemala: Centro Editorial "José de Pineda Ibarra". Ministerio de Educación Pública.

Gudykunst, William B. 1988. Language and ethnic identity. Philadelphia: Multilingual Matters Ltd.

Hawkins, John. 1984. Inverse images: The meaning of culture, ethnicity and family in postcolonial Guatemala. Albuquerque: University of New Mexico Press.

Heath, Shirley Brice. 1972. Telling tongues: Language policy in Mexico colony to nation. New York: Teachers College Press.

Henne, David M. 1964. Quiché dialect survey. ms.

Herman, Simon R. 1961. Explorations in the social psychology of language choice. Human Relations 14:149–164.

Hidalgo, M. 1986. Language contact, language loyalty, and language prejudice on the Mexican border. Language in Society 15:193–220.

Hile, Pat. n.d. A relevant message for the Quiché. ms.
Hill, Robert M., and John Monaghan. 1987. Continuities in highland Maya social organization: Ethnohistory in Sacapulas, Guatemala. Philadelphia: University of Pennsylvania Press.
Hunt, Eva, and June Nash. 1967. Local and territorial units. In Manning Nash (ed.), Social Anthropology, 253–282. Handbook of Middle American Indians 6. Austin: University of Texas Press.
Jones, Chester Lloyd. 1940/66. Guatemala past and present. New York: Russell and Russell.
Kaufman, Terrence Scott. 1974. Idiomas de Mesoamérica. Seminario de Integración Social Guatemalteca 33. Guatemala: Seminario de Integración Social Guatemalteca.
Kaufman, Terrence Scott. 1976. New Mayan languages in Guatemala: Sacapultec, Sipacapa and others. Mayan Linguistics 1:67–89.
Langan, Katherine A. 1990. Language proficiency use and attitudes in Santo Tomas Chichicastenango: A study of language competition. Ph.D. dissertation, Georgetown University.
LePage, Robert B., and Andrée Tabouret-Keller. 1985. Acts of identity. Cambridge: Cambridge University Press.
Lewis, M. Paul. 1993. Real men don't speak Quiché: Quiché ethnicity, Ki-che ethnic movement, K'iche' ethnic nationalism. Language Problems and Language Planning 17(1):37–54.
Lieberson, Stanley. 1961. A societal theory of race and ethnic relations. In Anwar S. Dil (ed.), Language diversity and language contact. Essays by Stanely Lieberson, 83–98. Stanford Calif.: Stanford University Press.
Mackey, William F. 1968. The description of bilingualism. In Joshua A. Fishman (ed.), Readings in the sociology of language, 554–584. The Hague: Mouton.
McAllister, I., and A. Mughan. 1984. The fate of language: Determinants of bilingualism in Wales. Ethnic and Racial Studies 7:321–341.
McArthur, Harry S. 1961. La estructura político-religiosa de Aguacatan. Guatemala Indígena 1(2):41–56.
McArthur, Harry S. 1969. El faccionalismo político-religioso en Aguacatan, Huehuetenango, 1966. In Roland H. Ebel (ed.), Cambio en tres communidades indígenas de Guatemala, 29–58. Guatemala: Seminario de Integración Social Guatemalteca.
Milroy, Lesley. 1980. Language and social networks. Baltimore, Md.: University Park Press.
Moore, Richard E. 1973. Historical dictionary of Guatemala. Metuchen, N.J.: Scarecrow Press.

Morren, Ronald C. 1988. Bilingual education curriculum development in Guatemala. Journal of Multilingual and Multicutlural Development 9(4):353–370.

Nyrop, Richard F., ed. 1983. Guatemala: A country study. Washington, D.C.: Headquarters, Department of the Army.

Paulston, Christina Bratt. 1987. Catalan and Occitan: Comparative test cases for a theory of language maintenance and shift. International Journal of the Sociology of Language 63:31–62.

Pettersen, Carmen L. 1976. The Maya of Guatemala, their life and dress. Guatemala City: Ixchel Museum. Seattle: distributed by the University of Washington Press.

Piel, Jean. 1989. Sajcabajá: muerte y resurrección de un pueblo de Guatemala, 1500–1970. Mexico: Centre d'etudes mexicaines et centramericaines; Guatemala: Seminario de Integración Social.

Pool, Jonathan. 1979. Language planning and identity planning. International Journal of the Sociology of Language 20:5–21.

Richards, Julia Becker. 1989. Mayan language planning for bilingual education in Guatemala. International Journal of the Sociology of Language 77:93–115.

Romaine, Suzanne. 1989. Bilingualism. Language in society 13. Oxford: Basil Blackwell.

Ross, J. A. 1979. Language and the mobilization of ethnic identity. In Howard Giles and Bernard Saint-Jacque (eds.), Language and ethnic relations, 1–13. New York: Pergamon Press.

Skinner-Klee, Jorge, ed. 1954. Legislación indigenista de Guatemala. México, D.F.: Instituto Indigenista Interamericano.

Stewart, Stephen O. 1984. Language planning and education in Guatemala. International Education Journal 1(1):21–38.

Tajfel, Henri. 1981. Human groups and social categories. Cambridge: Cambridge University Press.

Tajfel, Henri, ed. 1982. Social identity and intergroup behaviour. Cambridge: Cambridge University Press.

Tax, Sol. 1937. The municipios of the midwestern highlands of Guatemala. American Anthropologist 34:423–444.

Tax, Sol, and Robert Hinshaw. 1969. The Maya of the midwestern highlands. In Robert Wauchope (ed.), Handbook of Middle American Indians 7:69–100. Austin: University of Texas Press.

Troike, Rudolph. 1984. Proyecto bilingüe en Guatemala 1980–83. Una evaluación analítica y comparativa. Washington, D.C.: U.S. Agency for International Development.

Whetten, Nathan L. 1961. Guatemala, the land and the people. New Haven, Conn.: Yale University Press.

## SIL International
## Publications in Sociolinguistics
### Recent Publications

6     **K'iche': A study in the sociology of language** by M. Paul Lewis, 2001.
5     **The same but different: Language use and attitudes in four communities of Burkina Faso** by Stuart Showalter, 2001.
4     **Ashéninka stories of change** by Ronald James Anderson, 2000.
3     **Assessing ethnolinguistic vitality: Theory and practice** Gloria Kindell and M. Paul Lewis, eds., 1999.
2     **The early days of sociolinguistics: Memories and reflections** Christina Bratt Paulston and G. Richard Tucker, eds., 1997.
1     **North Sulawesi language survey** by Scott Merrifield and Martinus Selsa, 1996.

For further information or a full listing of SIL publications contact:

International Academic Bookstore
Summer Institute of Linguistics
7500 W. Camp Wisdom Road
Dallas, TX 75236-5699

Voice: 972-708-7404
Fax: 972-708-7363
Email: academic_books@sil.org
Internet: http://www.sil.org

www.ingramcontent.com/pod-product-compliance
Lightning Source LLC
Chambersburg PA
CBHW070243230426
43664CB00014B/2391